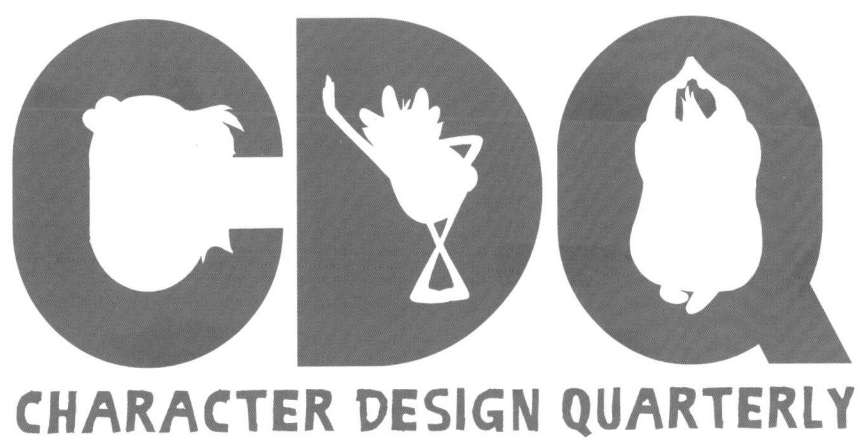

CHARACTER DESIGN QUARTERLY

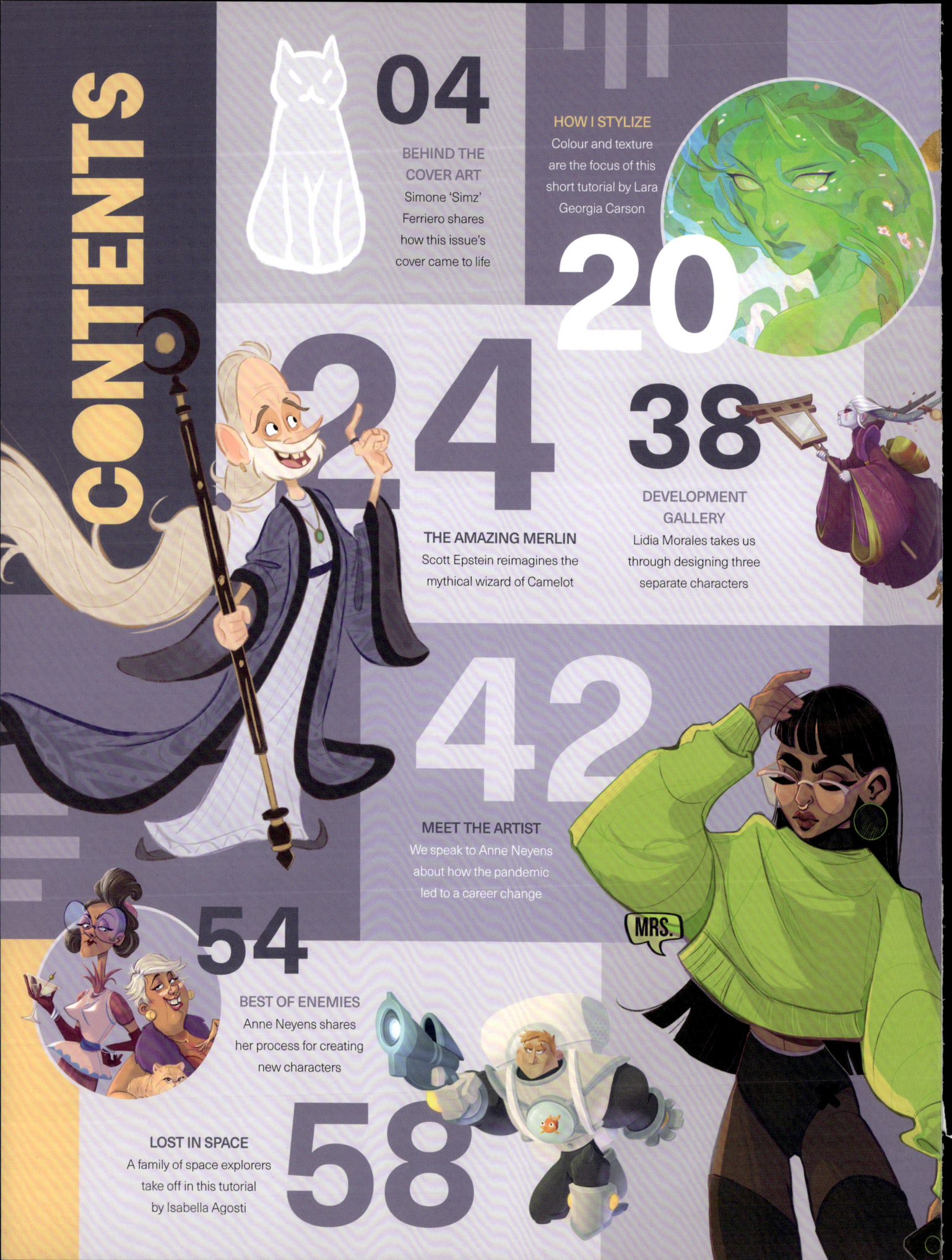

CONTENTS

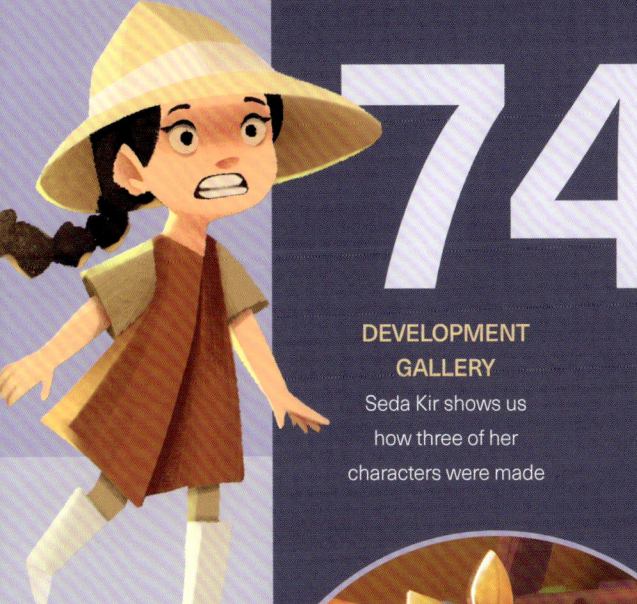

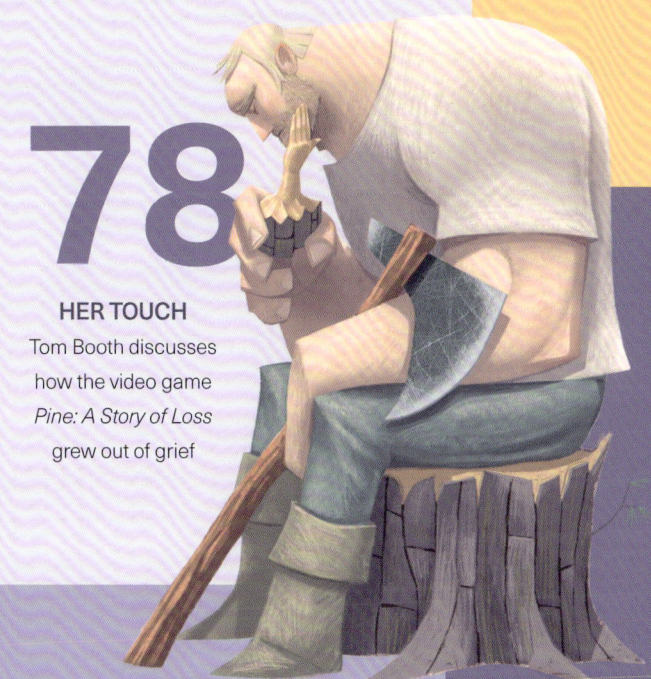

WELCOME TO
CHARACTER DESIGN QUARTERLY 34

The rise of social media brought a tidal wave of art and artists – finding your own unique style among so much can sometimes seem overwhelming. Our cover artist Simone 'Simz' Ferriero, has a style that stands out from the crowd – his iconic witches and ghost cats have earned him a massive following online. It was a pleasure to speak to Simz about his inspirations and learn how he put together our exclusive cover image.

Tom Booth and Najati Imam speaks to us about how the video game *Pine: A Story of Loss* came to life, from the first sketches, to a succesful Kickstarter, through to the game's release in 2024. We also talk with Anne Neyens about getting her break in the industy and her excitement at working on LEGO's *Piece by Piece*.

Elsewhere, Alberto Exposito creates a retro race driver, Scott Epstein interprets the myth of Merlin, and Isabella Agosti creates a family of space explorers. With our usual development galleries, 'Characterize This', and much more, there's bound to be something to inspire you in *CDQ 34*.

SAM DRAPER
EDITOR

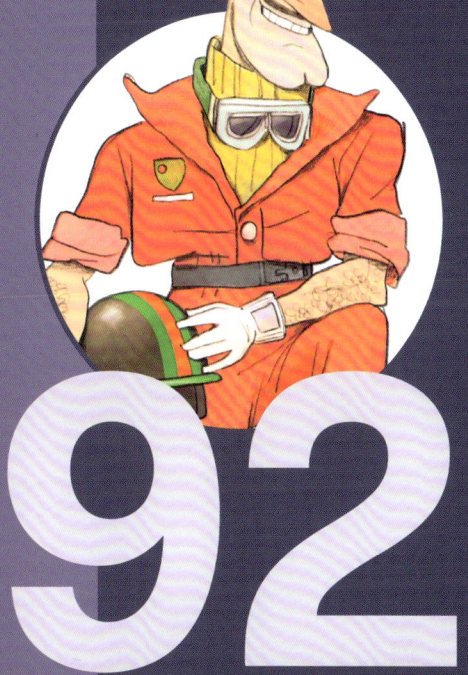

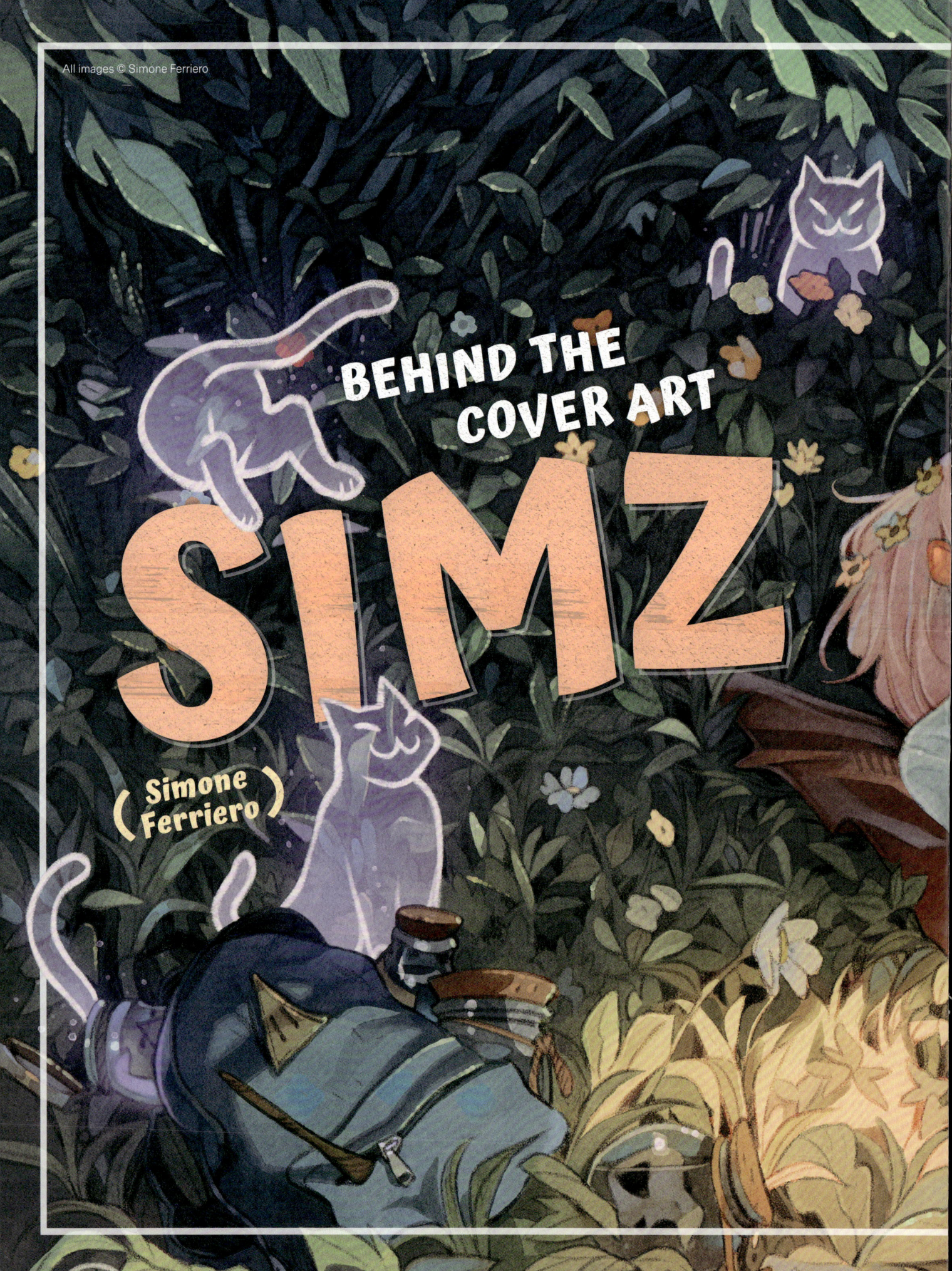

BEHIND THE
COVER ART

SIMZ

(Simone
Ferriero)

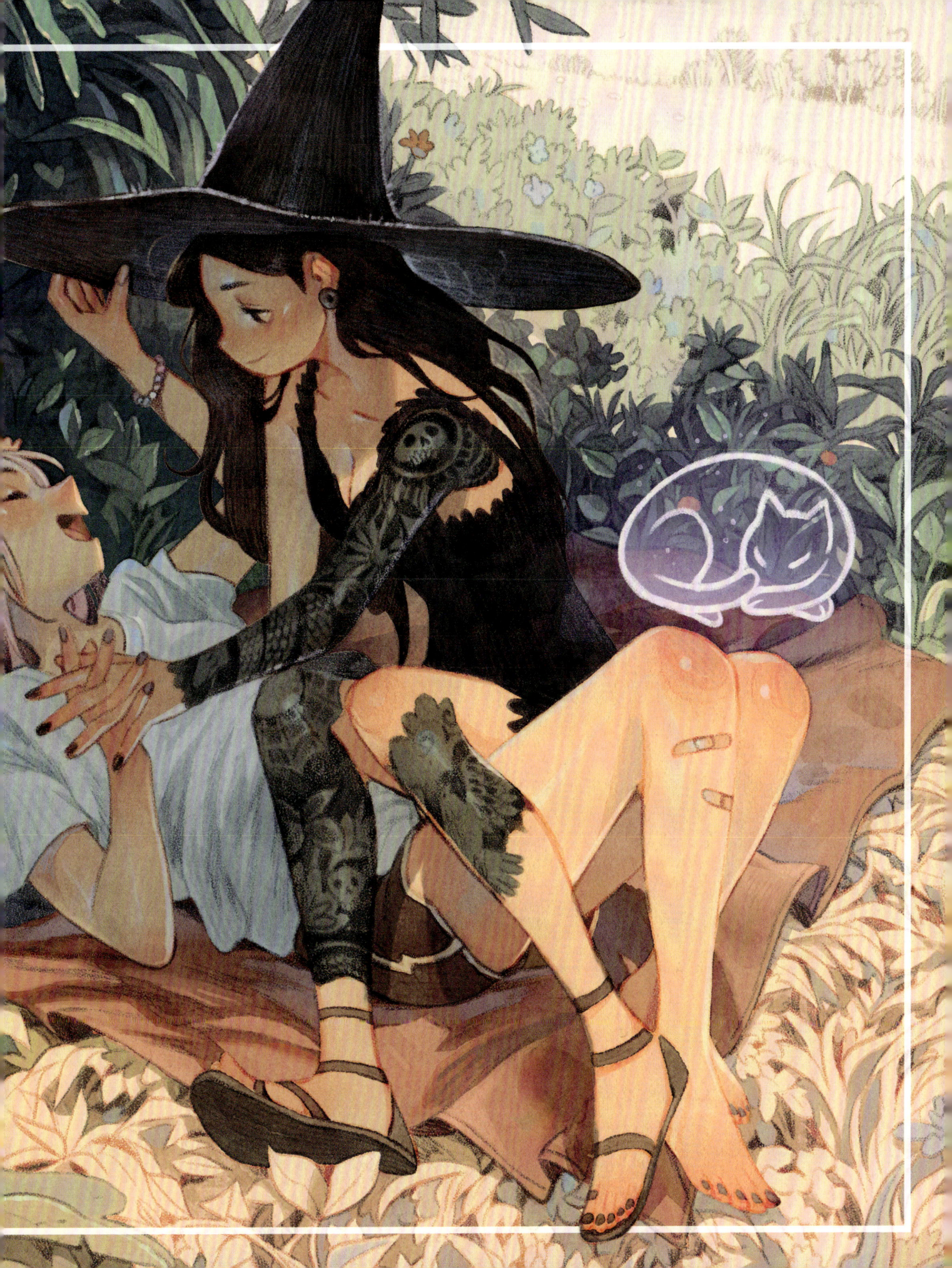

Hi Simone, welcome to *CDQ*. Can you start by telling our readers a little about your art journey so far?

Hi *CDQ*! My art journey started when I was still a kid, using my dad's pencils and paper scattered around the house. I used to draw a lot when I was in elementary school and I've never really stopped.

At the time, I didn't ever think of becoming a professional illustrator or comic-book artist, but I would often create small comics or drawings for friends and family. When I finished high school, I started getting my first paid work from friends, or friends of friends. This pushed me towards pursuing art in a more serious way and so I decided to go to art-school.

Although the course wasn't actually oriented towards illustration, it gave me a rudimentary understanding of how to approach the art world. Once I graduated, I had a brief experience in the industry as a graphic designer for video games – I left to pursue working as an independent artist. This decision led me to where I am today.

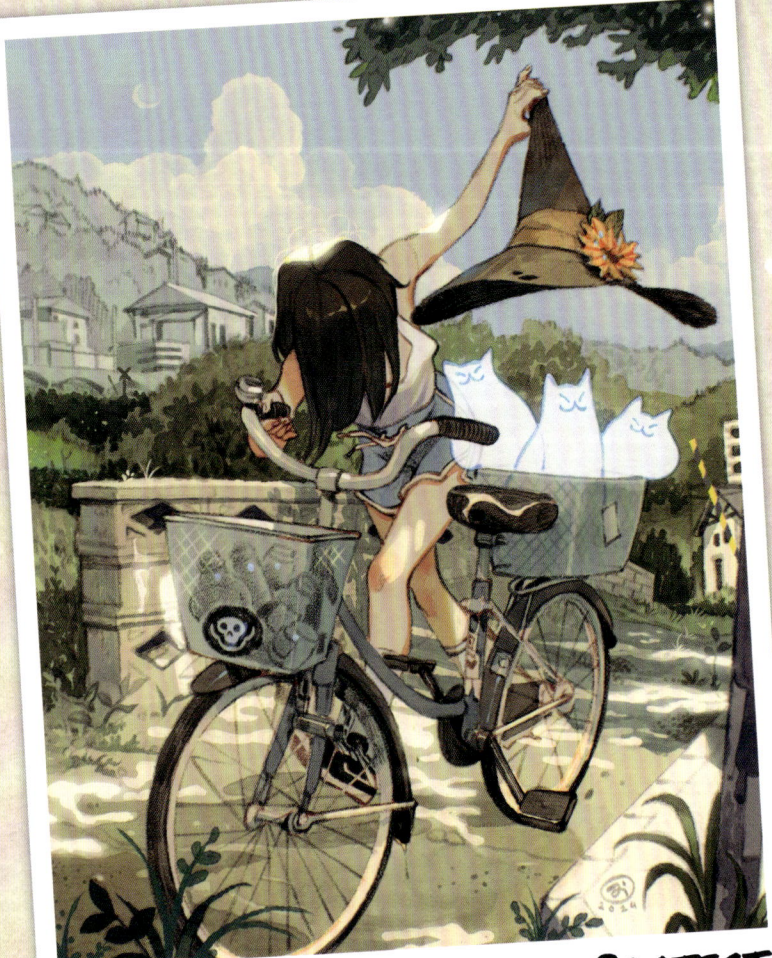

PROTECT

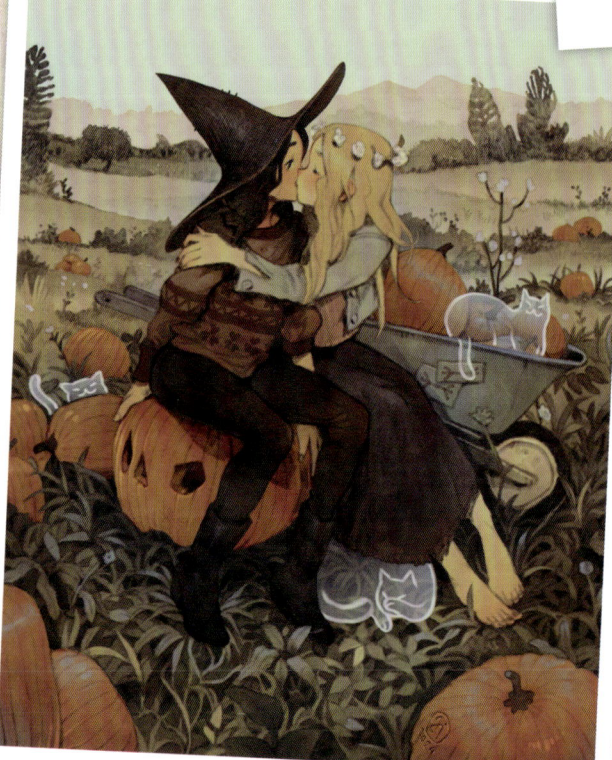

PUMPKIN PATCH

What would you say are the key elements of good character design?

When approaching any illustration, I think the part of the process that has the most impact is the initial design. A character, an illustration, or the page of a comic share their beginning as simple marks on a canvas, a two-dimensional representation made of lines and shapes. How we arrange all these elements is the main difference between a good or bad design. A character is not just about anatomy, details, pose, or how complex they are, it's about how we transform an interesting shape into something that happens to be a character.

I would say drawing the character using a visually powerful set of shapes is the most important aspect of their design. A character doesn't have to be complex or have a fancy haircut to be impressive or memorable, as long as it has a strong silhouette. You can see this in many of the most memorable character designs ever created. We don't love Mickey Mouse because his anatomy is correct or his clothes are well-drawn, but because the overall shape design is iconic, inspired, and perfectly fits the vibe of the world he inhabits.

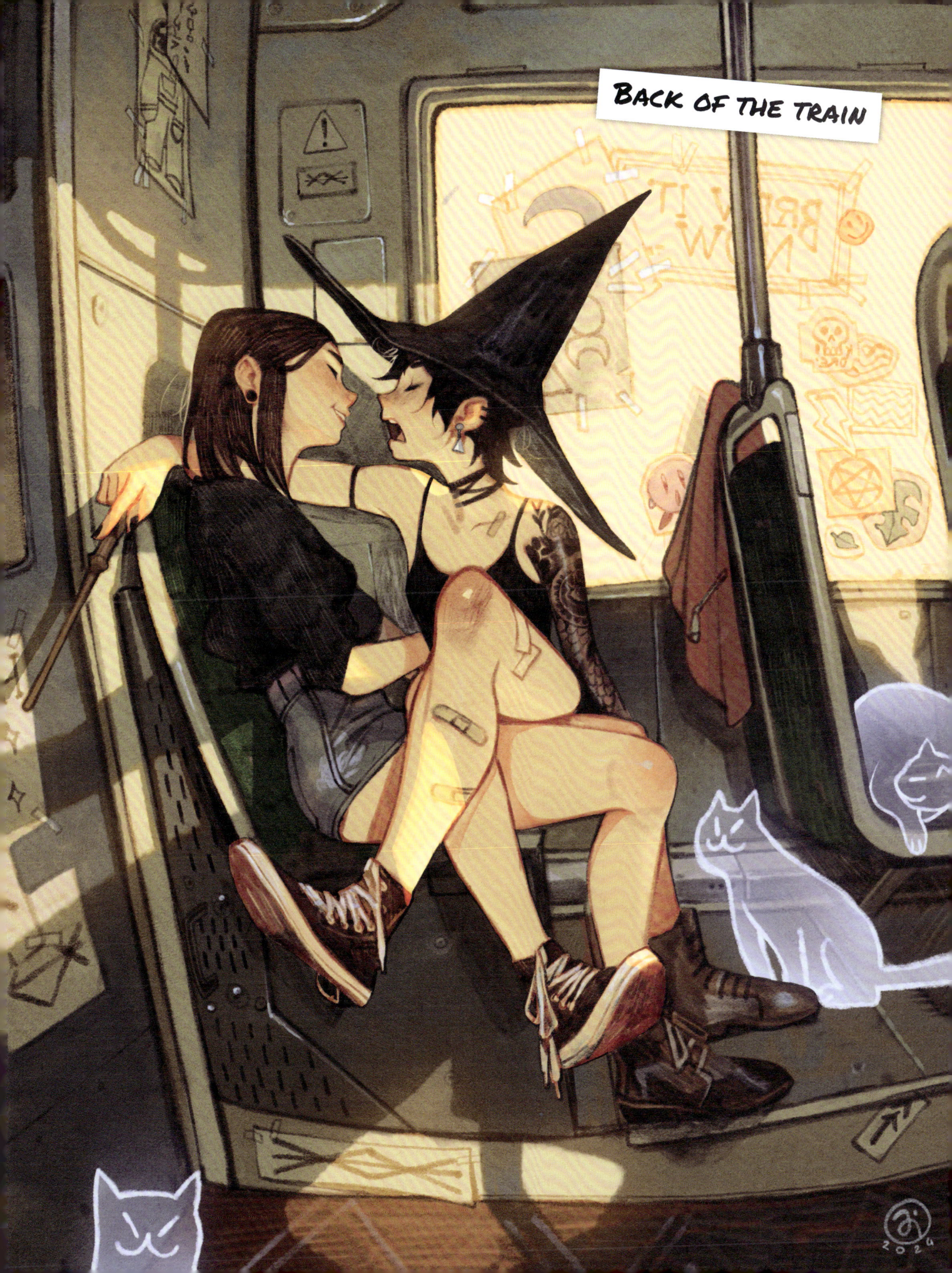

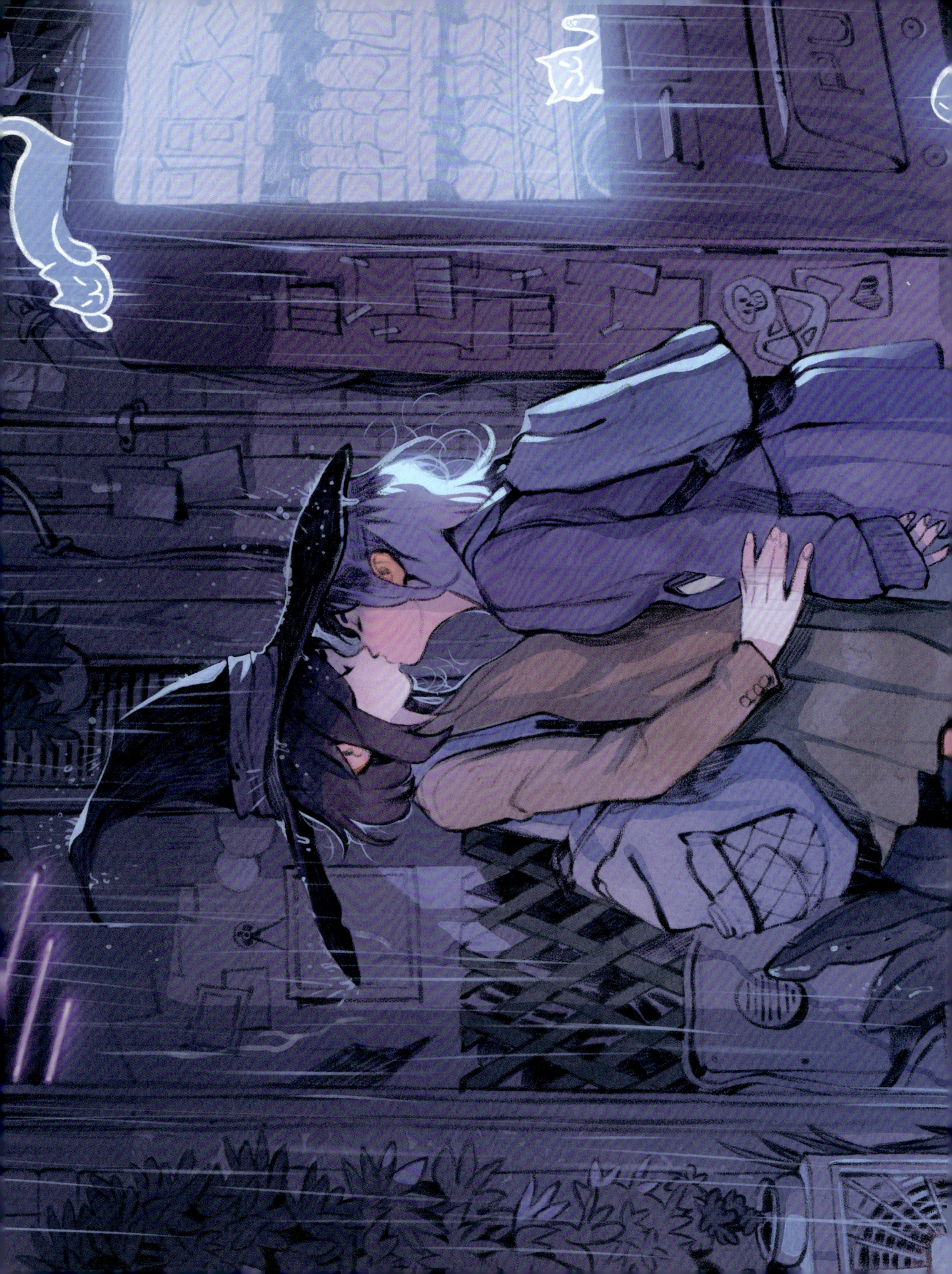

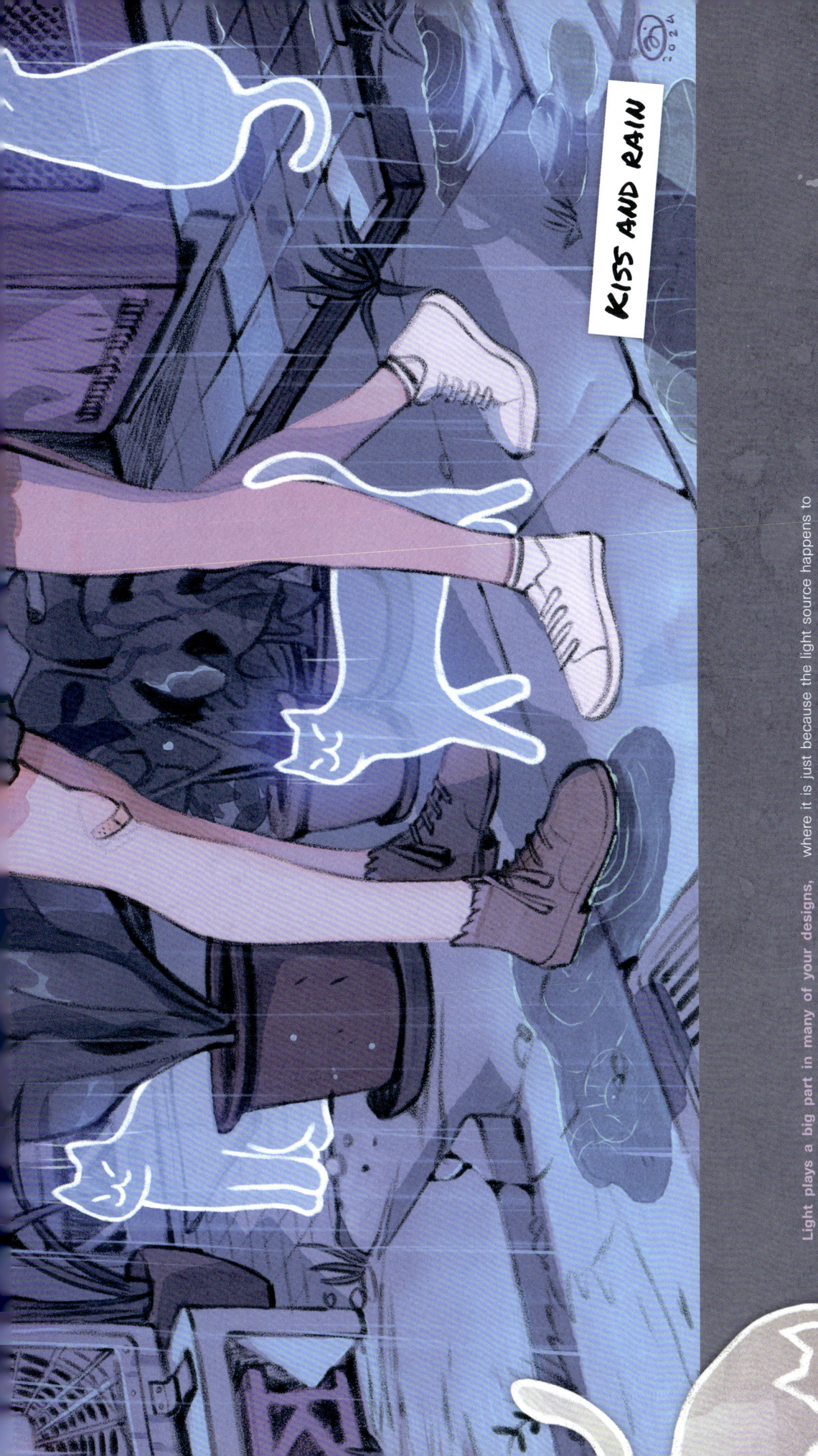

KISS AND RAIN

Light plays a big part in many of your designs, adding depth to your illustrations. Do you have any quick tips for learning to use light effectively?

I love drawing light first – that's the 'secret'. With many of my illustrations I basically work backwards. Often, the first thing that I think through is the colouring, followed by applying shadows, and finally I add highlights. The light I draw is not 'realistic'; by which I mean it's not where it is just because the light source happens to be there, it's very intentional. I make sure that the light is creating a fun shape or contrast in a certain area. Working in this way turns the lighting into another powerful design tool that makes every aspect of the illustration an important, well-thought out element of the overall design.

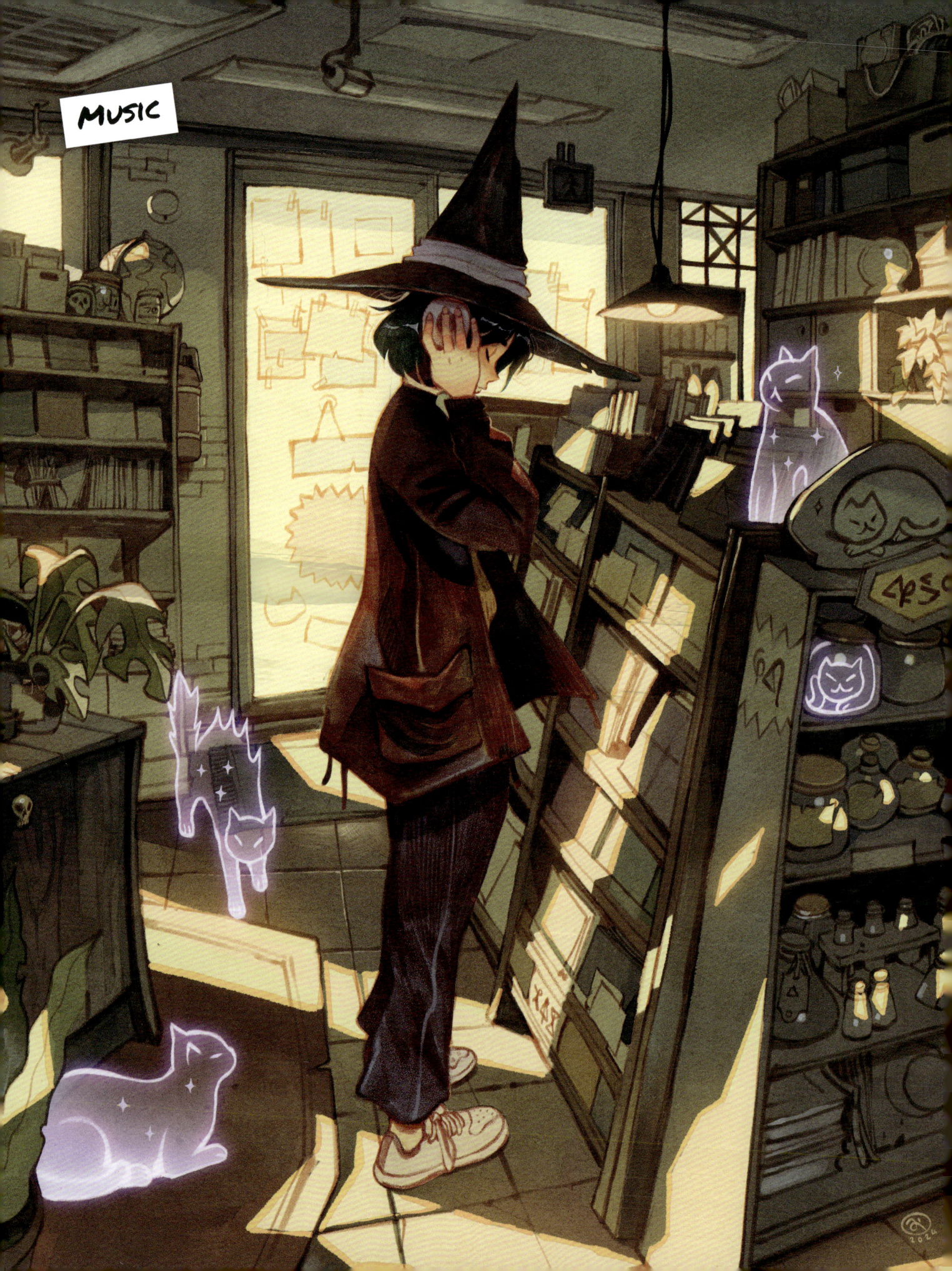

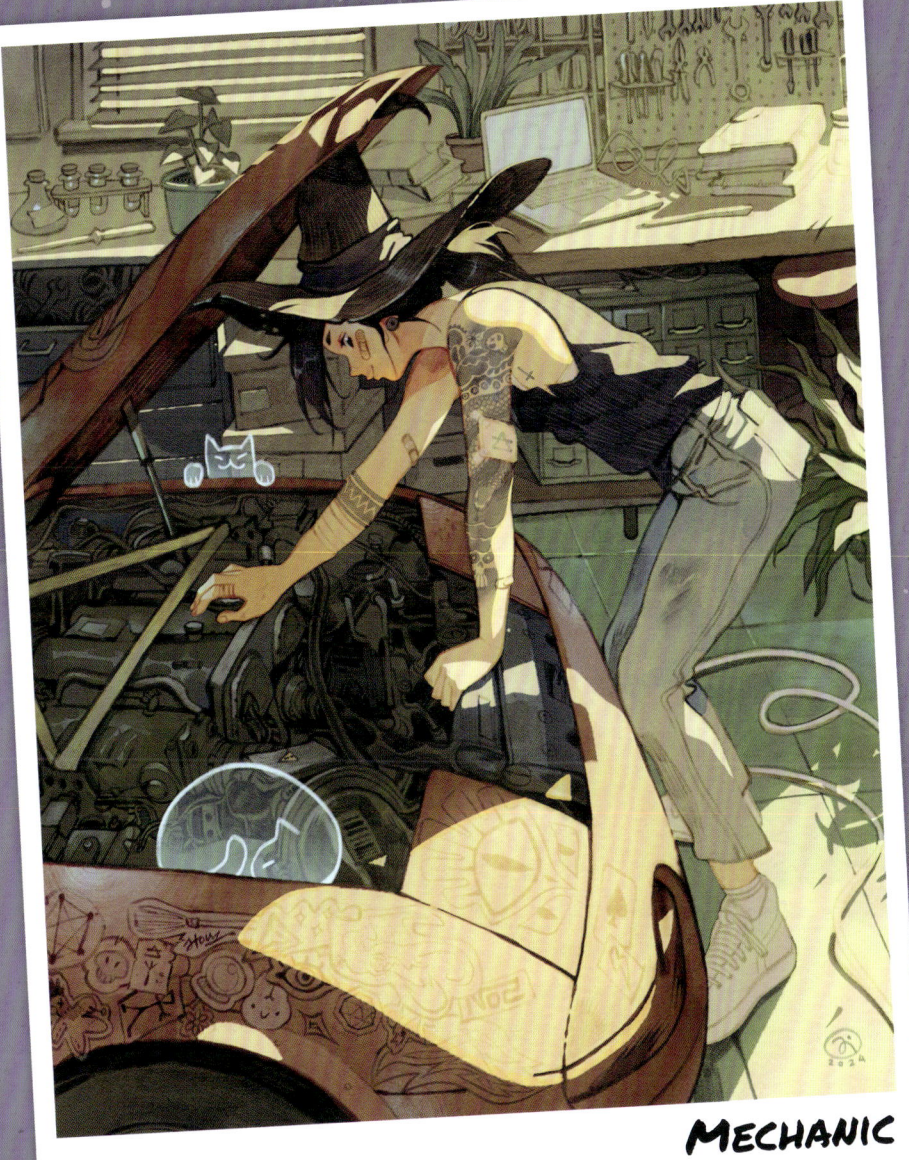

MECHANIC

'THE ONLY THING WE CAN ACTUALLY CONTROL IS THE QUALITY OF OUR WORK AND HOW CONSISTENTLY WE CAN PRODUCE ART'

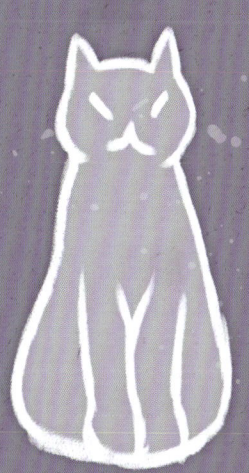

Do you have any advice for artists on how to get noticed online these days?

This is one of the questions I get asked on almost a daily basis, through my DMs and communities. I've spoken to hundreds of artists who ask me why their art isn't popular despite their best efforts, how they can beat the algorithm, and which social-media platform is the best for growth. I have always given the same answer – and unfortunately it isn't often what artists (and especially beginners) want to hear. The answer is: keep drawing and posting online. We could spend a lifetime trying to figure out the optimum posts per week, what style of content works best, what hashtags to use, and so on, but the reality is that there isn't a single technique that will work for everyone. The only thing we can actually control is the quality of our work and how consistently we can produce art. Wasting energy on something other than drawing, especially in the initial stages of a career, can be detrimental. If your gallery of work is powerful and unique then you increase the chance that people will be interested in what you produce. Likewise, when your work is refined enough that it can appeal to a large audience, then people will start to take notice – until then it will be hard to grow significantly, no matter how hard you try to work the system.

There is of course one other factor at play: luck. It definitely plays a part, but if we get a break and one of our pieces is seen by a massive audience, then we still need a gallery of stunning work to back up our fateful moment. If we consistently create quality work we are more likely to retain any audience we find, no matter how they come to our art, and gradually our popularity will grow.

How do you feel your art has evolved over time? Is it still evolving?

I think the biggest evolution is with my drawing. When I started, my approach was boring, clumsy, and generic. I played by the rules, which made me scared of many aspects of the art-making process. I went through a phase of drawing perspective grids for everything, building characters with circles and squares as various art books suggested. Slowly, I grew less afraid to push and pull lines, shapes, and designs. My only goal became to create great artwork and not worry about whether it was 'correct' or realistic.

My style continues to evolve, but with each new illustration the differences are harder to spot. There is a big leap from my early work to where I am now, but the curve of improvement has definitely flattened more recently. Evolving from piece to piece doesn't have to come at the expense of identity, and that's why good, sustainable growth happens gradually, over time.

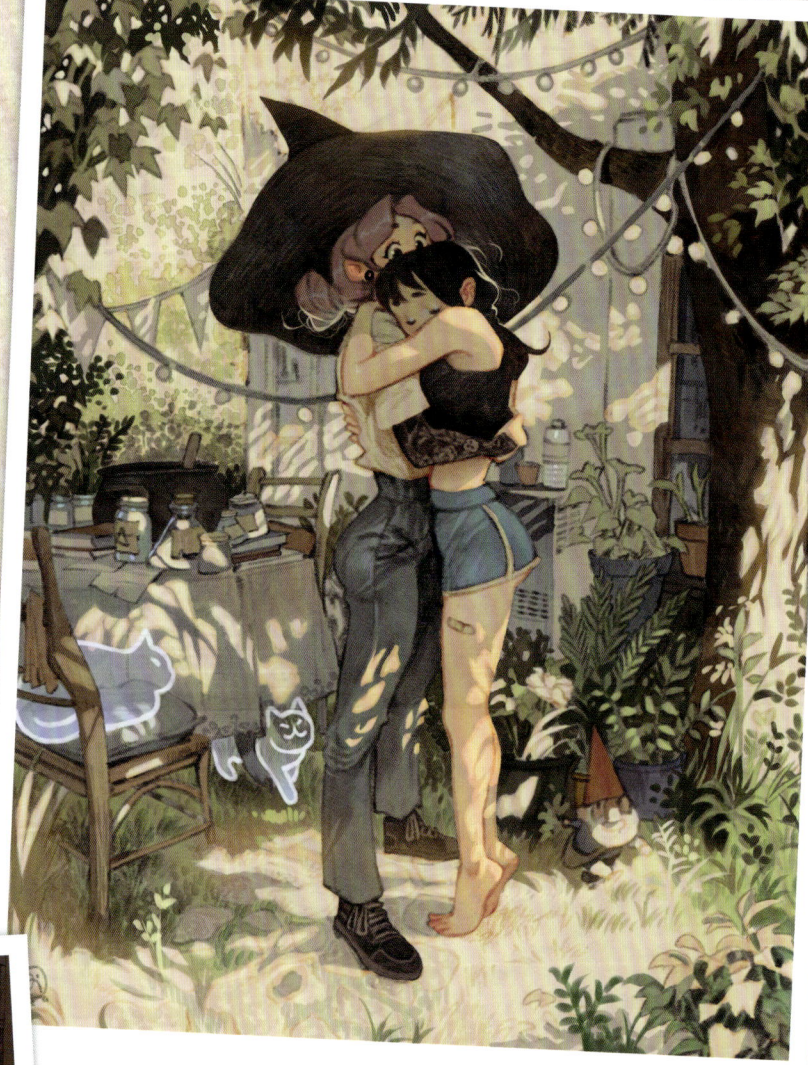

THANK YOU

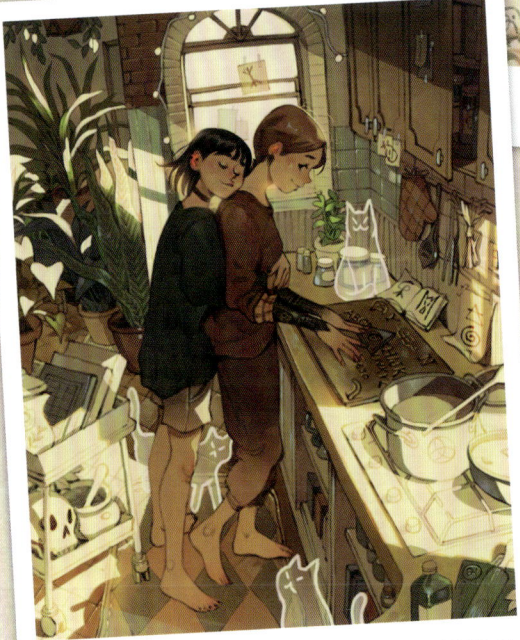

SUNDAY MORNING

Thank you for speaking to us Simone! Are there any upcoming projects we should look out for?

I'm currently working on several projects like my comic *Ghost Cats and Tea* that I've been developing for quite some time with the publisher Dupuis, and an art class that is going to be released soon on Coloso. I'm looking forward to seeing these collaborations come to life. I also had the honour to create the key art for *Witchbrook*, a video game developed by Chucklefish – I had a lot of fun working on this project so I'm looking forward to more chances to work on projects like this in the future.

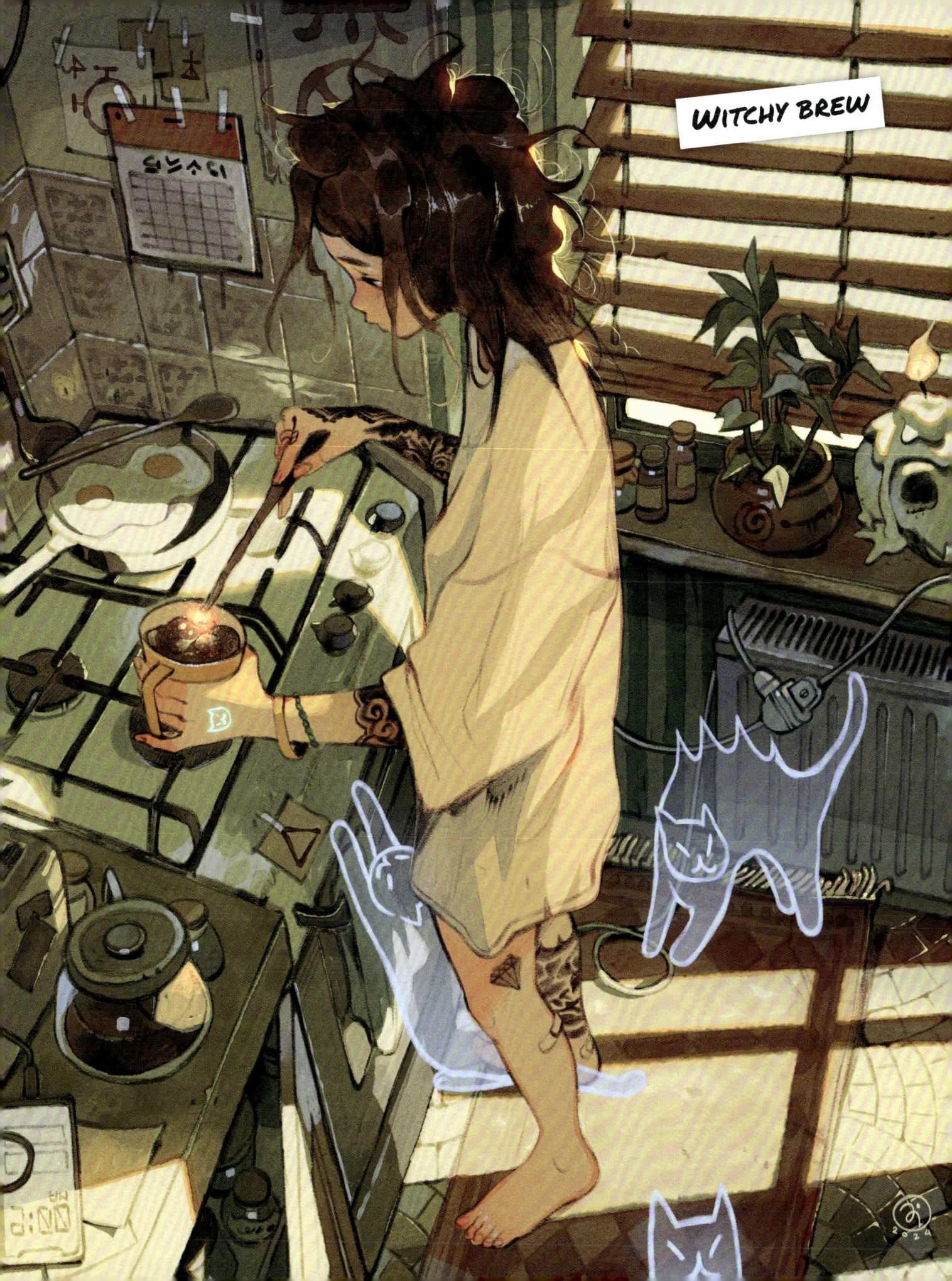

WITCHY BREW

CRAFTING THE COVER

In this tutorial I'll show you the key points that led me to create the illustration used for the cover of this issue of CDQ. I'm hopefully going to give you an idea of how to approach a complex scenario for something as challenging as a magazine cover. Working digitally, I'll show you what a typical sketch looks like and how to proceed from there, through the line art, colouring, and final touches. A cover is the first glimpse of a magazine so it's important for it to be as striking and impactful as possible, while still feeling personal and unique.

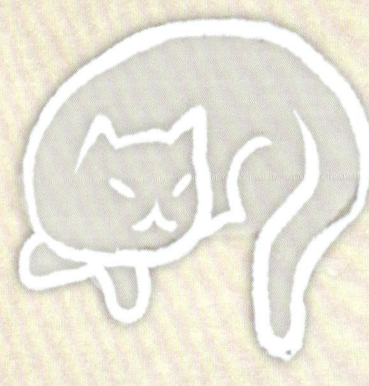

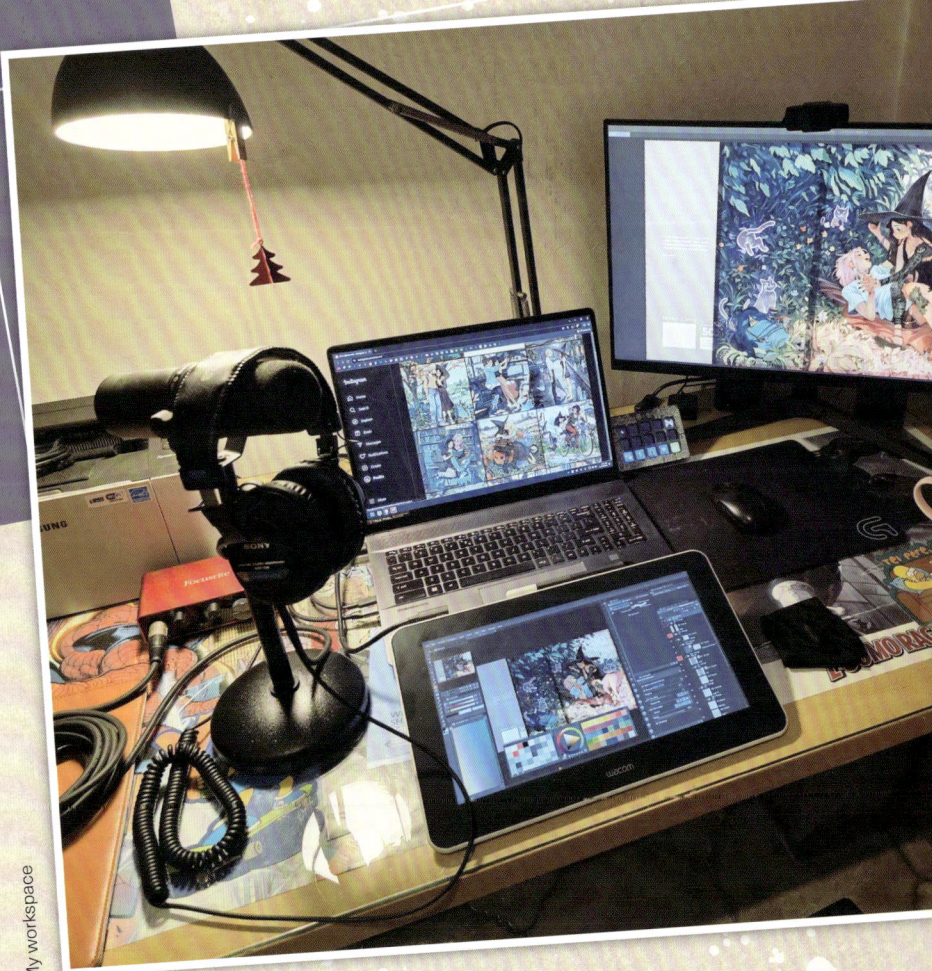

My workspace

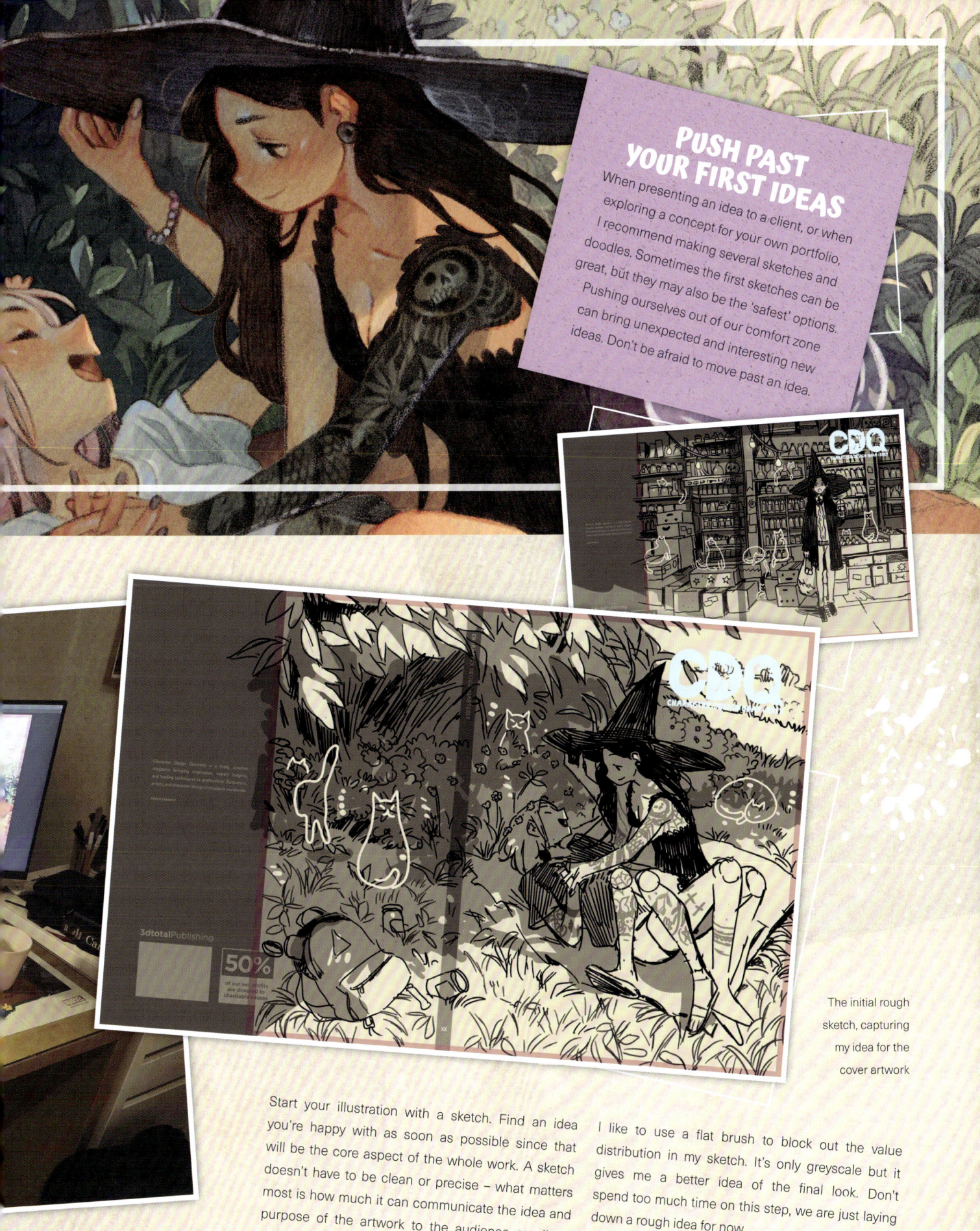

The initial rough sketch, capturing my idea for the cover artwork

Start your illustration with a sketch. Find an idea you're happy with as soon as possible since that will be the core aspect of the whole work. A sketch doesn't have to be clean or precise – what matters most is how much it can communicate the idea and purpose of the artwork to the audience or client.

I like to use a flat brush to block out the value distribution in my sketch. It's only greyscale but it gives me a better idea of the final look. Don't spend too much time on this step, we are just laying down a rough idea for now.

Once everyone is happy with the sketch, cleaning it up is no simple task. The goal from this point on is to move towards the final illustration without losing that spark we infused in the initial sketch. Every line has to contribute to a simplified, cleaner version of the sketch, while adding something special. Work on subtracting scribbles and unnecessary elements in favour of lines that sit just right, showing a lot with little. Remember to look at the overall picture from time to time, to make sure that the line weight is balanced across the canvas.

Refining the sketch with clean line art

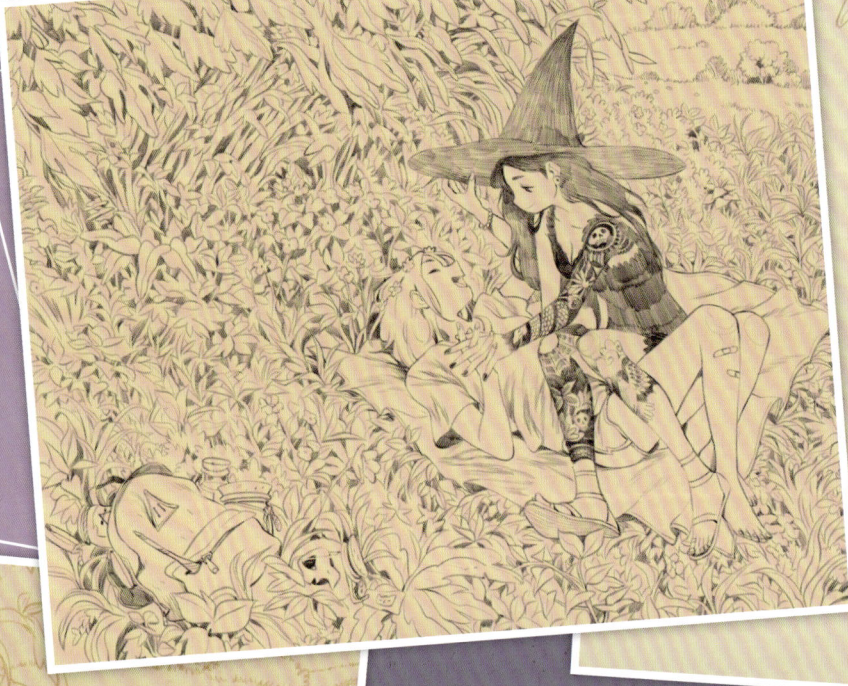

If colouring is one of the most technical parts of the process, selecting and masking areas based on the main subjects is the peak of it. Select the main elements (in this case the two witches), and create a mask out of them. This will make the colouring stage less daunting. Using folders within Clip Studio Paint to group the layers that apply to each mask will allow us to fill each section with colours and brushstrokes, constraining everything to the section within the mask. I create three main folders, one with the mask of the characters, one for the background below the characters, and one on the top for any element that will incorporate the entire artwork.

Masking the characters separates them from the background

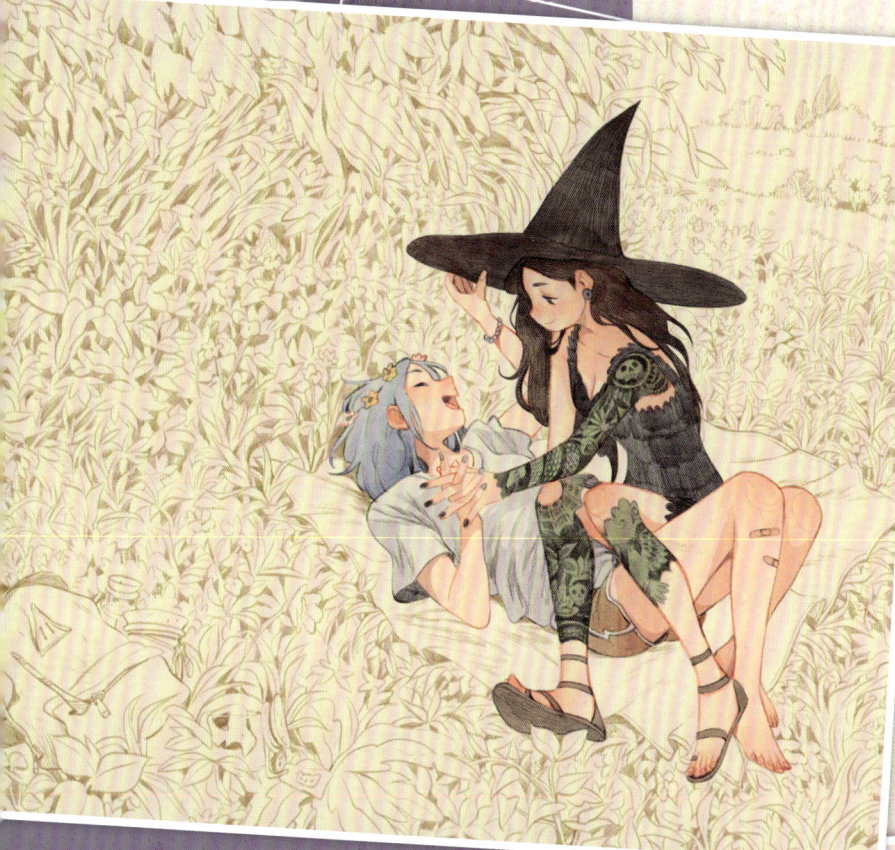

Start colouring the characters by choosing hues you think work best, but also making sure that the overall palette stays within a usable range. Picking random colours across the whole spectrum can work on a small illustration, but on a larger canvas it's hard to keep them all in harmony. Since there's a lot of greens and blues in this picture, adding pure reds, purples, or yellows could really confuse the viewer's attention. This can be used to our advantage in small quantities, but mustn't be overdone.

Adding the base colours of the characters to establish the overall palette of the illustration

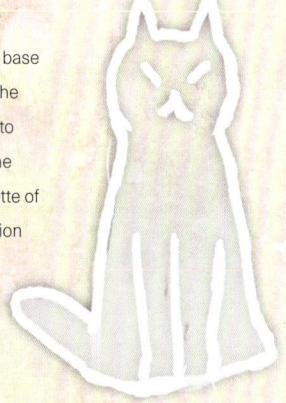

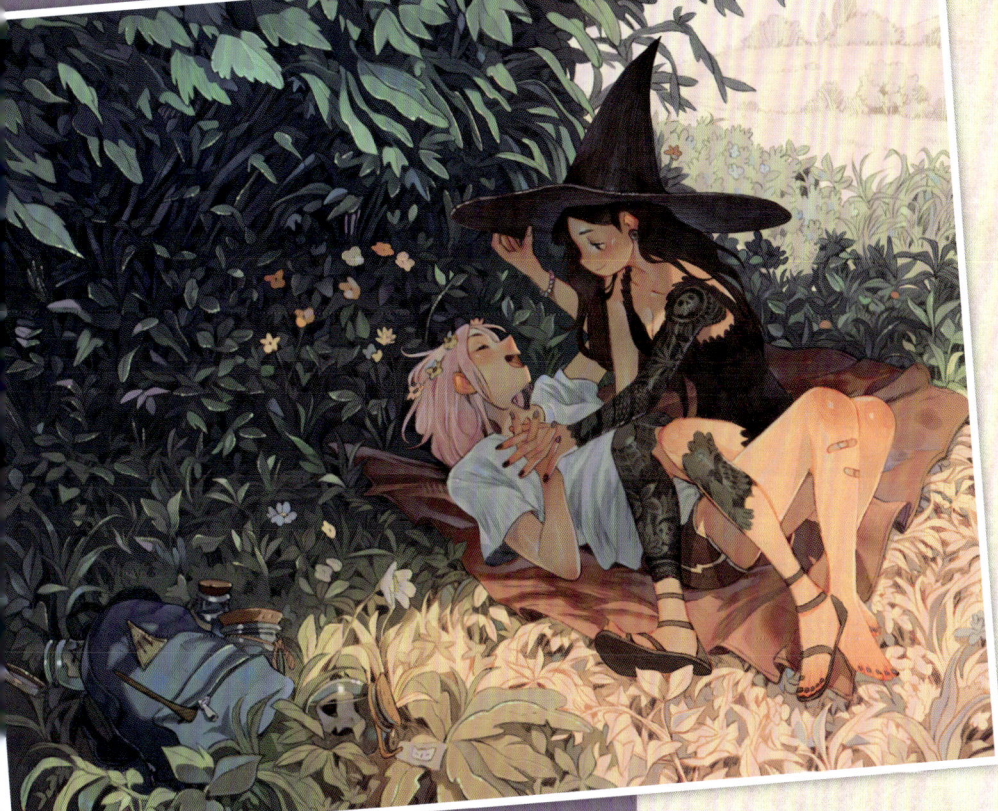

For most artists, the rendering step is probably the most time-consuming. There's infinite ways to colour artwork – in this case I followed an approach that went from flats, to highlights and shadows, and finally adding details and colour variations to add more vibrancy to the piece. On large works, it's tempting to use patterned and textured brushes as a shortcut, however I would discourage this, unless there's a very good reason for using them. Paying attention to details and having patience will always pay off in the end.

Rendering on two separate layers, one for the characters and one for the background

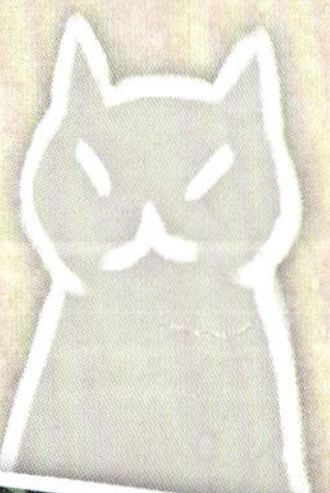

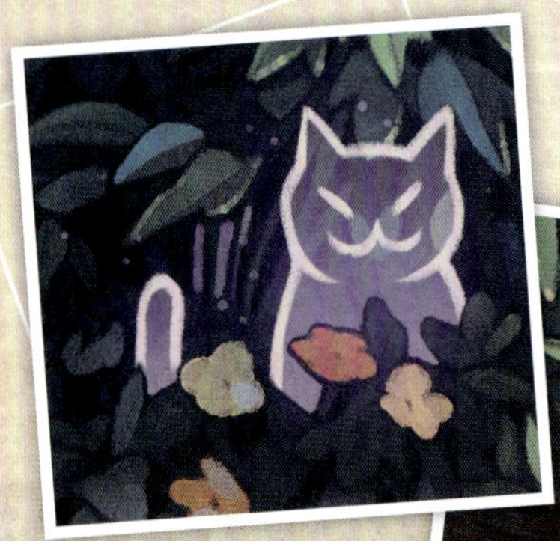

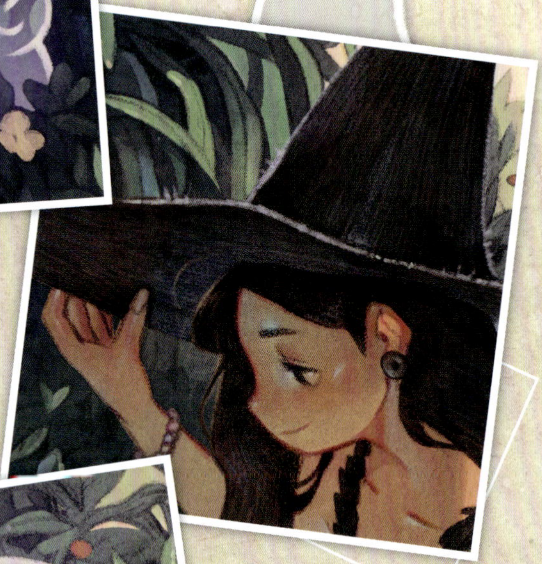

Adding final touches,
including rim light
on the characters
and ghost cats

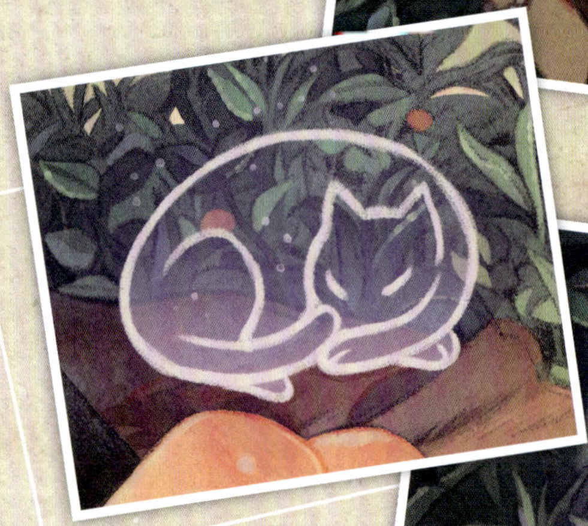

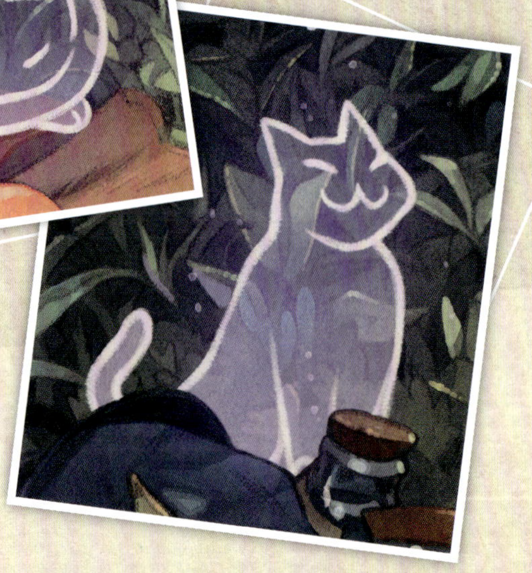

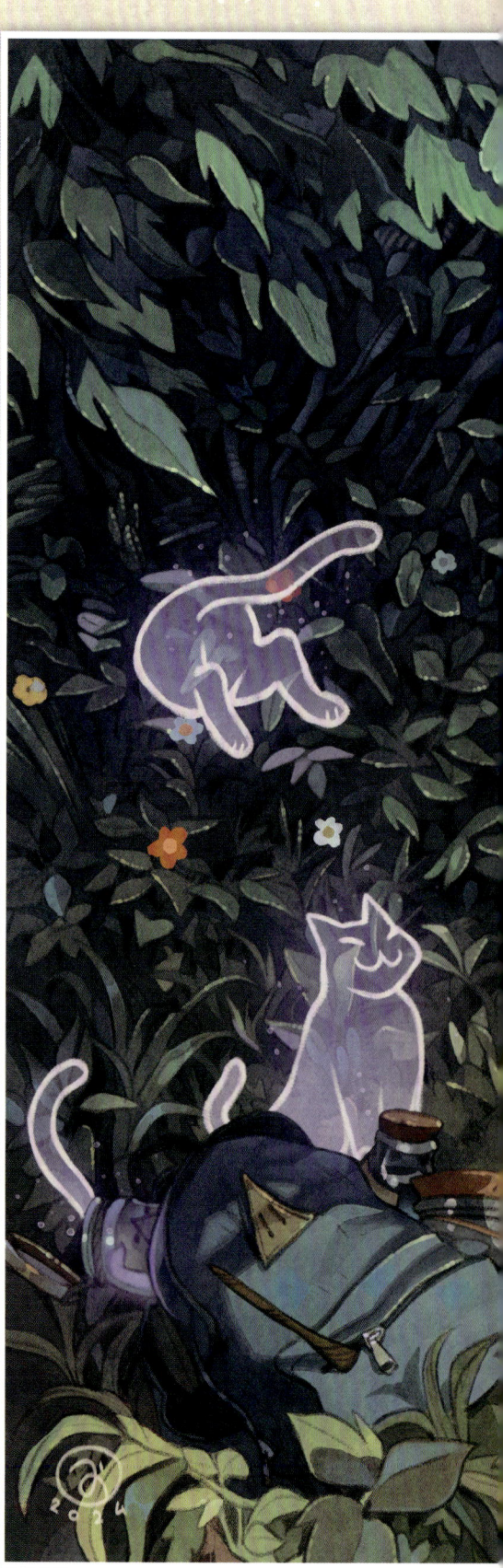

The final part of the process can make or break the illustration really quickly. With the render stage complete, we're now going to add fun highlights – in this case, ghost cats and sparkles. It can be tempting to fill the whole picture with colourful eye candy and glowing gradients, and that's exactly why we need to proceed with the utmost care and attention. Add the effects to a new layer or make a copy of the layer we're going to mess with. The keyword here is subtlety – we want to bring our artwork to life, rather than cover up mistakes or a boring undercolour. Keep switching between the artwork and the initial sketch to make sure that the energy has been retained and we didn't lose our direction along the way. And with that, the illustration is finished!

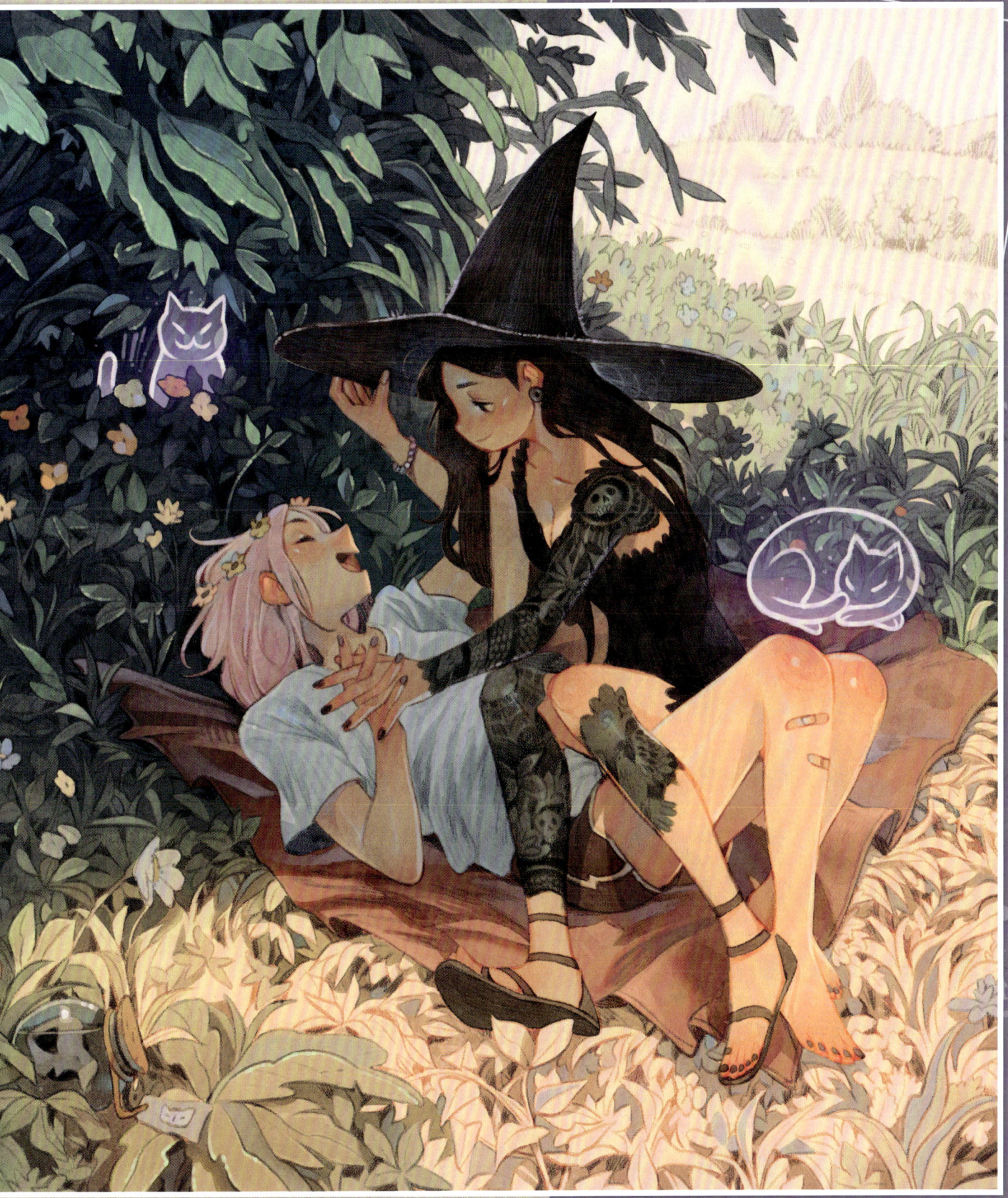

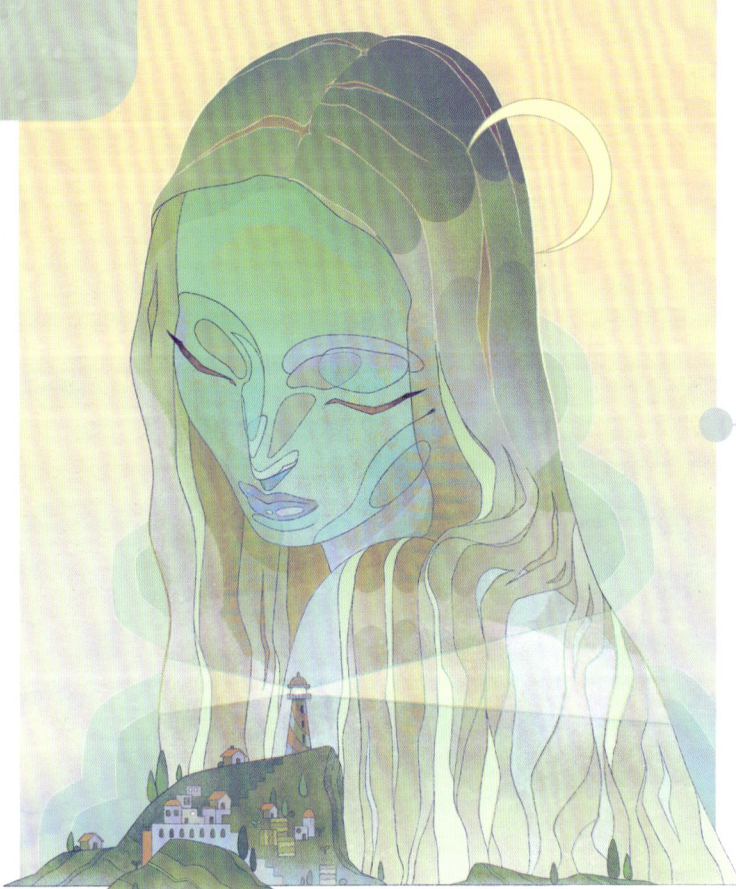

Don't be afraid to experiment with trying out different textured digital brushes. I like to experiment by filling the page with a texture, clipping it to the piece, and trying out different blending modes to create a subtle finish. Overlay and Multiply are tried and true options, but I find Luminosity and Pin Light to be great when using unusual textures, too.

HOW I STYLIZE

LARA GEORGIA CARSON

Stylization is something that comes naturally and eventually becomes a pretty intuitive process, but there are ways to guide you into finding what's important to you. Personally, colour and texture have always held the most interest to me – it's these aspects I experiment with the most, and so my style has been defined by my use of each of them. I actively try to personify emotions in my work, and even though I've landed on using colour in a way that suits me, style is in constant flux as we learn and absorb new techniques. Hopefully some of these tips will help uncover ways to push your style in your next pieces.

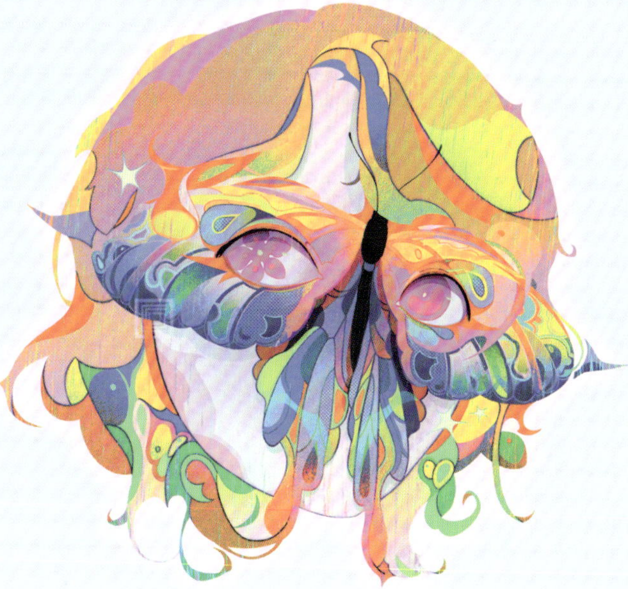

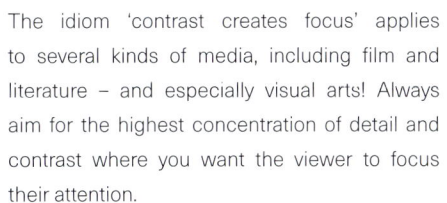

The idiom 'contrast creates focus' applies to several kinds of media, including film and literature – and especially visual arts! Always aim for the highest concentration of detail and contrast where you want the viewer to focus their attention.

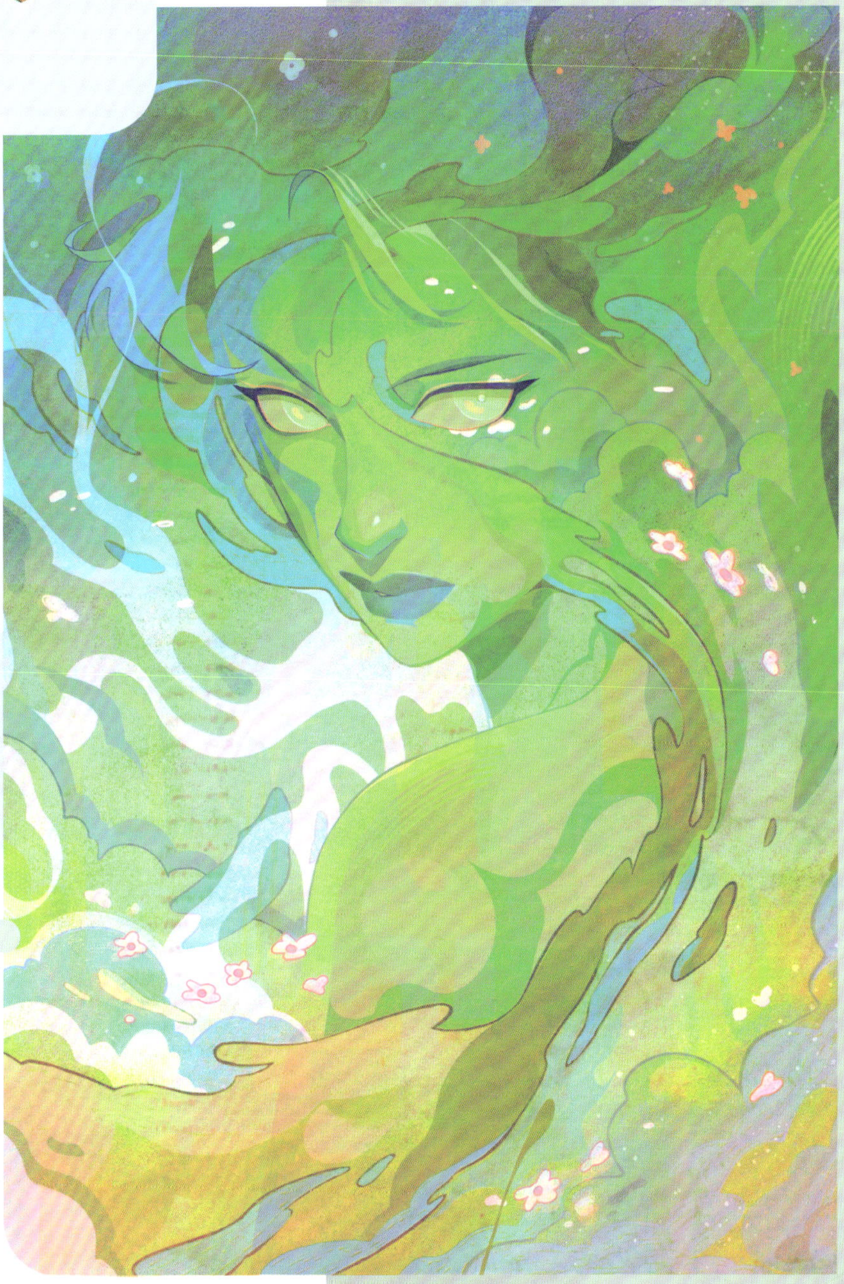

If the contrast isn't coming from the colour choices, then it should come from texture and level of detail. This piece is predominantly hues of green – by using a higher concentration of details I can still guide the viewer's eye to focus on the face area.

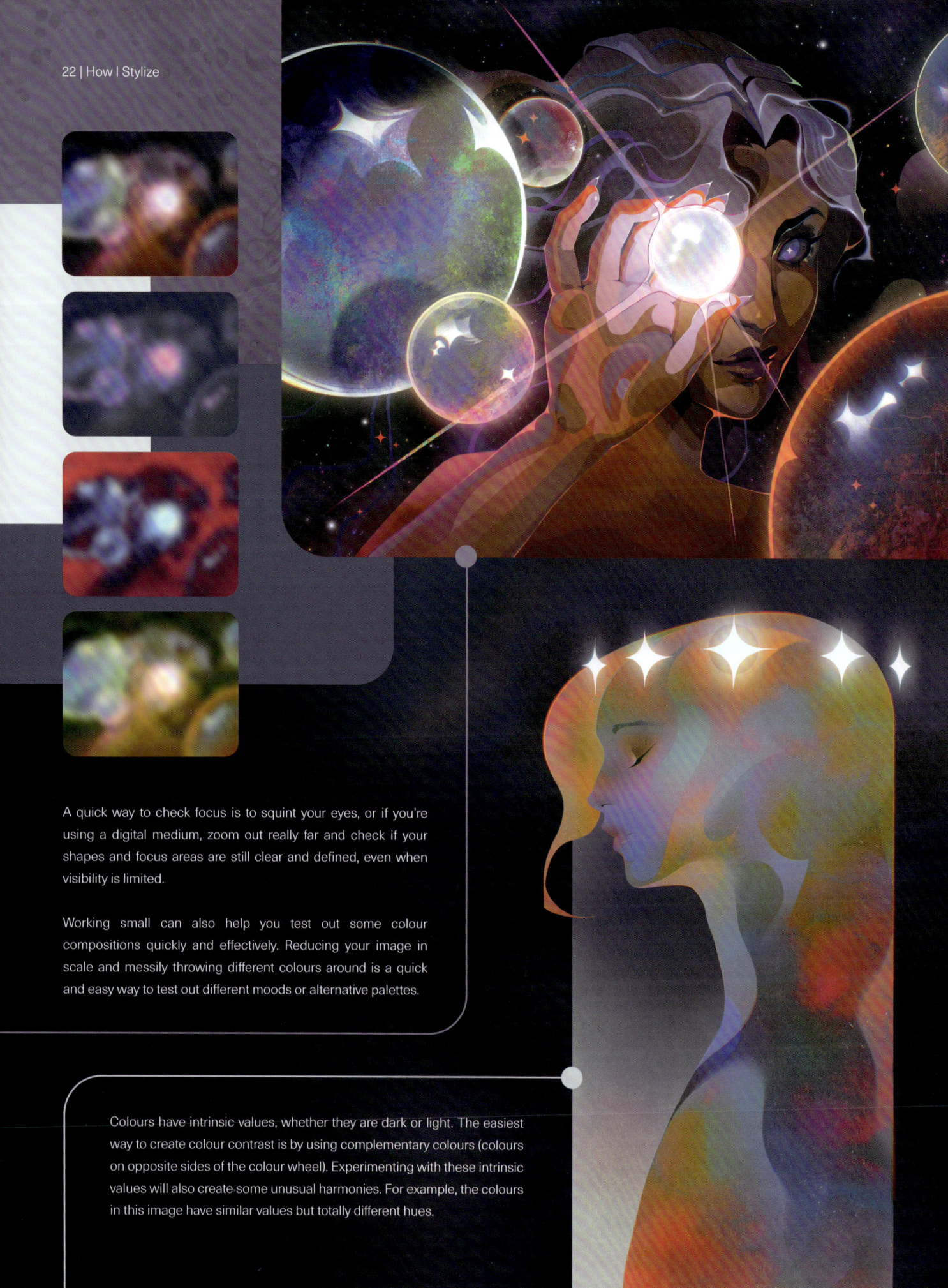

A quick way to check focus is to squint your eyes, or if you're using a digital medium, zoom out really far and check if your shapes and focus areas are still clear and defined, even when visibility is limited.

Working small can also help you test out some colour compositions quickly and effectively. Reducing your image in scale and messily throwing different colours around is a quick and easy way to test out different moods or alternative palettes.

Colours have intrinsic values, whether they are dark or light. The easiest way to create colour contrast is by using complementary colours (colours on opposite sides of the colour wheel). Experimenting with these intrinsic values will also create some unusual harmonies. For example, the colours in this image have similar values but totally different hues.

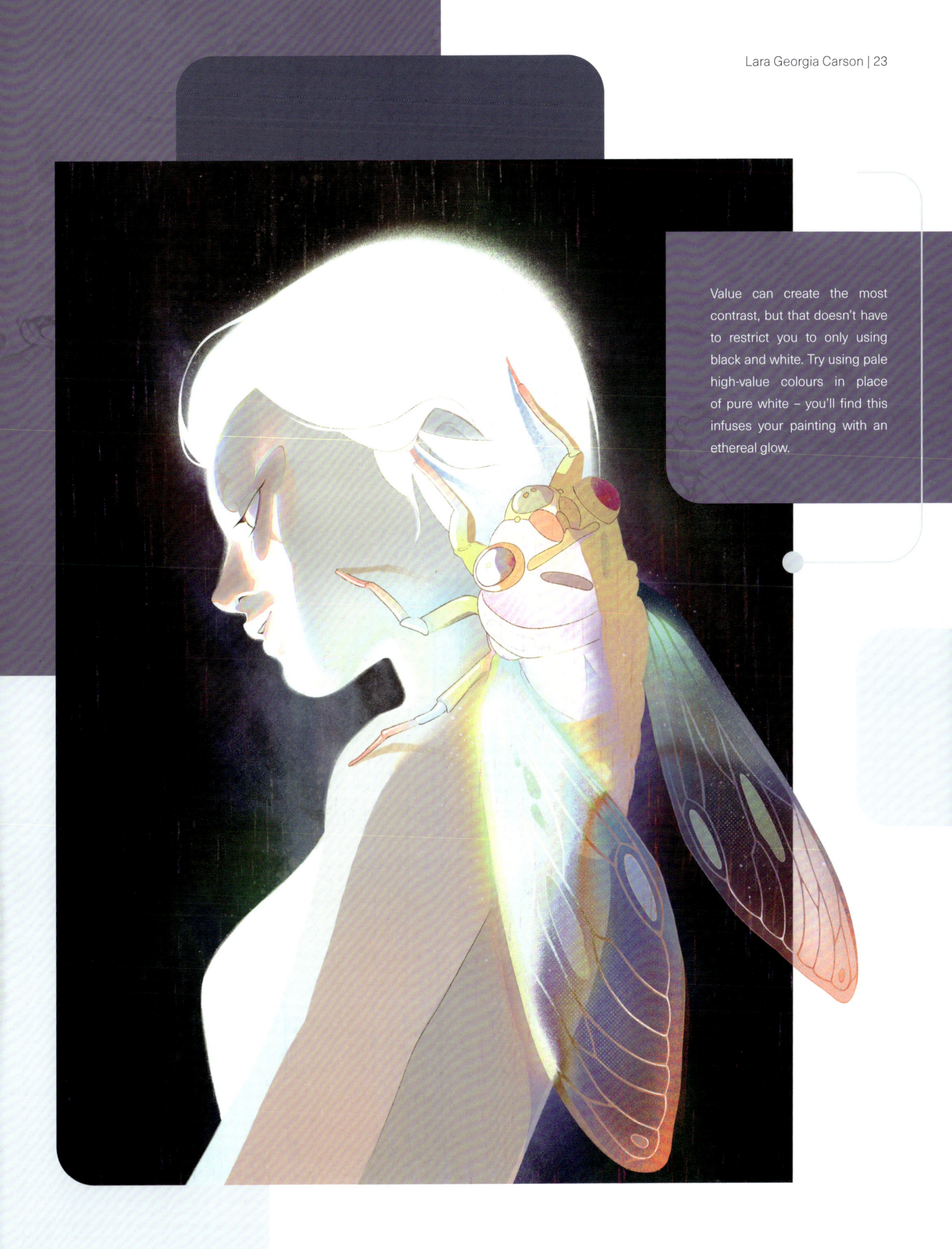

Value can create the most contrast, but that doesn't have to restrict you to only using black and white. Try using pale high-value colours in place of pure white – you'll find this infuses your painting with an ethereal glow.

THE AMAZING
MERLIN

Scott Epstein

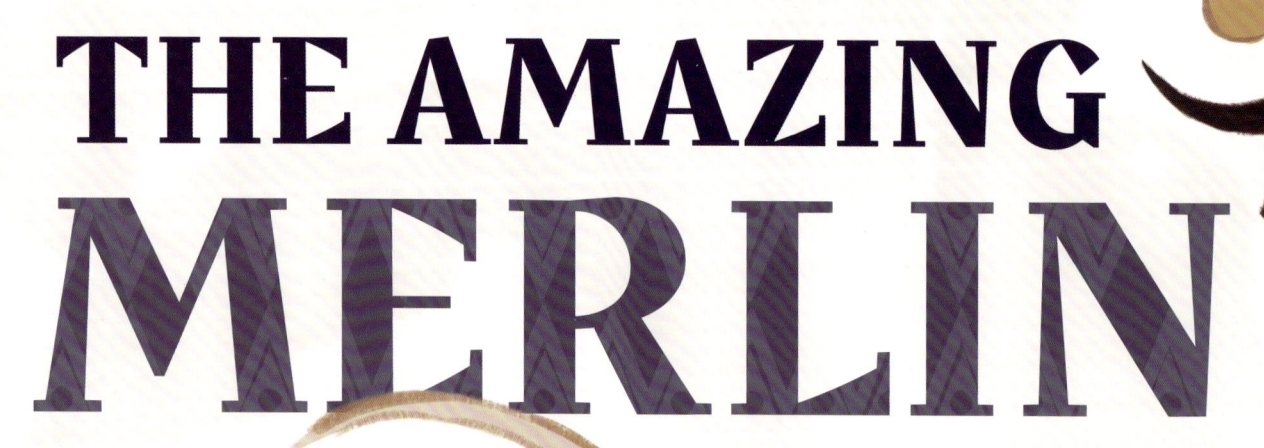

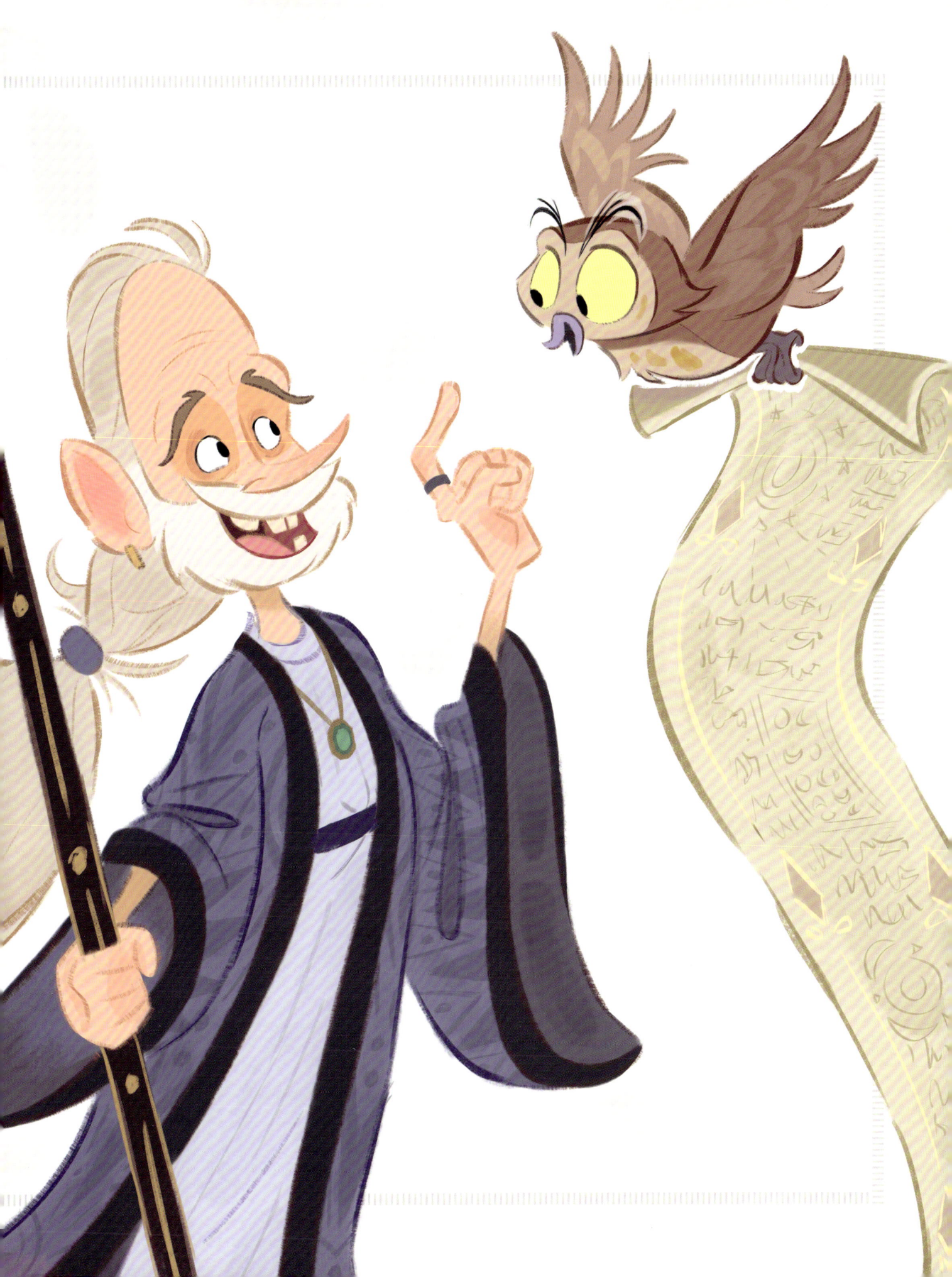

This tutorial will take you step-by step through the process of designing the wizard Merlin, one of my favourite characters in literature. I have a great love of fantasy and have always wanted to tackle this iconic character. We'll discuss different ways of 'finding'

his design, utilizing research, the 'block-in' method, and, above all, story-informed design choices. Though I am primarily working digitally, you can use any medium to achieve these designs.

While it may seem incredibly obvious to say, the first question that needs answering when designing a character is *who are they?* Before I think too much about what they look like and what they wear, I need to understand who they are both in the story and in relation to the characters around them. *What are the characters' goals? Their wants? Do they achieve them in the story? What is their place in society? Are they at peace with their lot in life? Do they perhaps see themselves one way, but society sees them another?* These questions will inform what a character looks like, what they wear, and how they act, so it's our job as designers to answer these questions before we start drawing.

As with many mythologized characters there's a lot of varying lore when it comes to Merlin. Versions of him include a human who went mad with power, an innocent baby born with unique gifts, a demon who rose from the depths of the earth, and so many more.

For this version I chose to design Merlin as a good-hearted, several-hundred-year-old wizard who's a bit zany and misunderstood by society, and so finds comfort in being a recluse. I imagine he'd spend many hours toiling away in his study, murmuring to himself (and his owl familiar, Archimedes) while reading ancient texts and practising magic. I picked the period of his life where he orchestrates the birth of the soon-to-be 'once and future king', Arthur. While I imagined in his early life his lifestyle was more 'of the earth', at this point he has acclimated to society and, though viewed as odd, is respected in the King's court. This affects his appearance, his costuming, and how he acts.

| Merlin! |

I begin by musing on personality traits and posing questions about the character to myself

- Zany, inquisitive
- wise, knowlegeable
- a bit of a recluse, he entertains himself through research and practicing magic
- has an owl familiar
- Want to design Merlin during the time of King Arthur's birth

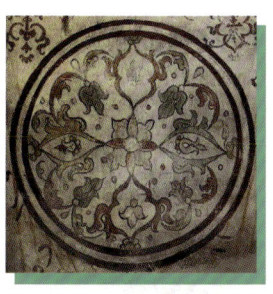
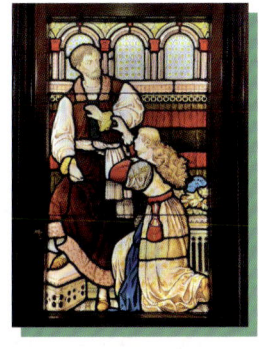
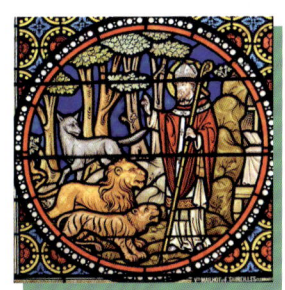

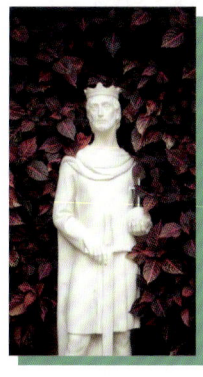
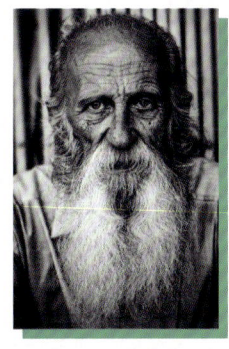
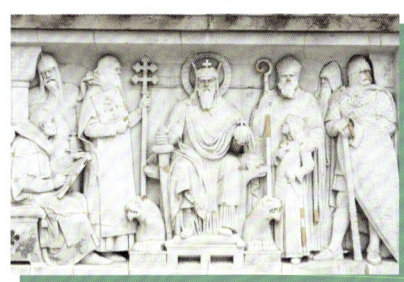

A small sample of the references I found; don't rush this step, you can find wonderful and inspiring resources if you do more than just a cursory search

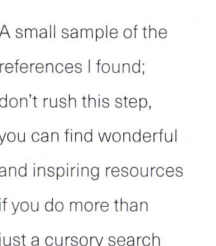
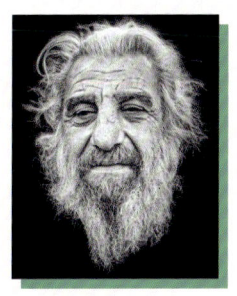
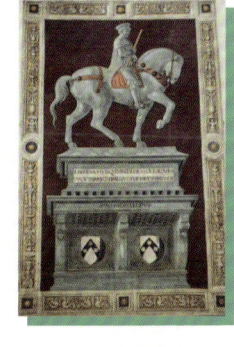
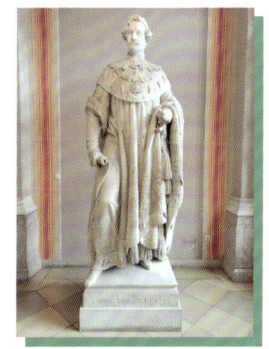

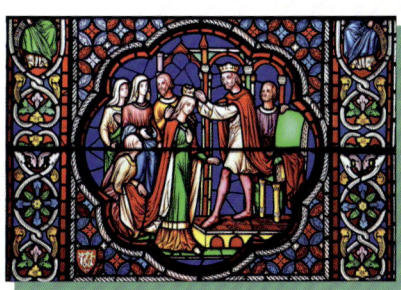
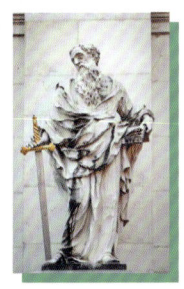
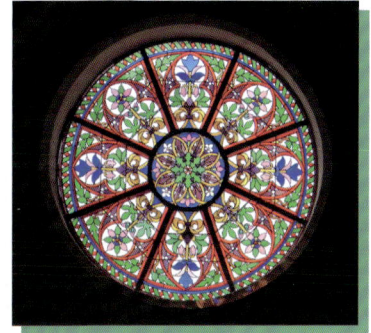

Once I've begun to understand who my character is, I then start the research process. I collect a wide range of resources and try to broaden my search outside of people, costumes, and items associated with the character. I try to find abstract or seemingly unrelated paintings and images that inspire feelings and shapes that evoke qualities of the character.

When it comes to designing period pieces, especially for the Middle Ages, resources can be tough to find. I take a lot of inspiration from sculptures, illuminated manuscripts, stained-glass windows, and paintings that were done either during the period, or more likely, created after the period as a way to preserve the information. There are times when it's important to be completely accurate to the period, but here I'm designing a fantasy world – it's okay to take some liberties in the name of fantasy and fun.

Once I have a good sense of my character and have distilled my research down to the pieces that most inspire me, it's time to start designing. I start with some head designs, getting a sense of the shapes and attributes I can use to embody my character, without having to worry about all the fuss of designing him in full. Plus, faces are my favourite things to draw, so I'll take any excuse to create a few!

The most important thing at this stage is to work loosely. We'll create millions of drawings to try to nail down the look of a character – well, okay, maybe not millions, but a *lot*. If I try to make every drawing beautiful and perfect I'll run out of time. So, it's important to find ways to create many iterations quickly, while showing a wide variety of shapes and features. To do this I use the block-in method.

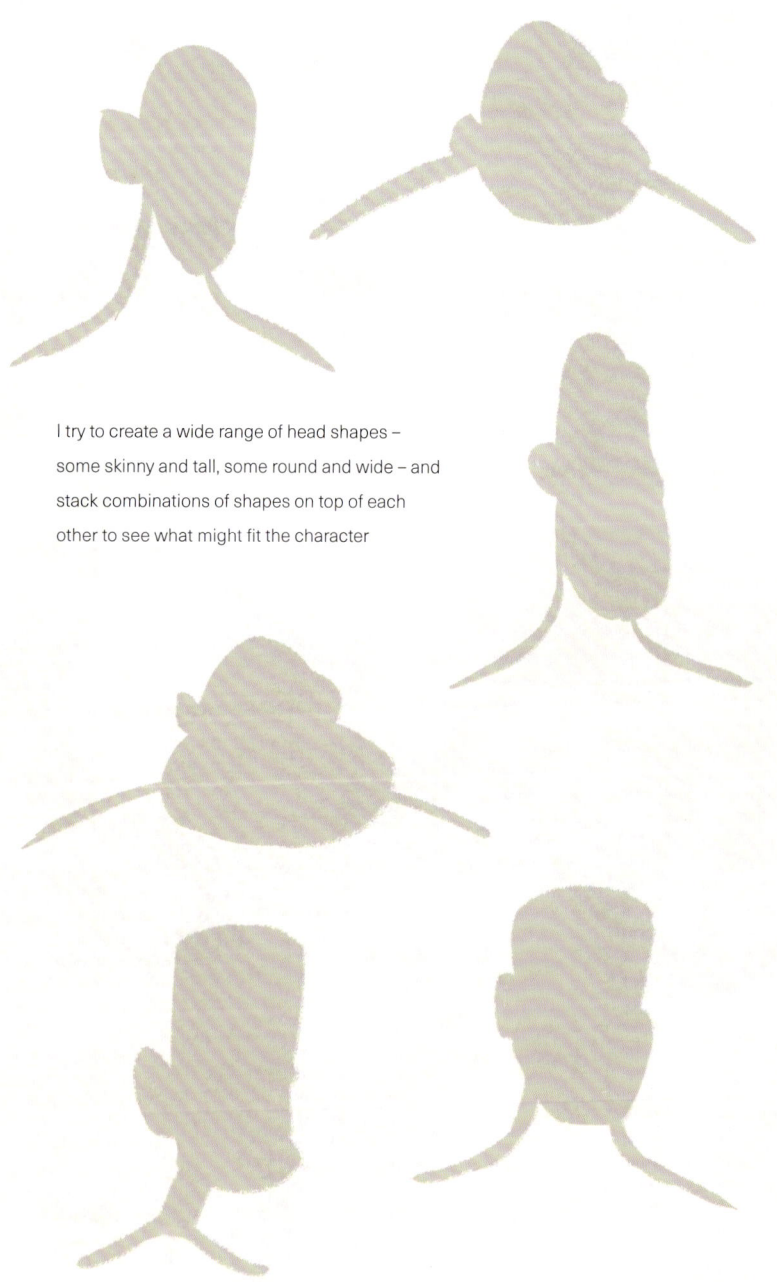

I try to create a wide range of head shapes – some skinny and tall, some round and wide – and stack combinations of shapes on top of each other to see what might fit the character

WHAT IS THE BLOCK-IN METHOD?

I'm so glad you asked! For whatever reason my brain can 'see' form better when I can wrap my imaginary construction lines around an existing shape, as opposed to drawing a bunch of lines to create a shape from scratch. So, while I could start with line drawings, I prefer the block-in method. I start by imagining heads as oddly shaped potatoes. I then lay down a blob of paint (or pixels) and 'sculpt' a head shape to be exactly what I want through painting and erasing. I find this a faster and more comprehensive process for my brain to follow than drawing a bunch of searching lines. However, the underlying thought process for the block-in method and drawing with lines is the same – in both I am constantly thinking about the form of the object.

Once I've laid in my base shapes, I start to indicate form. I draw two lines that wrap around the head shape: a vertical line to indicate my centre guideline and a horizontal line to indicate the base of the eyes. I then add small notch marks wrapping around the form to indicate the base of the nose and the centre of the mouth. Drawing these landmarks allows me to make changes easily and quickly at this stage. I can start to 'see' if the proportions are working the way I'd like them to, and if they aren't I can change it up quickly by adjusting the eye lines, the distance between the eyes, and the notch marks for the nose and mouth.

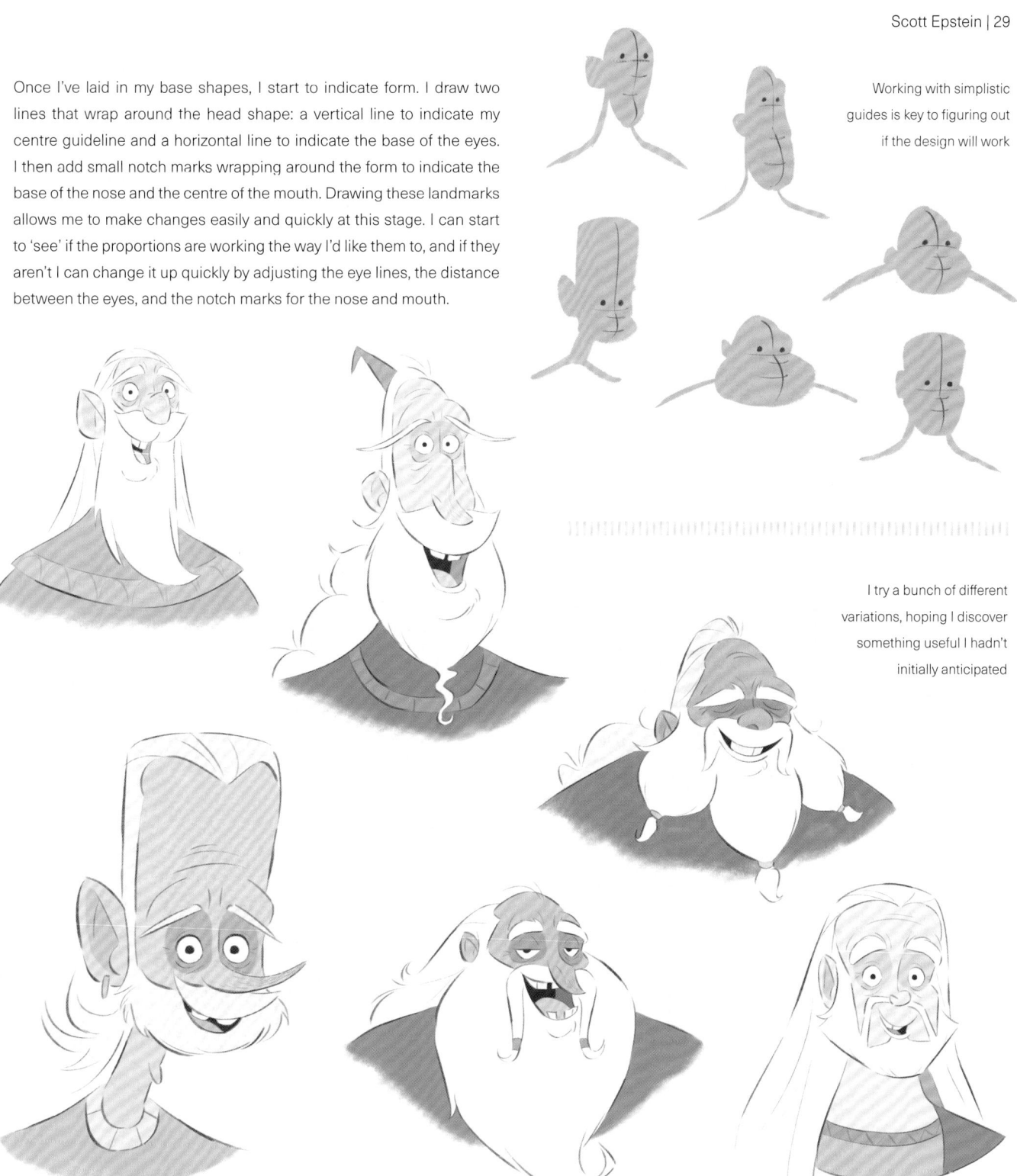

Working with simplistic guides is key to figuring out if the design will work

I try a bunch of different variations, hoping I discover something useful I hadn't initially anticipated

Now the fun part. Using the base guides I've created, I start to explore some head designs. Here's where I'll spend the bulk of my time, choosing features that might work for the character. Because Merlin is old, zany, and a bit of a recluse, I choose features like long hair, a lightly unkempt beard, imperfect teeth, eyebrows in need of a tweezer, and so on. I also begin to indicate costuming with hints at tunics and robes.

At this point I'm still exploring all options, so I want to cast as wide a net as possible in terms of design. It's better to provide many options to your director, production designer, or art director than just one or two. As beautiful as a drawing may be, if it doesn't work for the character or the story, then it's no good. Providing a wide array of options allows for more discussion and helps better inform the final design.

STYLIZING DESIGNS USING PROPORTIONS

There's nothing wrong with splitting proportions evenly (shown in red below) but I prefer to stylize and push them a *lot* further, so I use the 'thirds' method. The theory behind this is that you concentrate most of the important detail and focus of a design within a small range, roughly one third, and the rest of the design in the remaining two thirds. I apply this method to faces as well as bodies. For a head I may choose to place the facial features in the top third of the shape, creating a large chin, or I may choose to place the facial features in the bottom third, creating a large forehead.

The same goes for full bodies. I often like to use the waist as the splitting point – maybe I'll give a character a really short torso and super long legs, or vice versa. Or maybe they have a long neck, or even hardly any neck at all. The possibilities are endless.

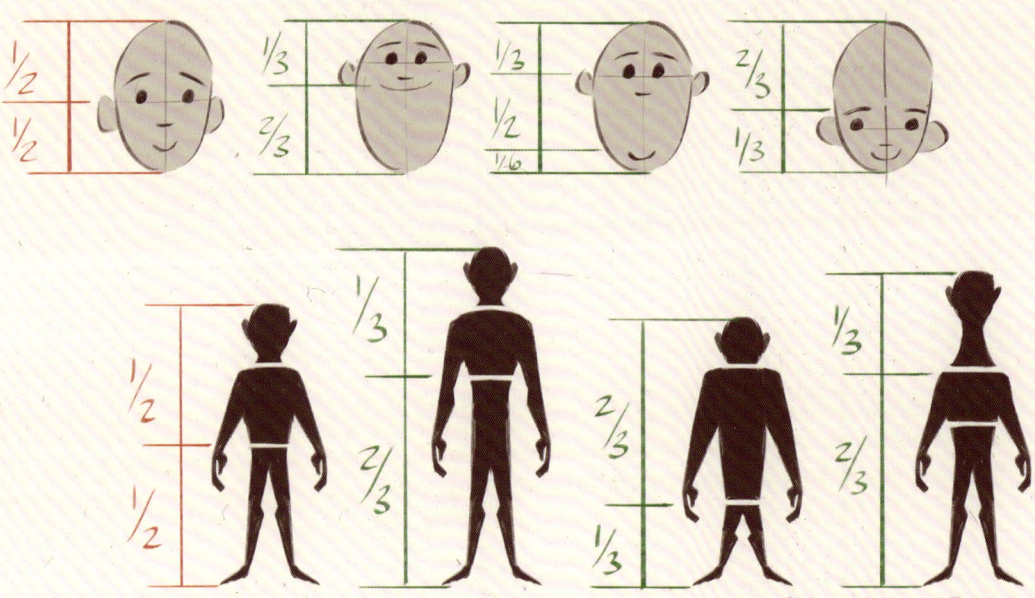

After exploring a bunch of head designs, I move on to full-body explorations. First I consider the gesture I want the character to be acting out. To avoid drawing a stiff figure, I lay in a quick and fast example. Whether it's just a wireframe or a full block-in, here I'm making sure that there's movement and energy in the pose and that the figure feels balanced and grounded. Second, I consider any props that will support the design, like the spell book and fireball.

Third, I look at the silhouette, and if I haven't blocked in my shape design from the get-go, I'll do so here. I'm making sure that the pose is still readable with the anatomy and costuming added. Finally, I tie everything together, fleshing out the final shapes, anatomy, costuming, and props. The goal is that even with everything else added on top of the initial wireframe, the essence of my initial gesture and action still reads.

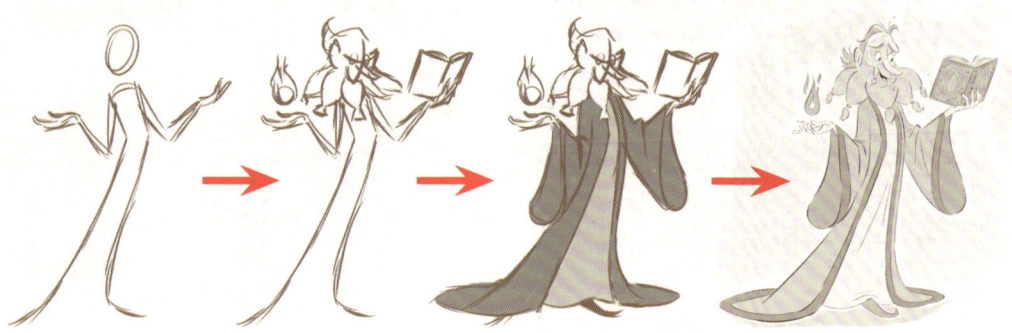

As much fun as it is to just draw heads, there's more to a character than just a pretty face

As with the head designs, my first pass at full-body explorations often focus more on exploring character and shape design rather than on fully posed, story-driven moments. For Merlin there are many elements to put together all at once – hair, beard, staff, and robe, all of which are uniquely designed and can easily compete with each other visually if I'm not careful. Starting with a few more shape-based designs helps me learn how I can start combining these elements together.

While these designs may not have dramatic poses, I still want to make sure they exude character and personality

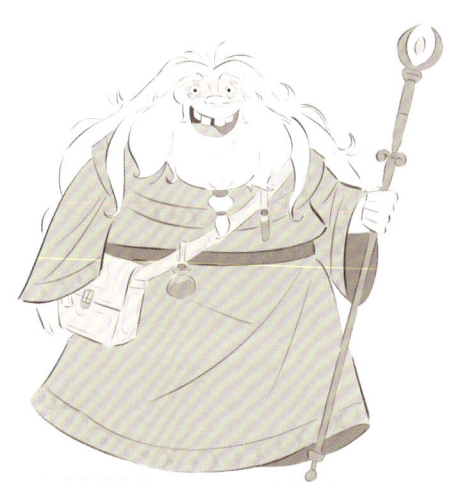
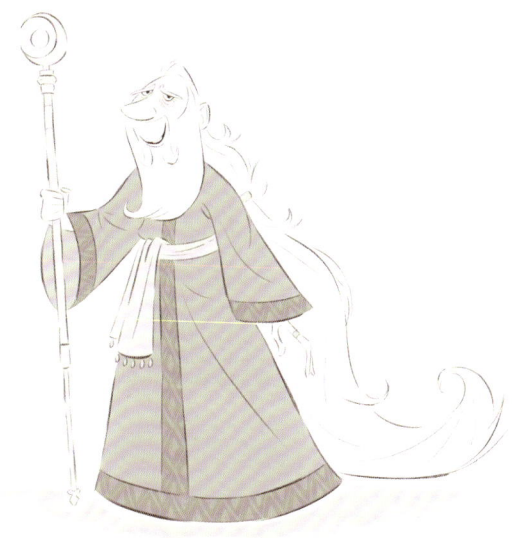

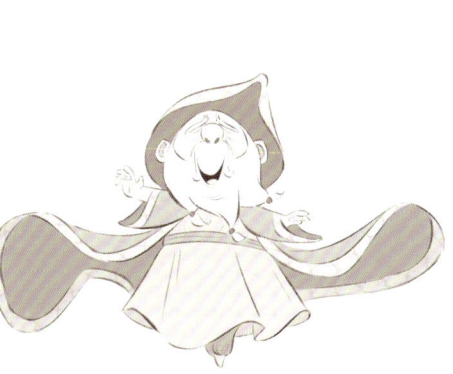
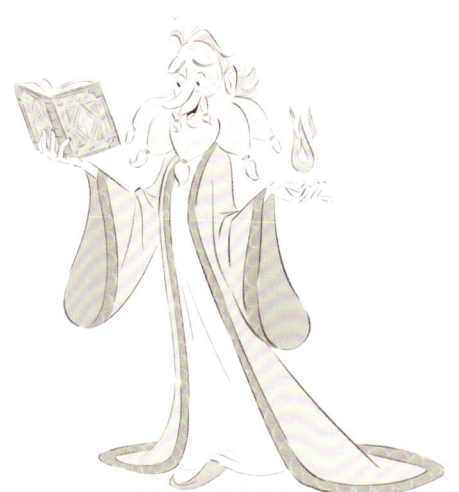

Your best asset as a designer is your ability to think in terms of story

Now that I've begun to understand ways to combine the complex elements needed to design Merlin, I start creating a few more options that not only contain interesting shape design and character choices, but also show a bit more acting, using a story-inspired moment. I start to imagine things Merlin might be doing around his study – practising levitation or casting spells from a book. These are the types of drawings I get most excited about presenting to a director, because here we can hopefully start to see how the character might appear on screen. As designers in entertainment, we're not just making standalone still images, we're creating moving, breathing, living characters – characters who jump around, laugh and cry, and light up a screen. I try to imbue every drawing, a static shape-focused pose or a story-based one, with acting and personality. A beautiful design cannot save a drawing that is devoid of these things.

I like to explore a mixture of
options with different heights,
weights, facial and body features,
posture, and costumes

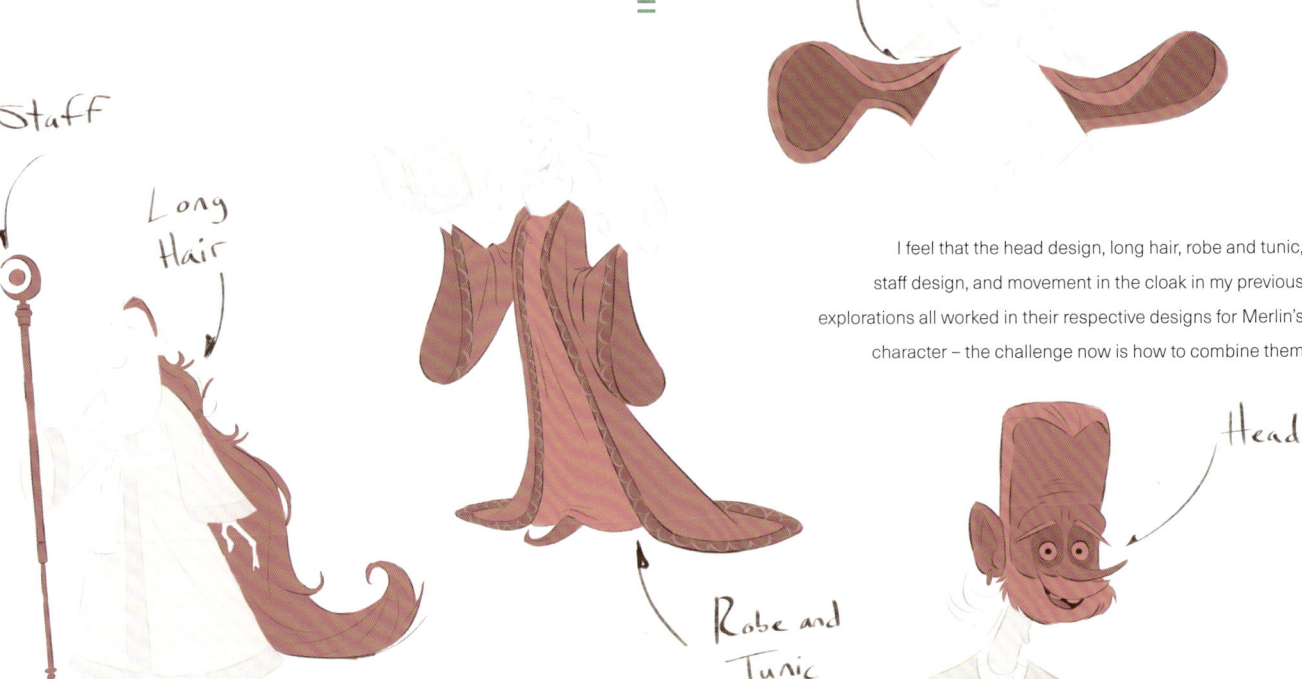

It's important to explore and provide a wide array of full-body designs. If I don't feel I've done my due diligence in exploring a range of ideas, how can I be sure that I've successfully 'found' the character in my design? Sometimes your very first design is the one that's most successful and that's wonderful! But more often than not, your first design is based on a surface-level understanding of your character, using stereotypes and iconography as opposed to something that is unique to this particular interpretation. Exploring your options also helps you understand what *doesn't* work just as much as what *does* work, all leading to a better final design.

While sometimes you 'find' the character in one of your initial exploratory drawings, oftentimes it will take a little longer. Throughout the exploration process you've likely learned about what does and doesn't work for the character. In this instance, I feel like I haven't quite nailed Merlin's design yet, but that I can combine many of my early explorations to create something I'm happy with.

Movement
in cloak

I feel that the head design, long hair, robe and tunic,
staff design, and movement in the cloak in my previous
explorations all worked in their respective designs for Merlin's
character – the challenge now is how to combine them

Staff

Long
Hair

Robe and
Tunic

Head

'HIS HAIR IS IMPOSSIBLY LONG, TO SHOW HE MAINTAINS HIS INDIVIDUALITY'

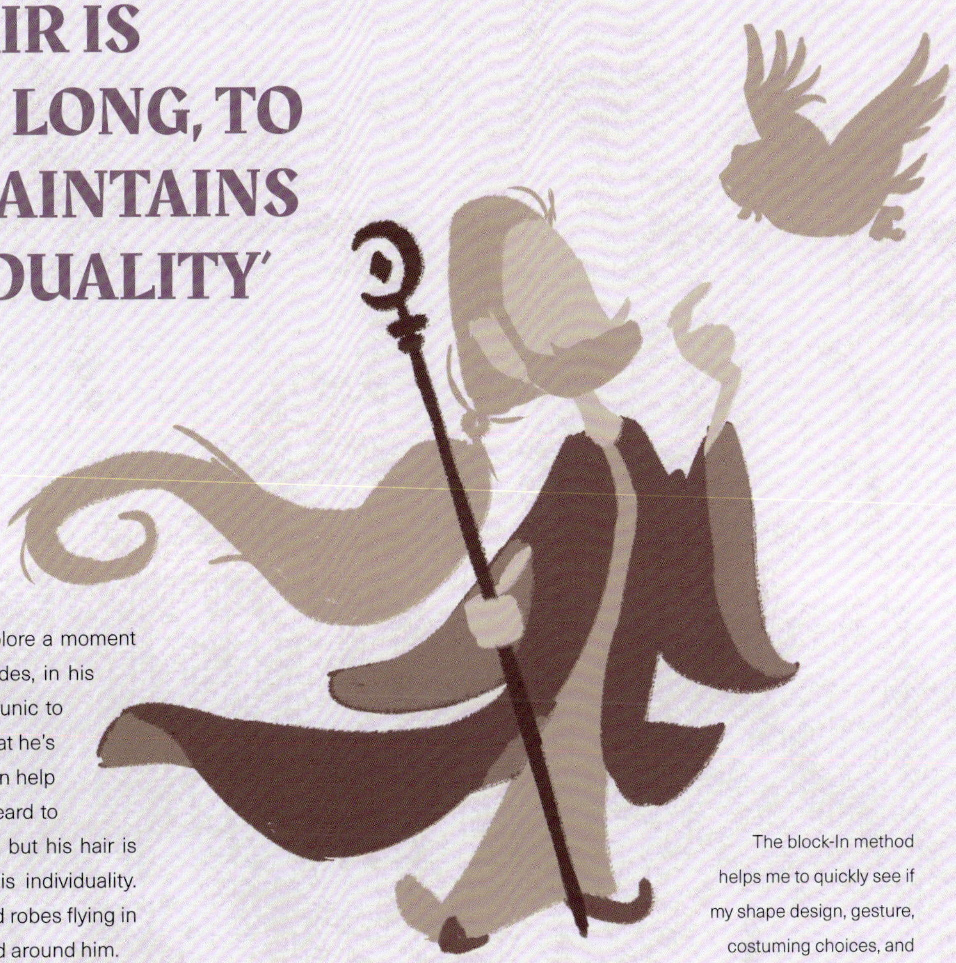

For my final design of Merlin I want to explore a moment of him talking to his owl familiar, Archimedes, in his study. I dress him in flowing robes and a tunic to give him a distinguished air and to show that he's a respected member of society. His hair can help tell the story, too – I give him a trimmed beard to show he's trying to acclimate to court life, but his hair is impossibly long, to show he maintains his individuality. To add a sense of magic, I draw his hair and robes flying in a small gust of seemingly ever-present wind around him.

The block-In method helps me to quickly see if my shape design, gesture, costuming choices, and posing are all working

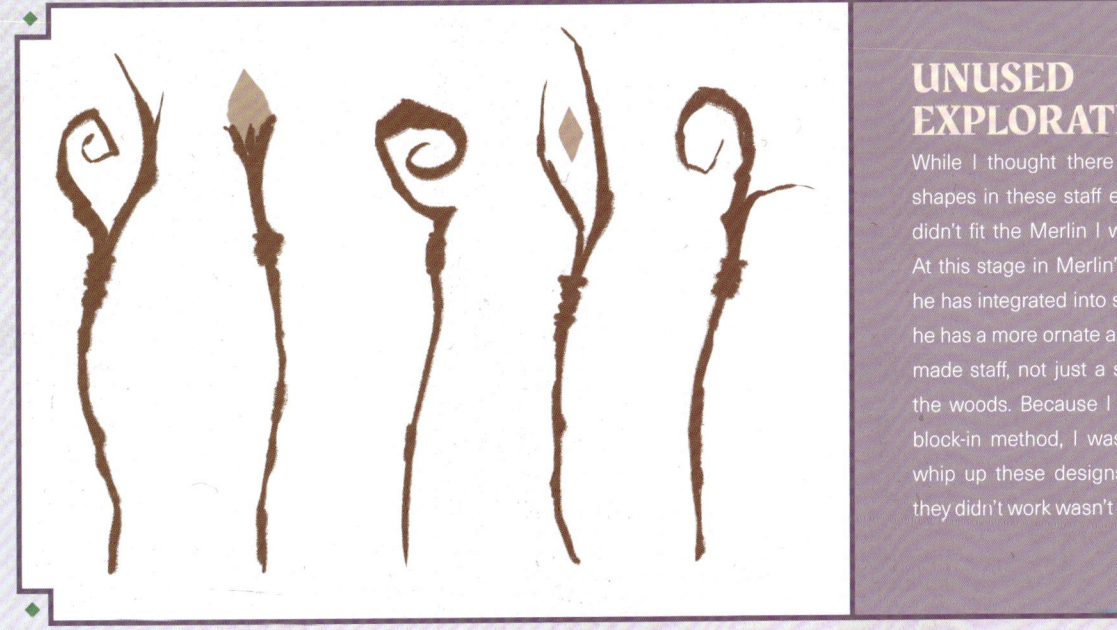

UNUSED EXPLORATIONS

While I thought there were some fun shapes in these staff explorations, they didn't fit the Merlin I wanted to create. At this stage in Merlin's story, now that he has integrated into society, I imagine he has a more ornate and mystical man-made staff, not just a stick he found in the woods. Because I worked with the block-in method, I was able to quickly whip up these designs, so finding out they didn't work wasn't too much hassle.

Using my block-in as reference, I start to flesh out Merlin's design. In this phase I want to make final decisions on facial features, costuming, props, and storytelling. I keep my lines loose, but clear. Because of the block-in I don't need to do as many 'searching' lines – I've already figured it out. I can use this time to focus instead on specific choices and redesigning elements from my previous explorations. I change elements of the staff, robe, and hair, and create my design for Archimedes the owl. While I do like Archimedes' design in this drawing, if I was creating this character for a commercial project, I'd go through the same full design process for the owl as I have for Merlin. But that's for another tutorial!

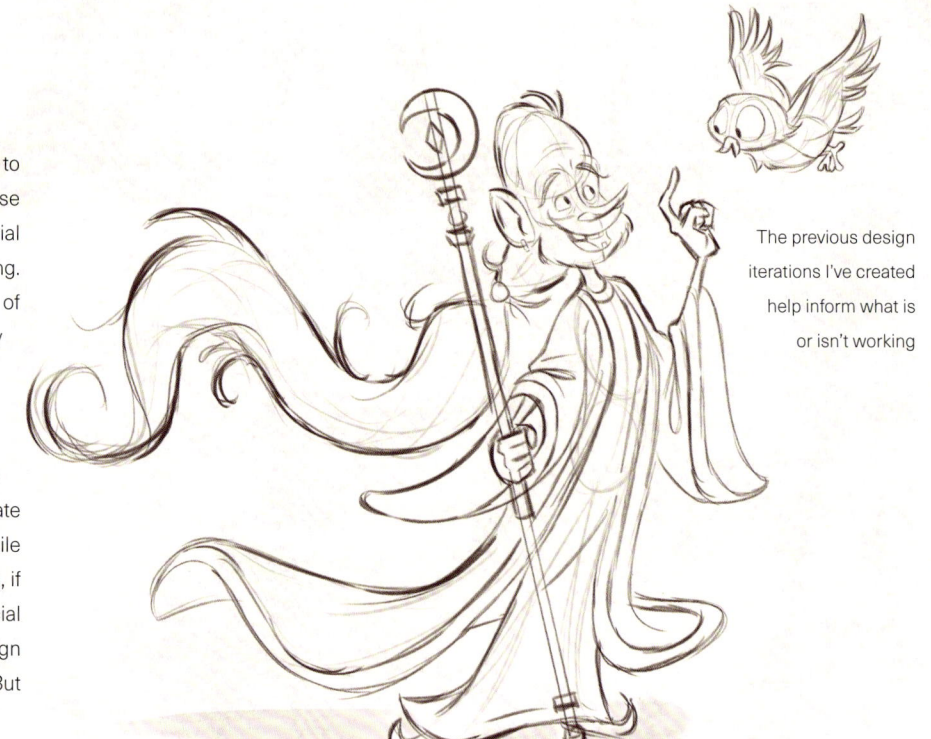

The previous design iterations I've created help inform what is or isn't working

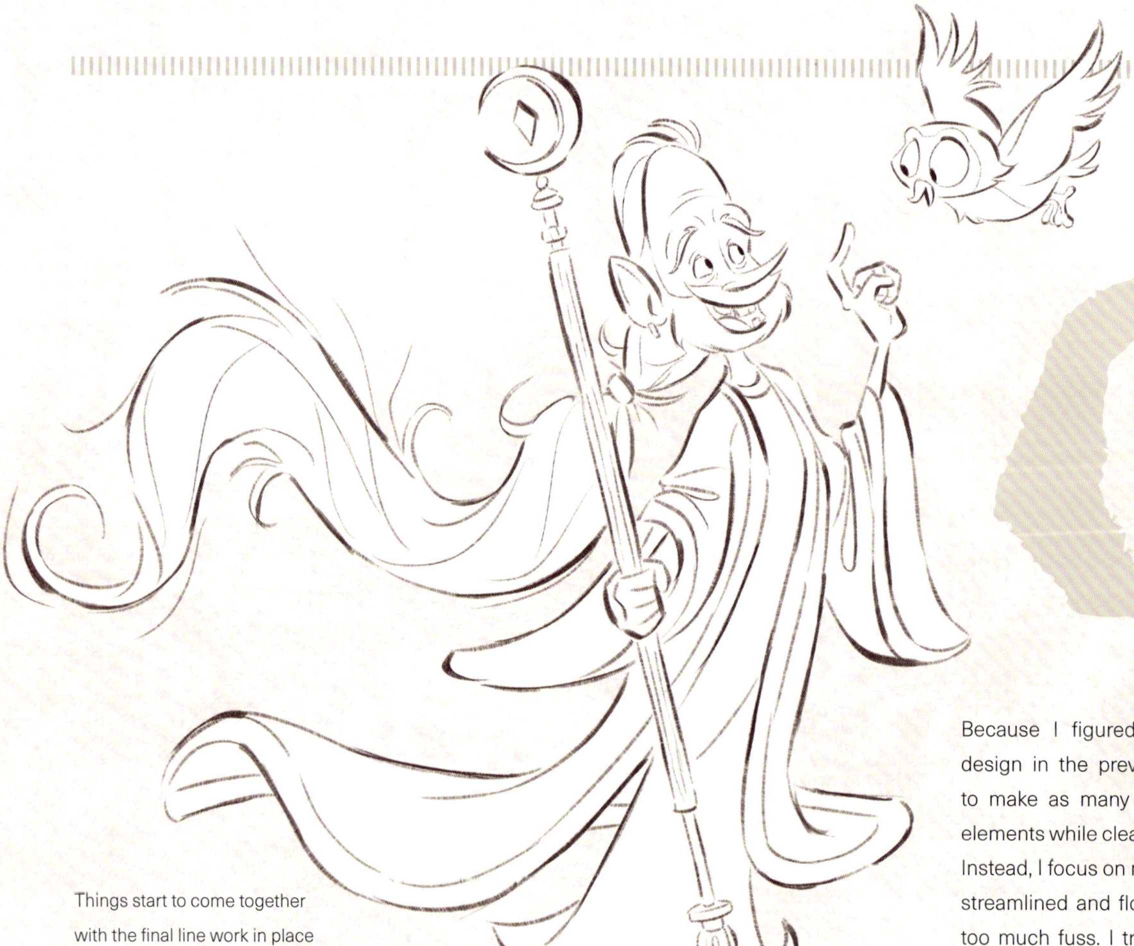

Things start to come together with the final line work in place

Because I figured out the majority of my design in the previous passes, I don't have to make as many decisions about the final elements while cleaning up my rough drawing. Instead, I focus on making sure my shapes are streamlined and flow together nicely without too much fuss. I try to maintain gesture and energy through my strokes while still keeping the integrity of the forms underneath.

KEEPING THE ENERGY GOING

One of the pitfalls of creating final line work is that you can often lose the energy of your rough sketch. There's nothing wrong with a super clean line, but I like to maintain a little more energy by using a brush that outputs dynamic pressure (thin to thick lines and vice versa) and by including small breaks in between my lines. This helps my final line work feel looser and not as overworked, keeping some of the energy from my rough sketches, while still being clear.

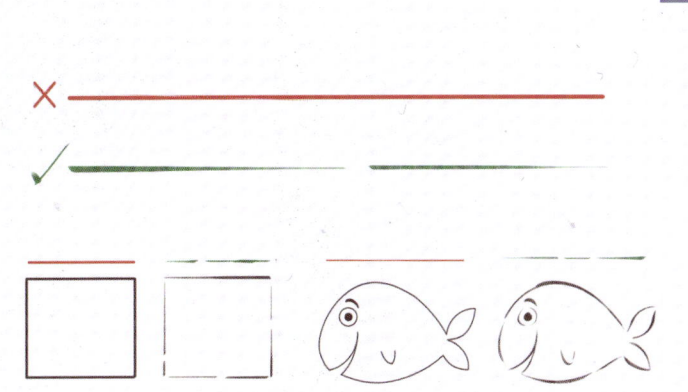

The last step before the final piece is to work out my local colours (the colour before it's affected by light) and values (the contrast of how dark or light each piece looks next to another). It's a nightmare trying to adjust hue (the base colour of an object), saturation (the intensity of the colour), and values when I've already rendered and textured my final colour piece. These small thumbnails help me quickly formulate a game plan, allowing me to try several different colour options quickly. And again, the more options I can show my art director, the better.

Spend the time to explore different colour variations with solid values before you start your final piece

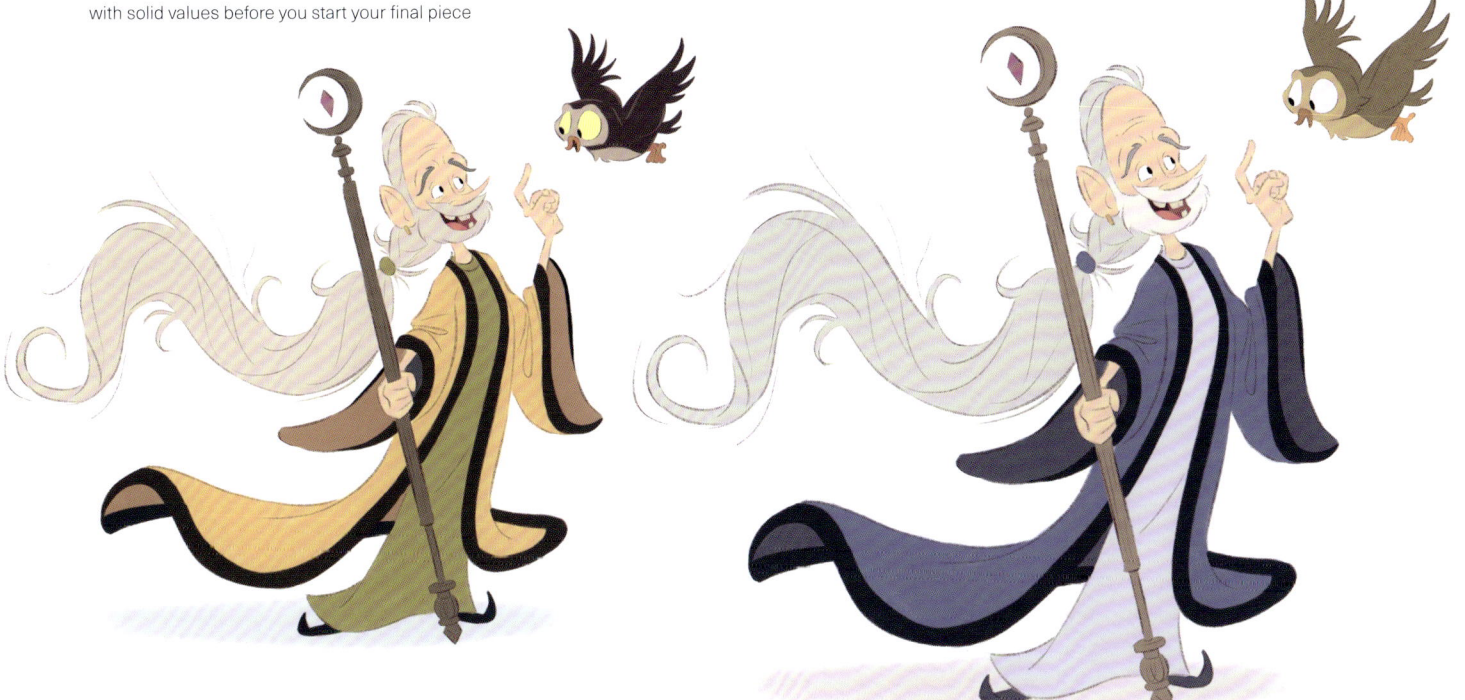

Finally, the culmination of all of the work we've done. I select one of my colour schemes and apply it to the final piece. You'll notice there are a few new additions to the design – even as I move to my 'final' stage I'm still thinking about how I can improve the character and narrative. I felt like I could push the storytelling moment even further by having Archimedes hold a magic scroll that he and Merlin are discussing. I've also added some jewellery (in the form of a ring and a mystical amulet) to further add to Merlin's character.

The best piece of advice I can give is to never be afraid to change your designs and drawings to better imbue story and character in them. Story is the most important aspect of what we do and every design decision we make is in service of it. Explore, be bold, and revel in making story-informed choices. If you do, you'll create a living, breathing character right before your very eyes.

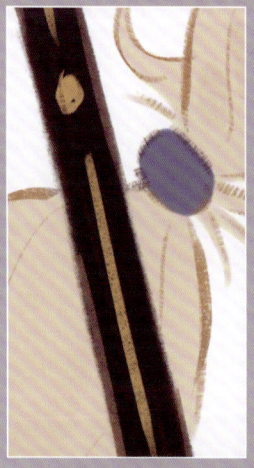
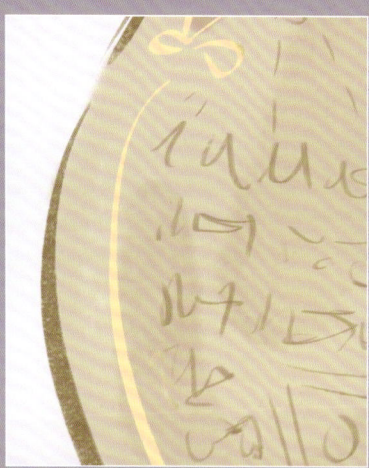

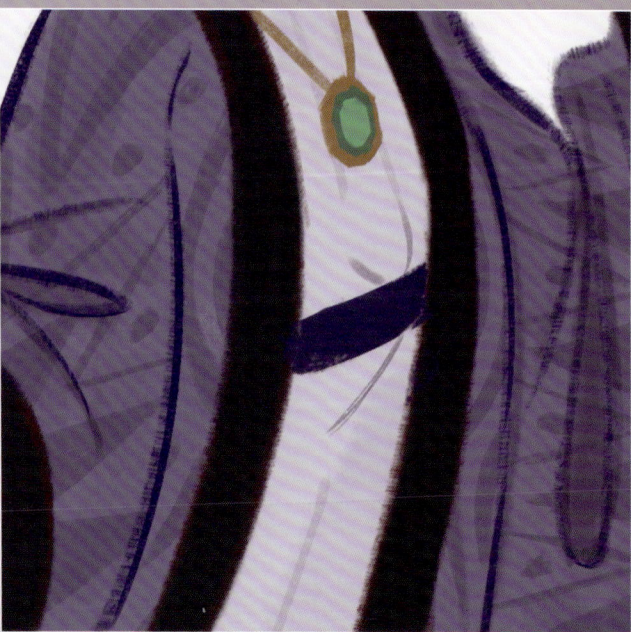

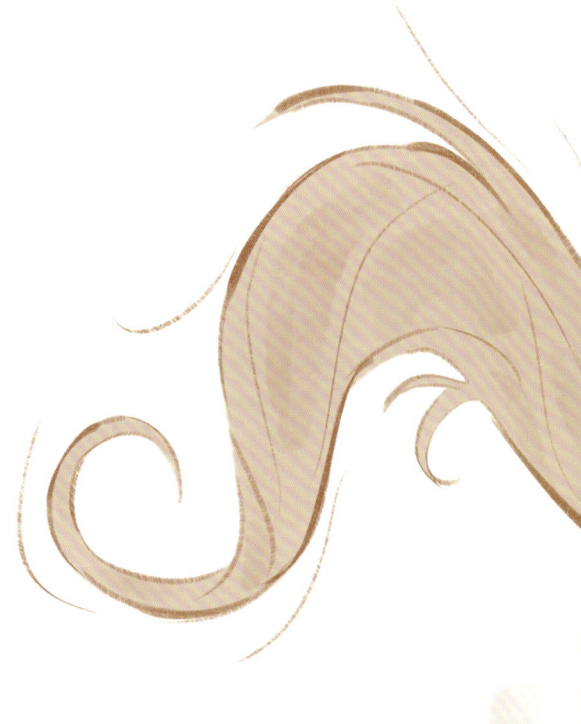

I add my finishing details to the image, including patterns to clothing and some textural brush strokes, so my designs aren't too flat

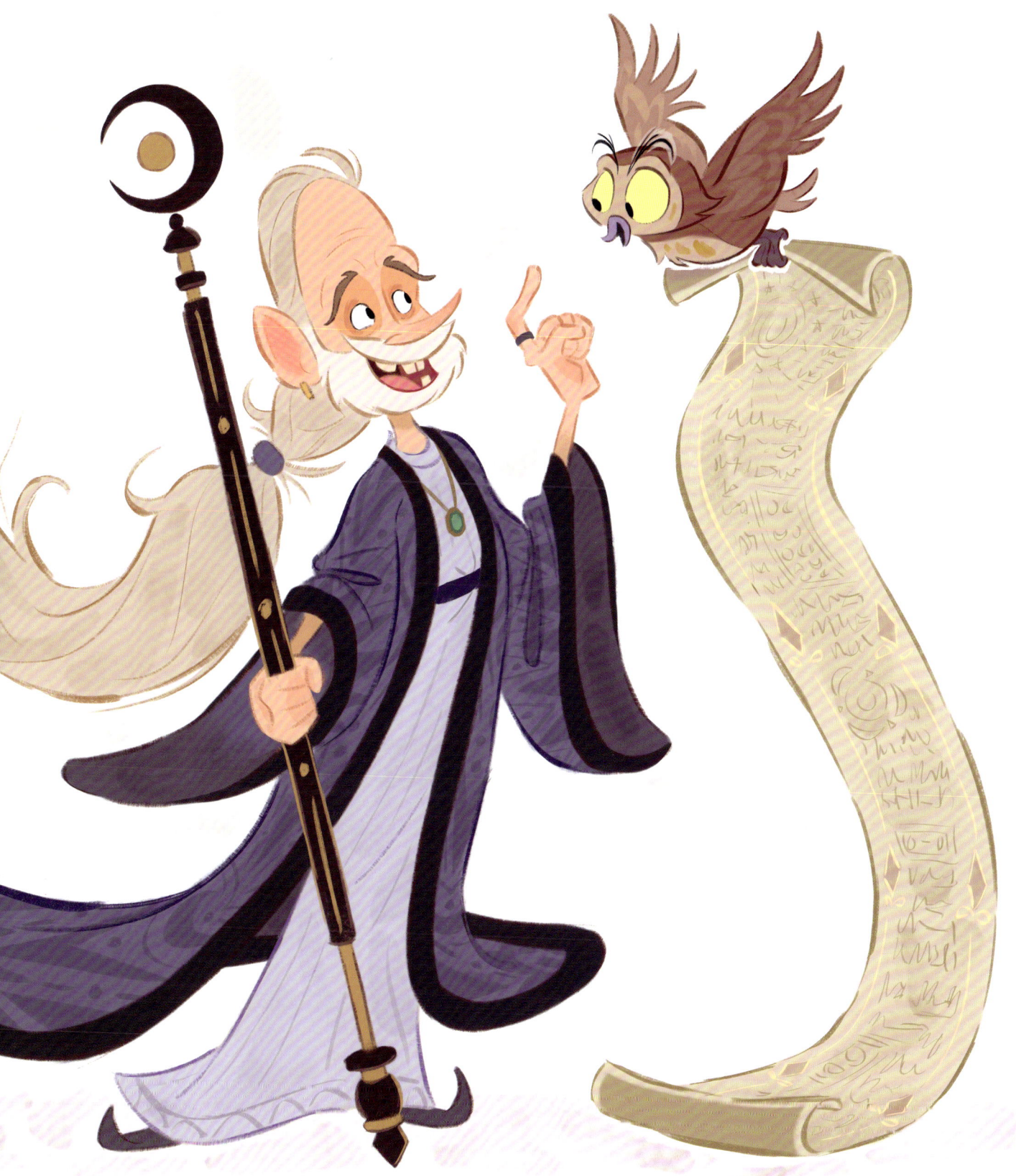

DEVELOPMENT GALLERY
LIDIA MORALES

My artwork focuses on creating magical worlds full of vibrant colours and powerful characters. In both my professional and personal work, I seek to evoke a sense of wonder, mystery, and even humour through my drawings and the stories they tell, inviting the viewer to connect with their own emotions. For me, the creative process always involves a journey into my inner universe, so I consider myself an explorer who is always looking for adventures and new discoveries.

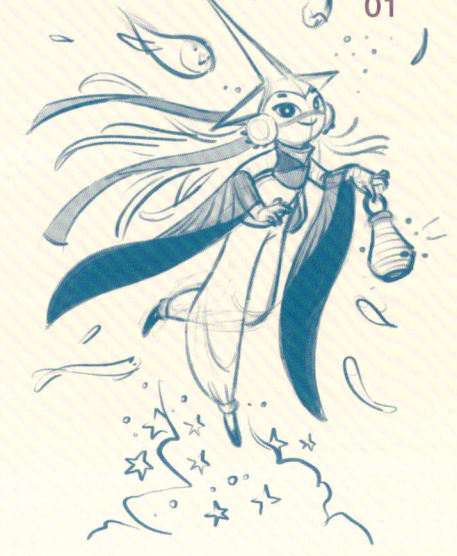

01

01. I drew several rough sketches before finalizing this one, in which I defined the character's proportions. My main goal was to represent a guiding star lighting the way forward, using a dynamic composition with all elements pointing towards the centre.

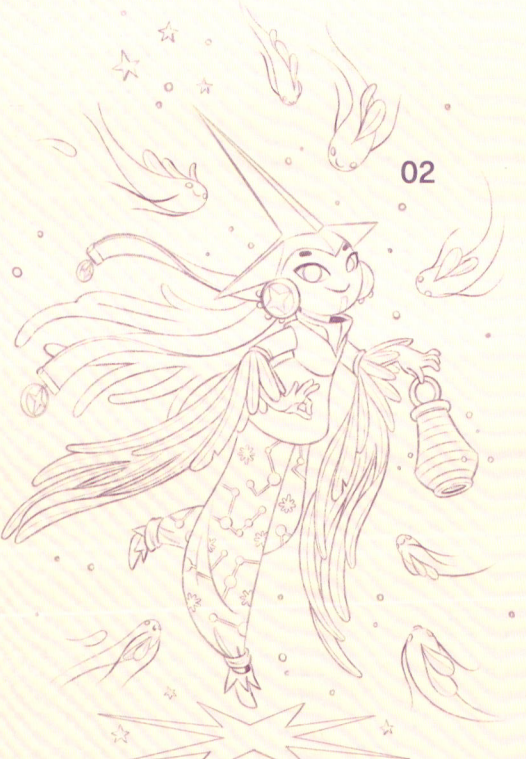

02

02. I didn't want lines to show in the final image, but I still I worked on the clean-up to make sure the character was polished and the result visually cohesive. I also tweaked, improved, and added details that weren't present in the sketch.

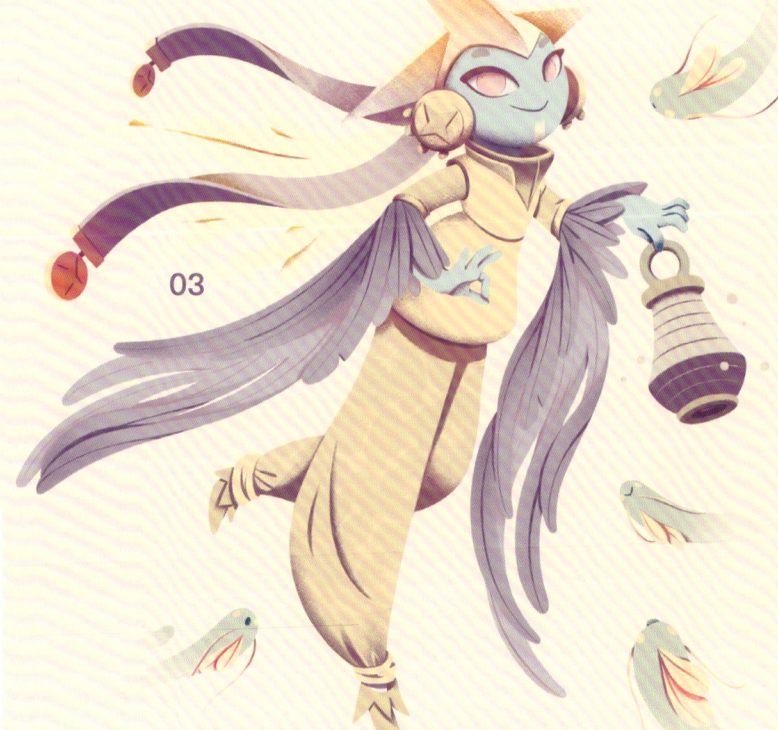

03

03. After carefully finishing the colour-blocking (thanks to the clean-up) I added a light, low-opacity layer over the base colours. This made it easier to apply shadows on a top layer, emphasizing the three-dimensionality of the feathered sleeves and overlapping clothes.

04. Finally, I added light effects on the guide's head and the stars in the background, giving the illustration a touch of magic, and a more charming ambience. The finishing touch was to apply a paper texture to give it a handmade feel.

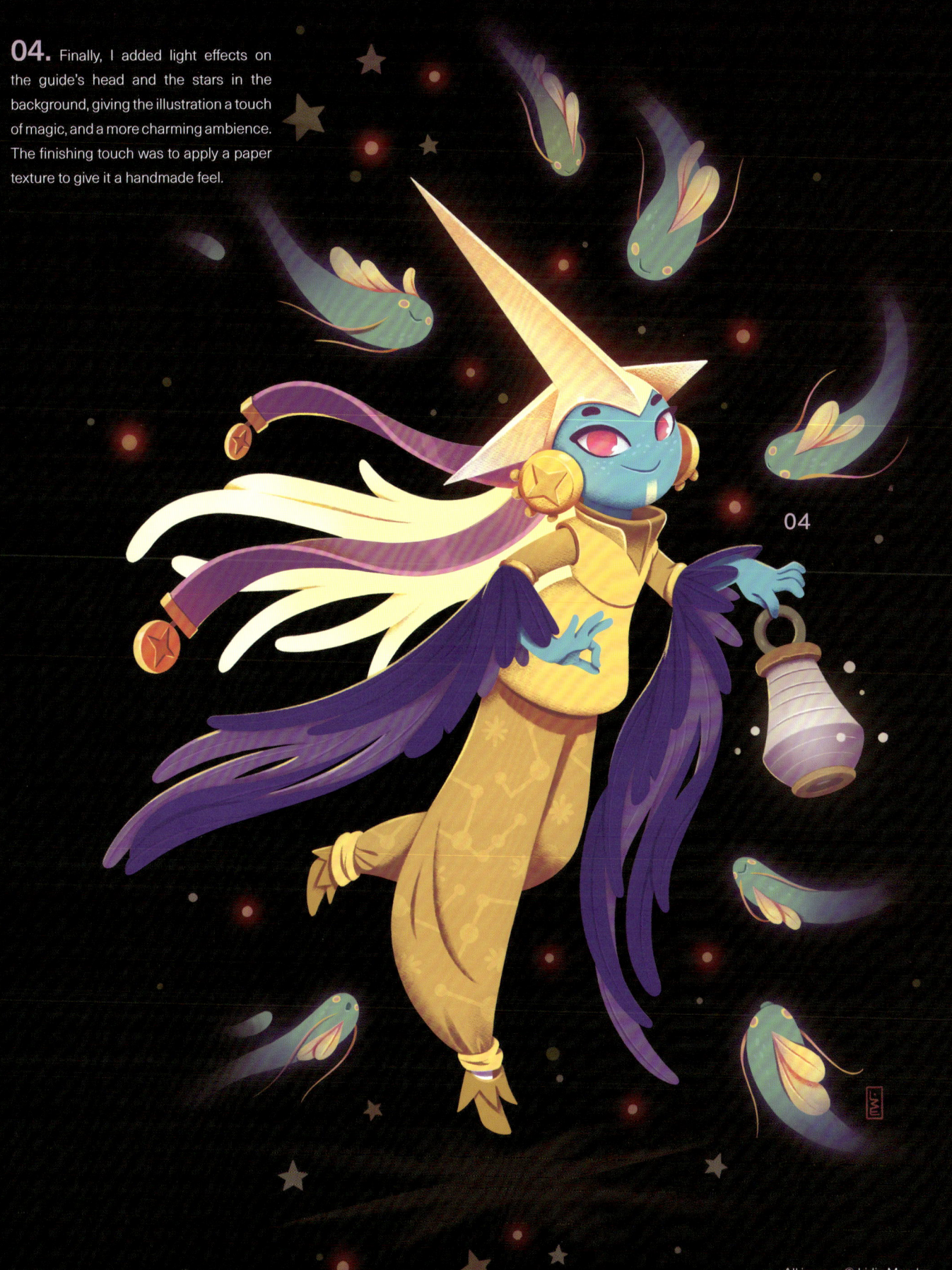

04

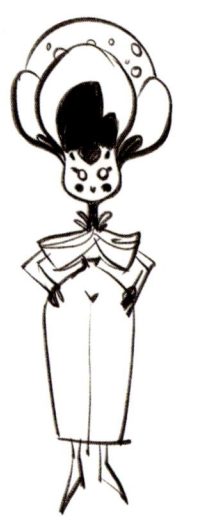

01

02

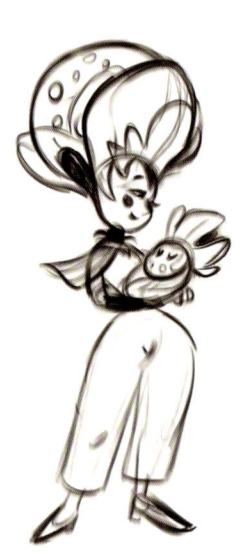

03

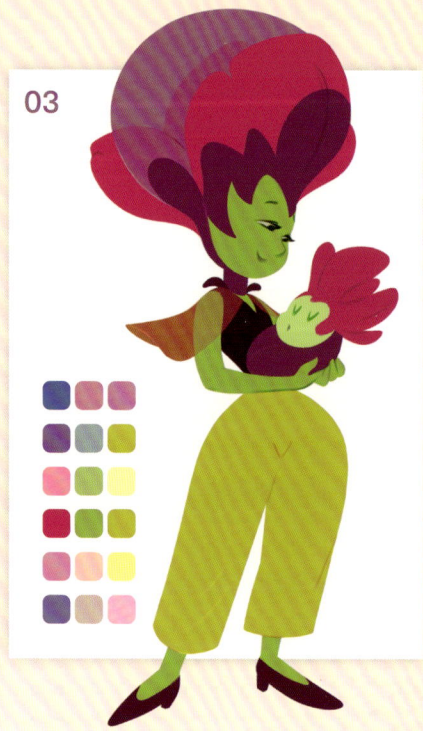

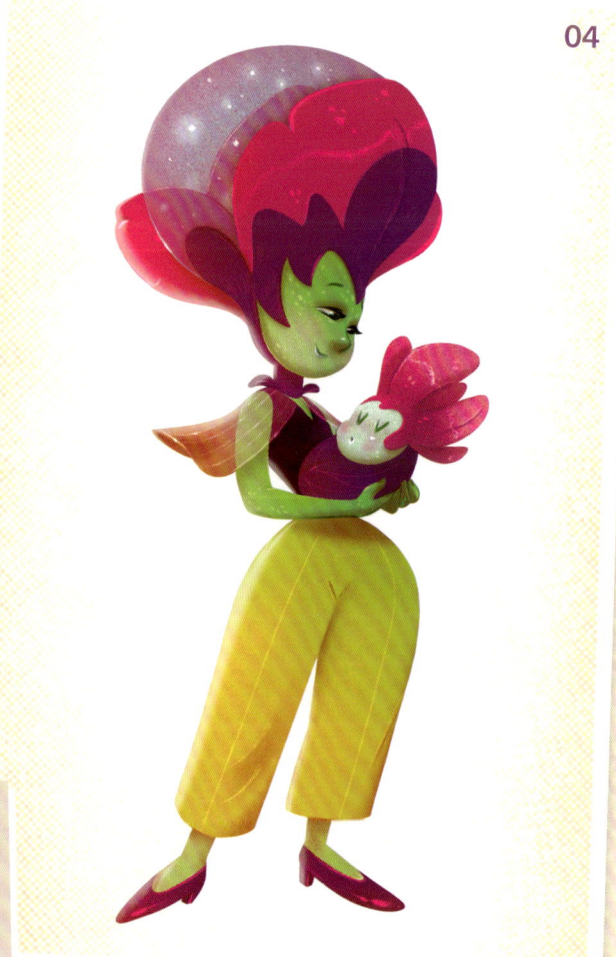

04

01. Sometimes I look for inspiration on my iPad, bringing to life forgotten ideas hidden among the files. In this case, I decided to develop this quick sketch of a flower woman, whose basic structure seemed interesting to me.

02. In this first step, I worked on the original character's story and style. I introduced a second character (her little son-bud) and positioned them both in a three-quarter view, applying volume and perspective to add depth to the composition.

03. After experimenting with different colour ranges, I chose this warm palette to evoke the feelings of tenderness and comfort that I wanted the image to convey.

04. I particularly enjoyed the final step of this illustration, which involved adding shadows, details, and textures. I played with lighting to create an atmosphere that enhances the narrative of the illustration, which is a key element for me.

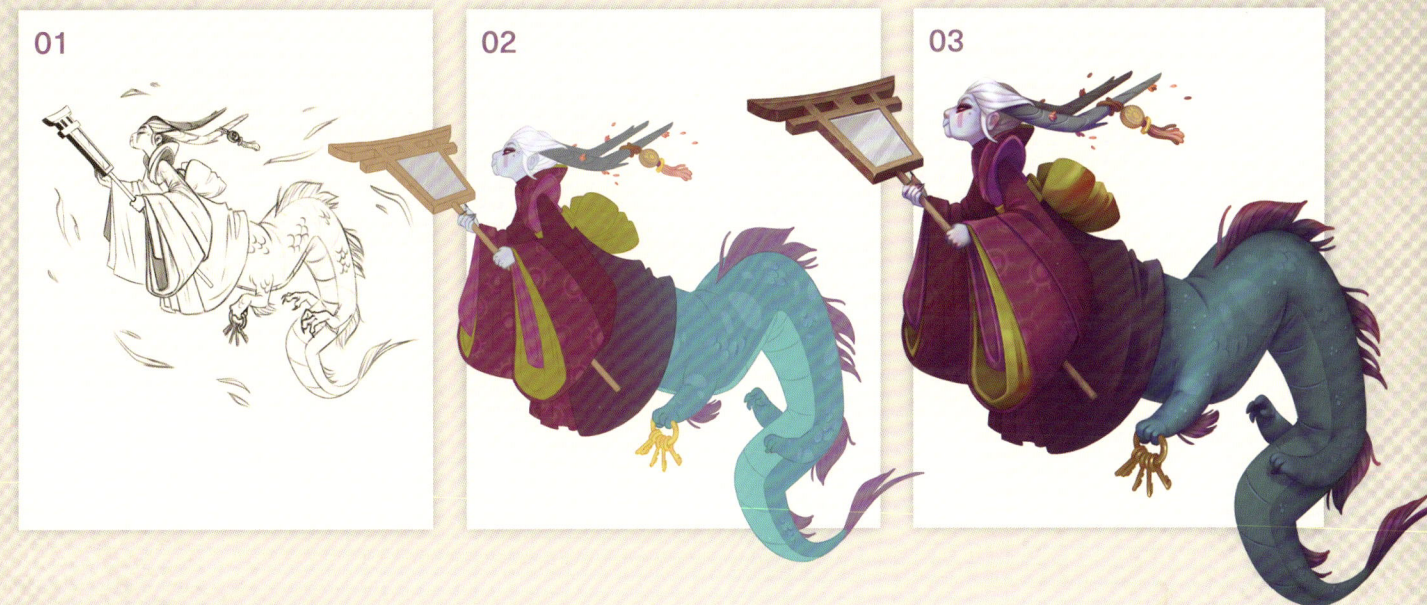

01. My main aim while exploring this hybrid was to create a dynamic shape that embodied both power and mystery. I also faced the challenge of making sure the character looked three-dimensional, despite the view being from the side.

02. I cleaned up the drawing, maintaining the three-dimensionality while adjusting proportions, such as the claws. I applied local colours with a gradient from warm to cooler tones within the character, and added the kimono pattern and skin spots to the tail.

03. In the rendering phase, I focused on ambient occlusion, creating various layers of shadow to emphasize darker areas. I also worked on the lighting, considering diverse refraction of light on different materials to highlight certain textures, like the keys and kimono.

04. For the final image, I added detail to the hair, colour gradients, and effects to bring dynamism to the composition. I used rim light and a halo for depth and included her face's reflection in the mirror to add an eerie touch.

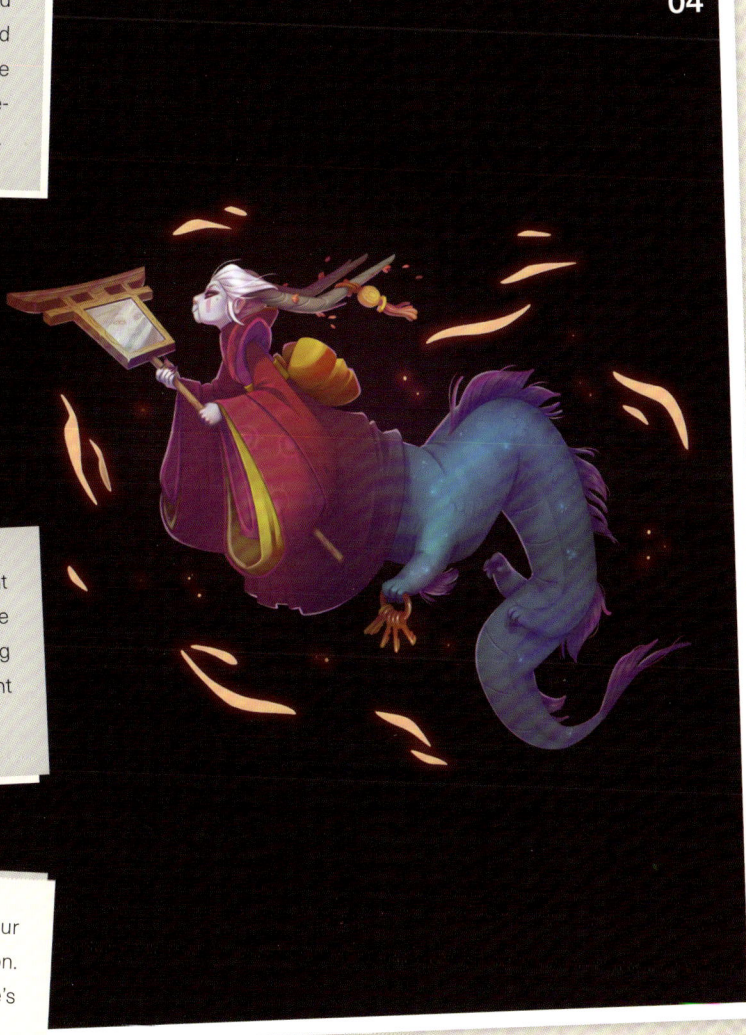

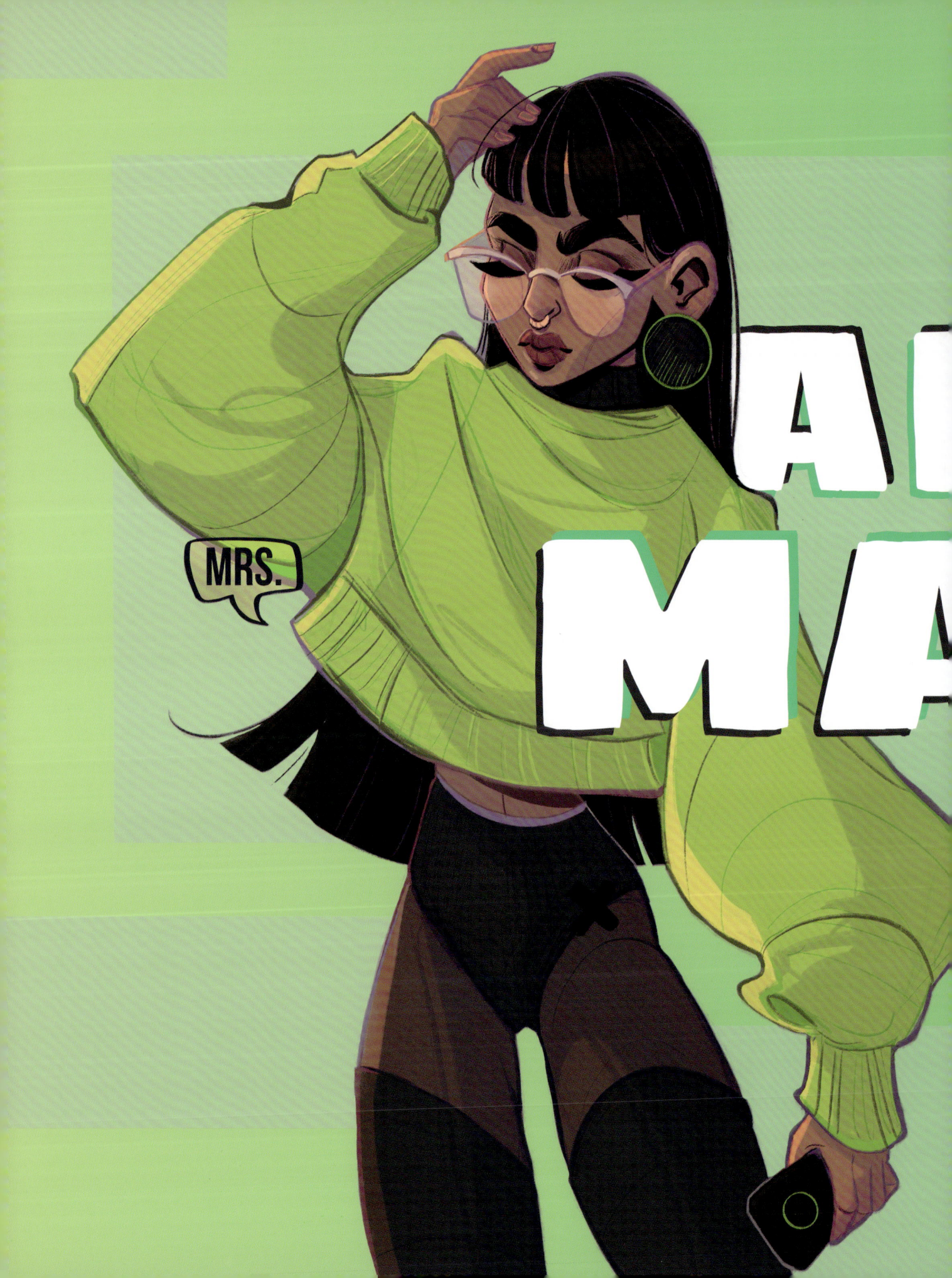

MEET THE ARTIST:

ANNIE MATION

Anne Neyens (aka Annie Mation) speaks to us about her inspirations, influences, and experiences in the industry.

Hi Anne, welcome to *CDQ*! Could you start by telling our readers a little about yourself?

Hi *CDQ*, Thanks for having me! I'm Anne Neyens, a Belgian artist who recently moved to the Netherlands. After graduating as an animator I got a teaching qualification and started teaching art. Although I loved mentoring others, I didn't really feel artistically challenged in that job. Then the pandemic happened – suddenly we had to work from home, and animation studios started to consider hiring artists from all over the world to work for them remotely. This opened doors for me and I was very lucky that Zebu Animation Studios found me on LinkedIn. At Zebu I learned how to work in a studio environment. Three years later and I had my name in the credits for *LEGO DREAMZzz* and Pharrell Williams' biopic, *Piece by Piece*!

This piece is from a project about the different stages of a relationship; I taught myself how to draw gorgeous men from David Ardinaryas Lojaya – there's no one who does it better!

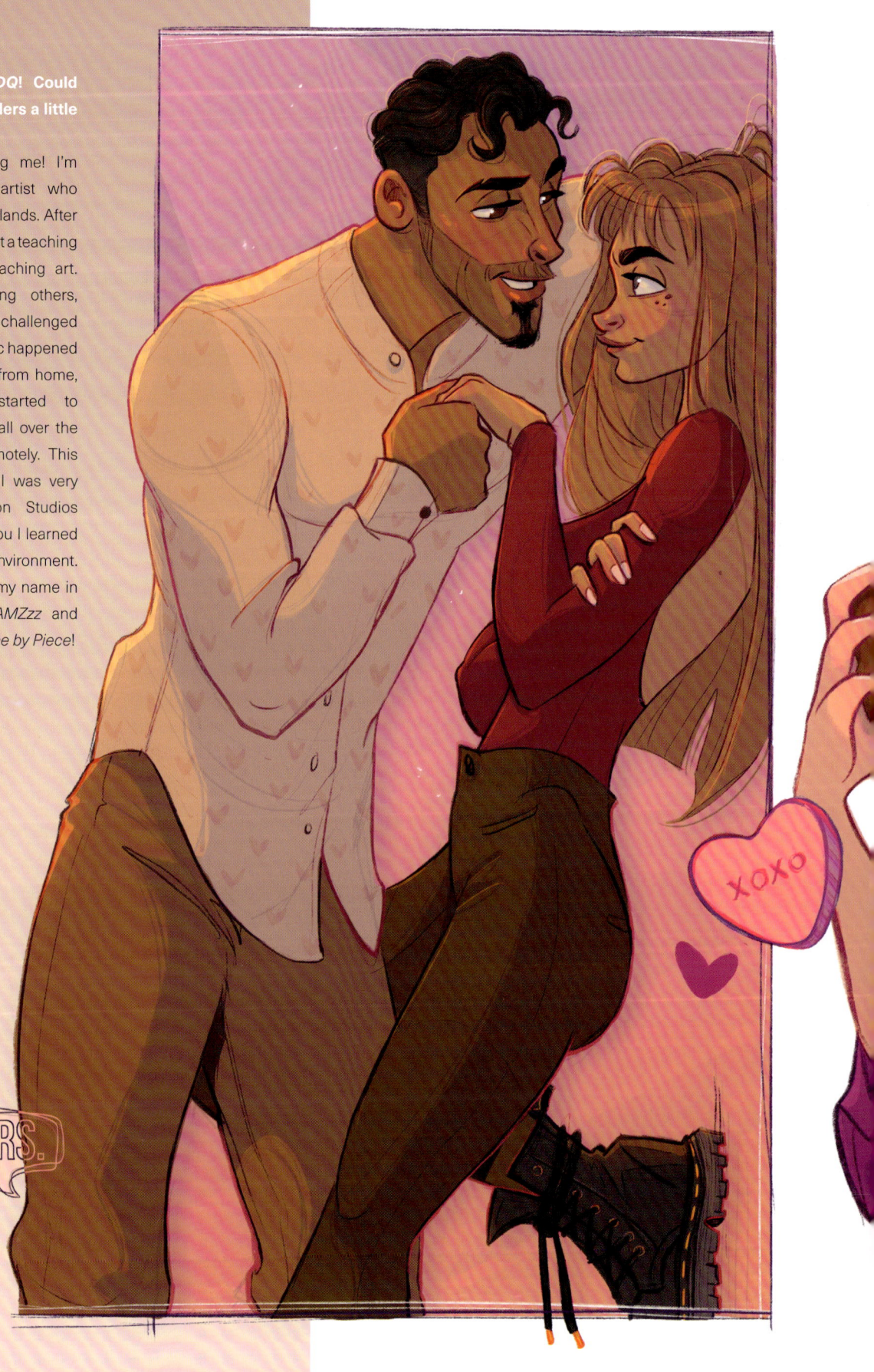

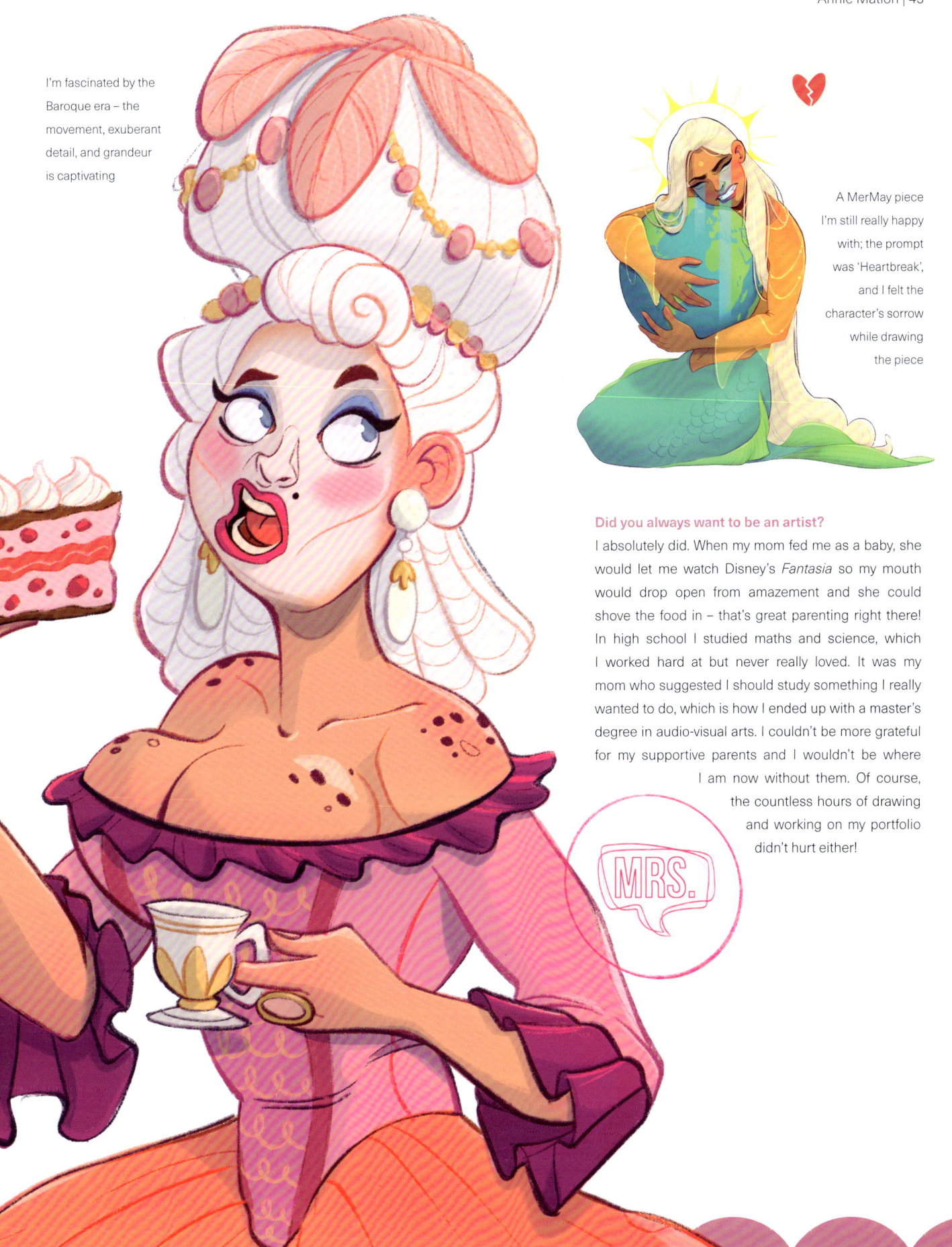

I'm fascinated by the Baroque era – the movement, exuberant detail, and grandeur is captivating

A MerMay piece I'm still really happy with; the prompt was 'Heartbreak', and I felt the character's sorrow while drawing the piece

Did you always want to be an artist?

I absolutely did. When my mom fed me as a baby, she would let me watch Disney's *Fantasia* so my mouth would drop open from amazement and she could shove the food in – that's great parenting right there! In high school I studied maths and science, which I worked hard at but never really loved. It was my mom who suggested I should study something I really wanted to do, which is how I ended up with a master's degree in audio-visual arts. I couldn't be more grateful for my supportive parents and I wouldn't be where I am now without them. Of course, the countless hours of drawing and working on my portfolio didn't hurt either!

As you mentioned, you've worked on several LEGO projects – what are the challenges of working in that universe?
LEGO DREAMZzz was a particularly fun project to work on. I remember when I heard I would be creating designs for a LEGO series, I had some doubts about my skills because my personal artwork is usually very organic and 'flowy'. Suddenly, I had to design with rigid bricks in mind. I was reassured when my art director told me *LEGO DREAMZzz* would take place in a world where the sets and props had curves and organic shapes, like the Ninjago universe. Honestly, it was the perfect project to ease me into working in the LEGO style.

When it came to working on Pharrell Williams' *Piece by Piece*, I actually had to build my props and characters with LEGO bricks – it was the most fun I've ever had working on a project. I had to pinch myself when I was digitally building Pharrell's Ferrari with LEGO bricks, following the actual LEGO instructions. Later in the project I got to do the character designs for some of Pharrell's outfits and many of his exceptional friends. Turning Morgan Neville, Teddy Riley, Gwen Stefani, Mariah Carey, Madonna, and many others into LEGO minifigures has been the highlight of my career so far.

This piece was from a series of illustrations about the different stages of a relationship; it started as a commission that was unfortunately cancelled, but the series is still very close to my heart

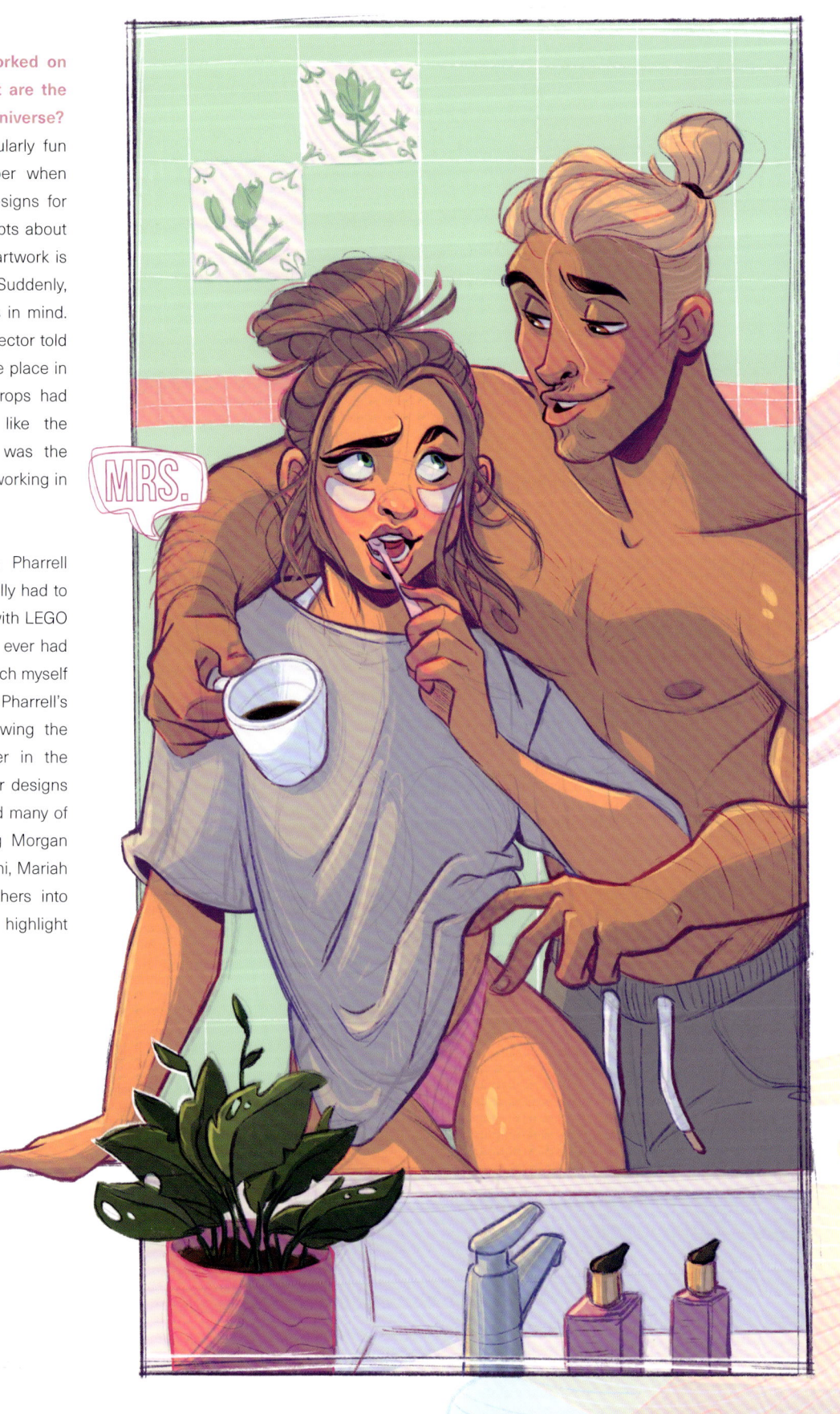

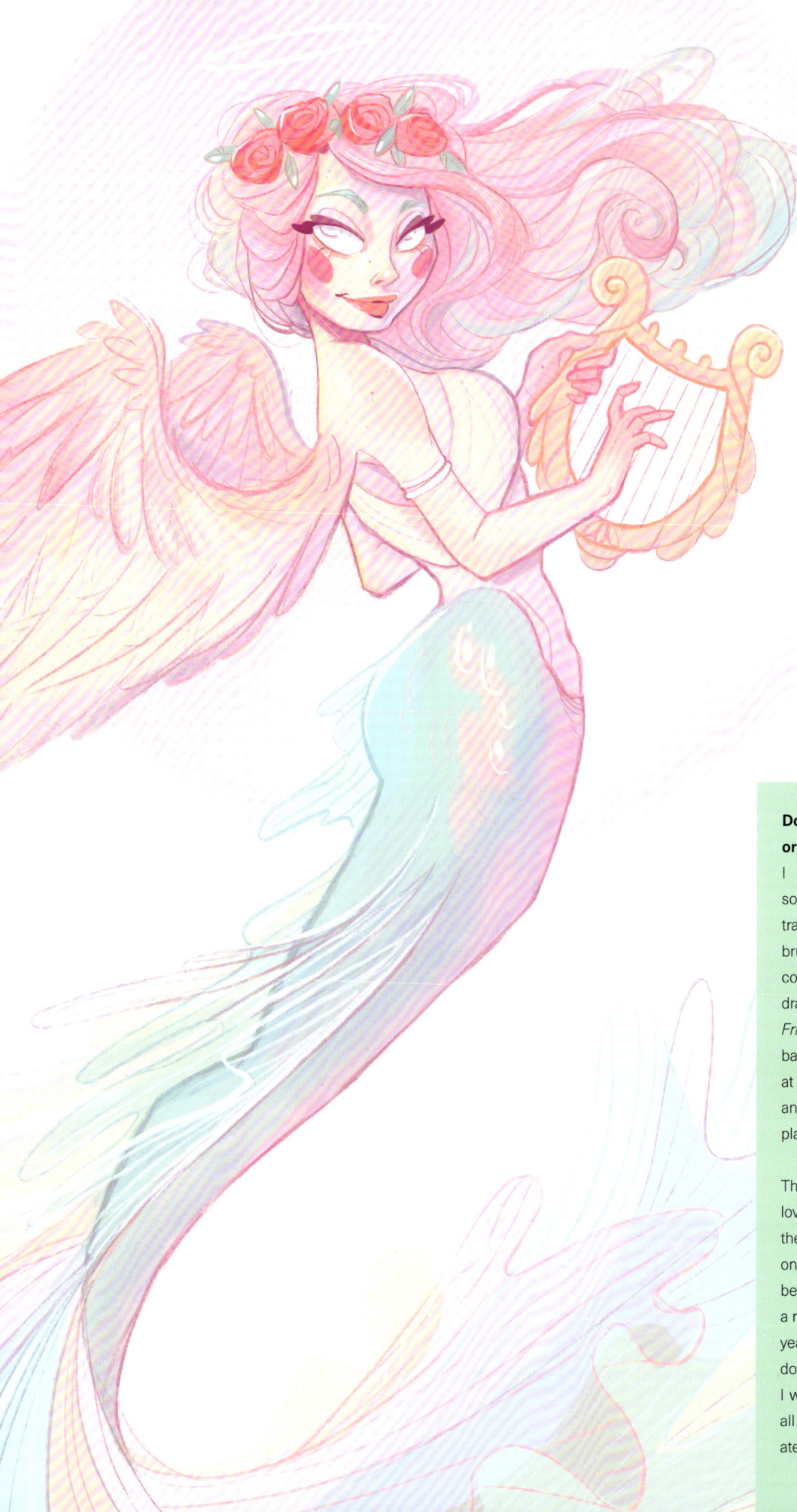

I often paint with very deep, rich colours and I wanted to try something different - I think this character design suits these soft, powdery pastels

Do you prefer to work traditionally or digitally?

I prefer to work digitally because sometimes I can be a bit lazy – working traditionally means cleaning your brushes. I adore curling up on my couch with my iPad on a pillow and drawing for hours, while a season of *Friends* or *The Simpsons* plays in the background. I can sometimes look at a painting of mine from years ago and remember the episode that was playing when I created it – weird!

That being said, occasionally I do also love to paint traditionally. I haven't had the opportunity to work with acrylics on a large canvas for a while, as I'm 'in-between ateliers' at the moment, due to a renovation. Funny how you suddenly yearn for making a mess when you don't have the space to do it! I guess I will be cleaning those brushes after all in a few months, when my new atelier is finished.

Who are the biggest influences on your style?

I guess no artsy 90s kid will ever be able to answer this question without mentioning Disney – those Disney Classics were life-changing for so many of us. I also remember having the habit of literally 'judging books by their cover' – the painted covers for R.L. Stine's *Goosebumps* series and the illustrations of Belgian artist Jan Bosschaert spoke to me, and I still adore my collection. When social media became a thing it kickstarted my love for digital art. Seeing so many amazing artists creating brilliant work was like witnessing magic and I had to understand how to do it. Social media legends like Loish, Pernille Ørum, Peter Straubel, and David Ardinaryas Lojaya – whom you all definitely know – keep inspiring me to be better every day.

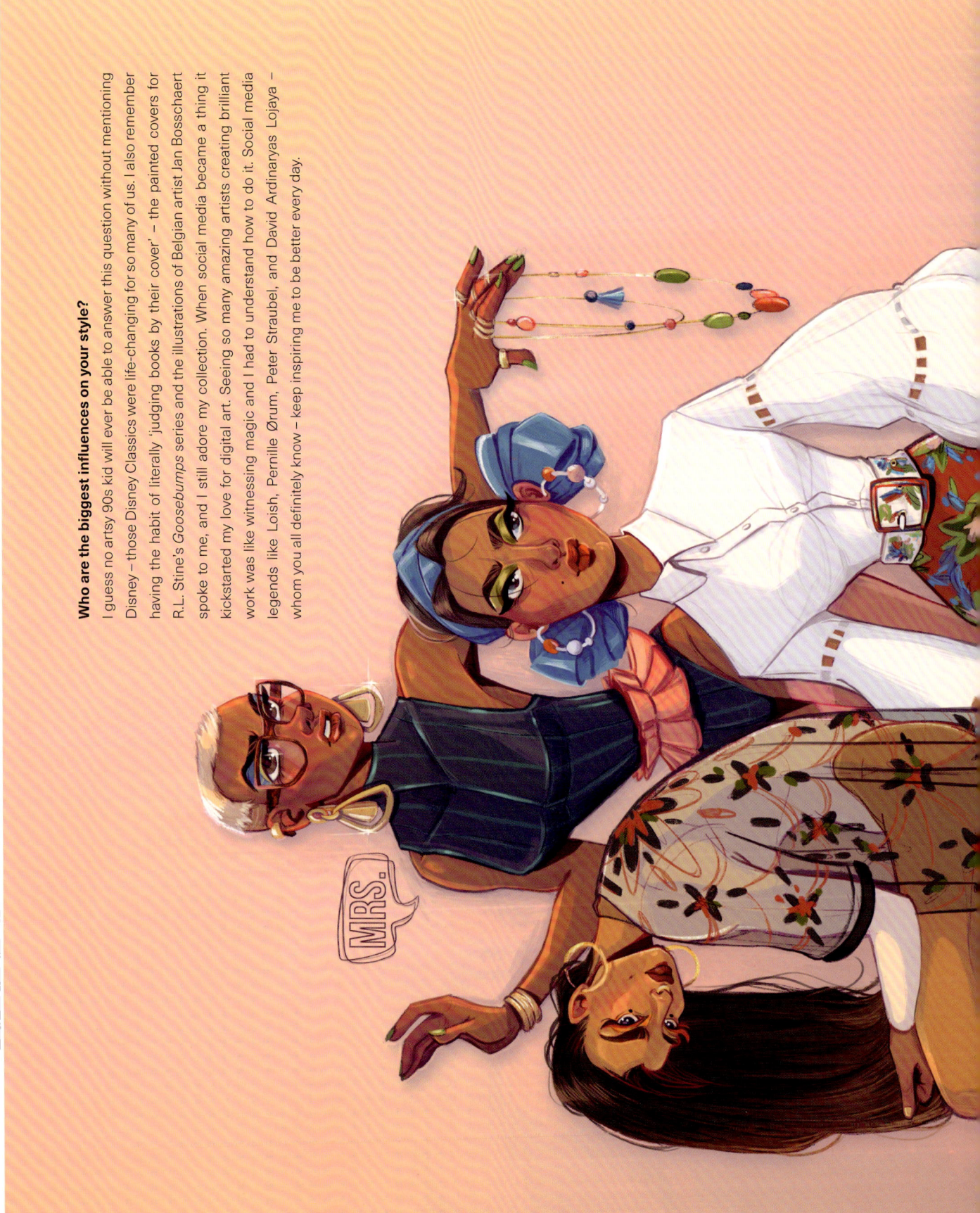

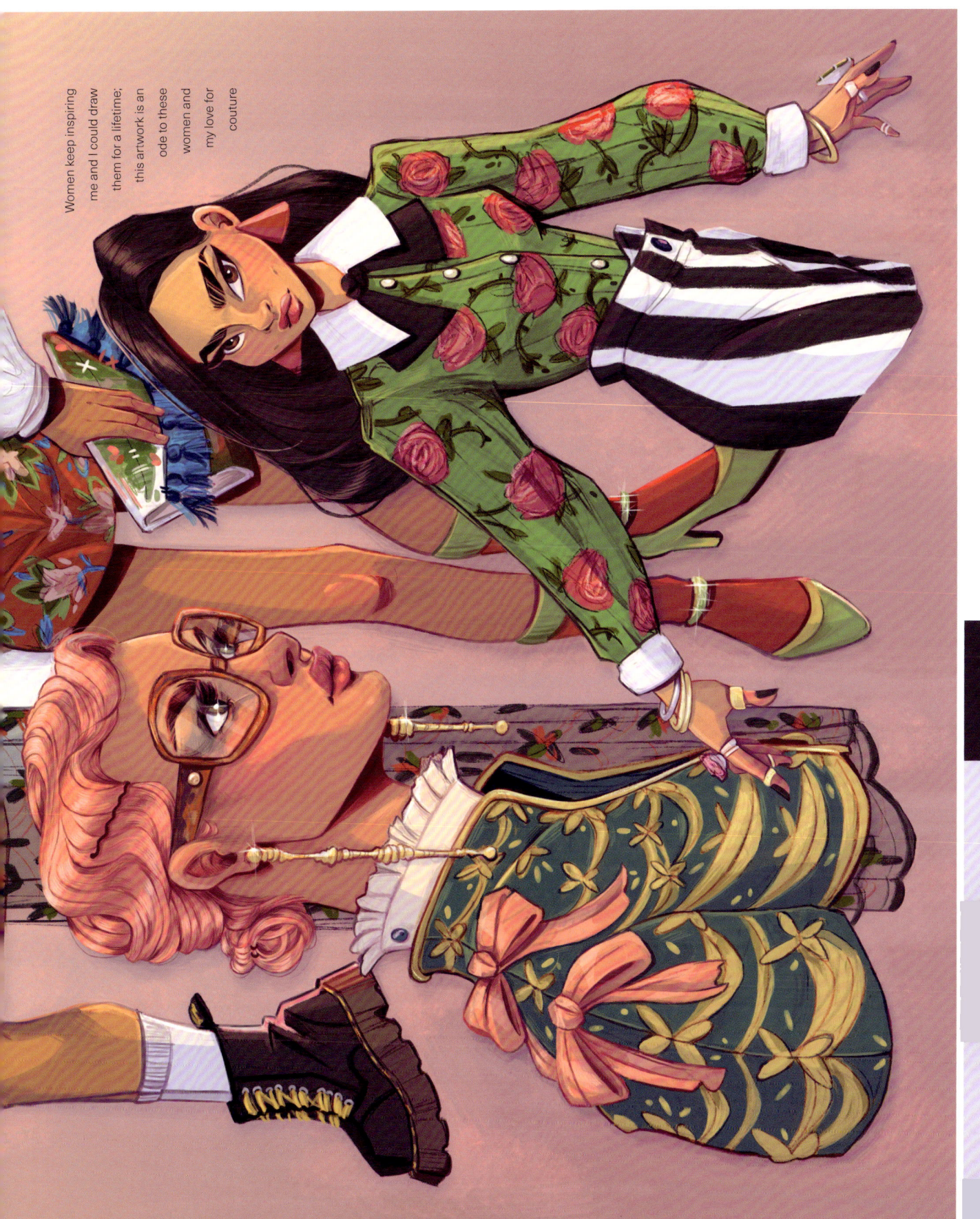

Women keep inspiring me and I could draw them for a lifetime; this artwork is an ode to these women and my love for couture

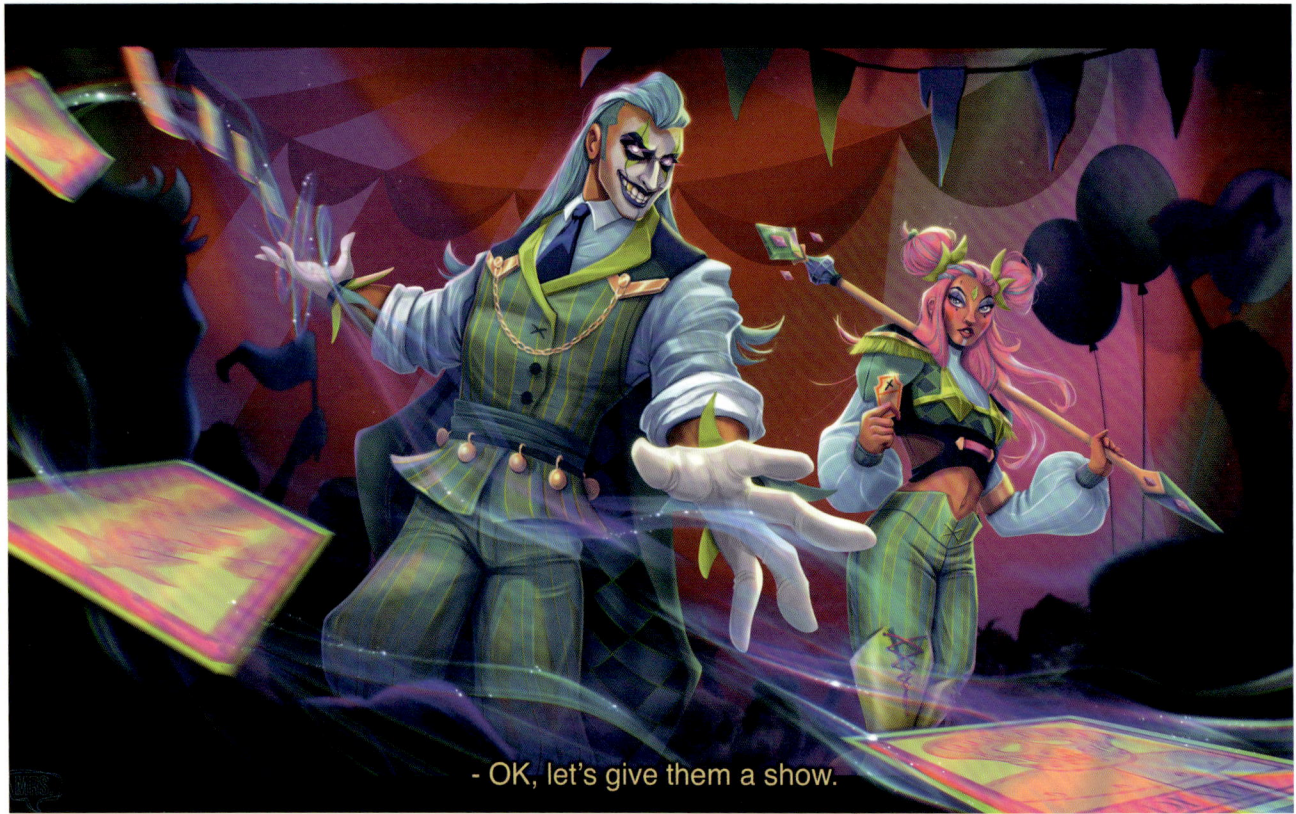

- OK, let's give them a show.

I took a deep dive into splash art and this was the result of the study; it taught me a lot about composition and lighting

What are the key elements of creating a memorable character design?

I think a great character design is readable, funny, and maybe even tugs a bit at your heartstrings. I think it's amazing when you're able to tell within seconds who the character is, based on its design. Does the character have a colourful personality or are they rather moody? Maybe their clothes or features tell you something about their hobbies, career, or family. A scar could tell you something about their past. If the character makes you laugh, I consider that a success. Characters can be multidimensional these days – their personalities are not black and white. Someone truly, deeply evil could still have a sweet affection for something or someone – those sorts of characters are fascinating.

And what is the most important skill to have when working in character design?

It's important to keep pushing yourself further than your first idea. It's something I learned from teaching art to teenagers – your first idea is not always your best idea. I noticed that the kids in my class always just started drawing any idea that came to mind, and when I asked them to give the theme a bit more thought, it always bothered them immensely. Those that did brainstorm a bit further seemed more pleased with their artwork in the end. Some trial, error, and hard work will pay off. That's why making rough thumbnails or sketches while brainstorming for ideas is so important. And it's a good warm-up at the same time!

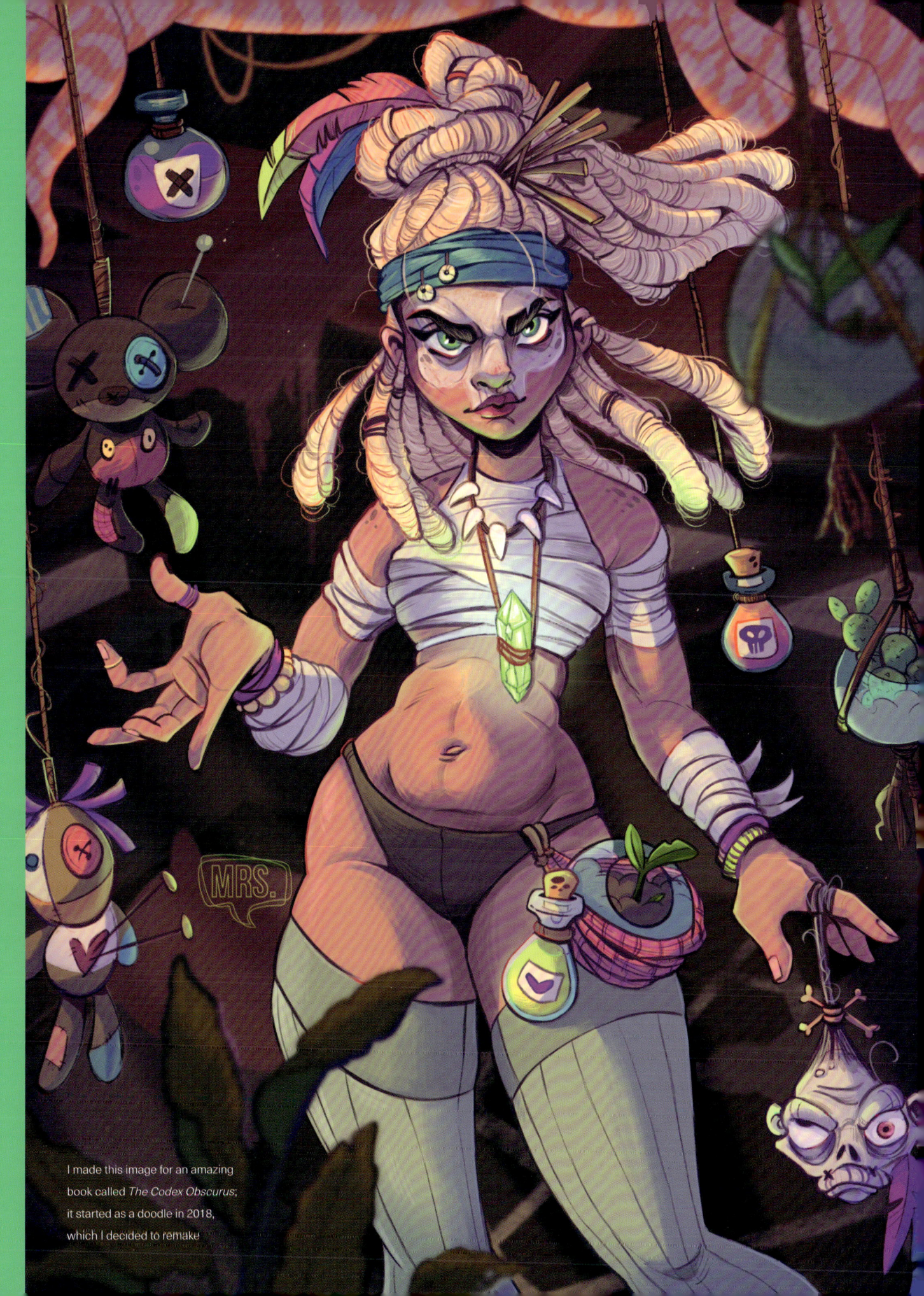

I made this image for an amazing book called *The Codex Obscurus*; it started as a doodle in 2018, which I decided to remake

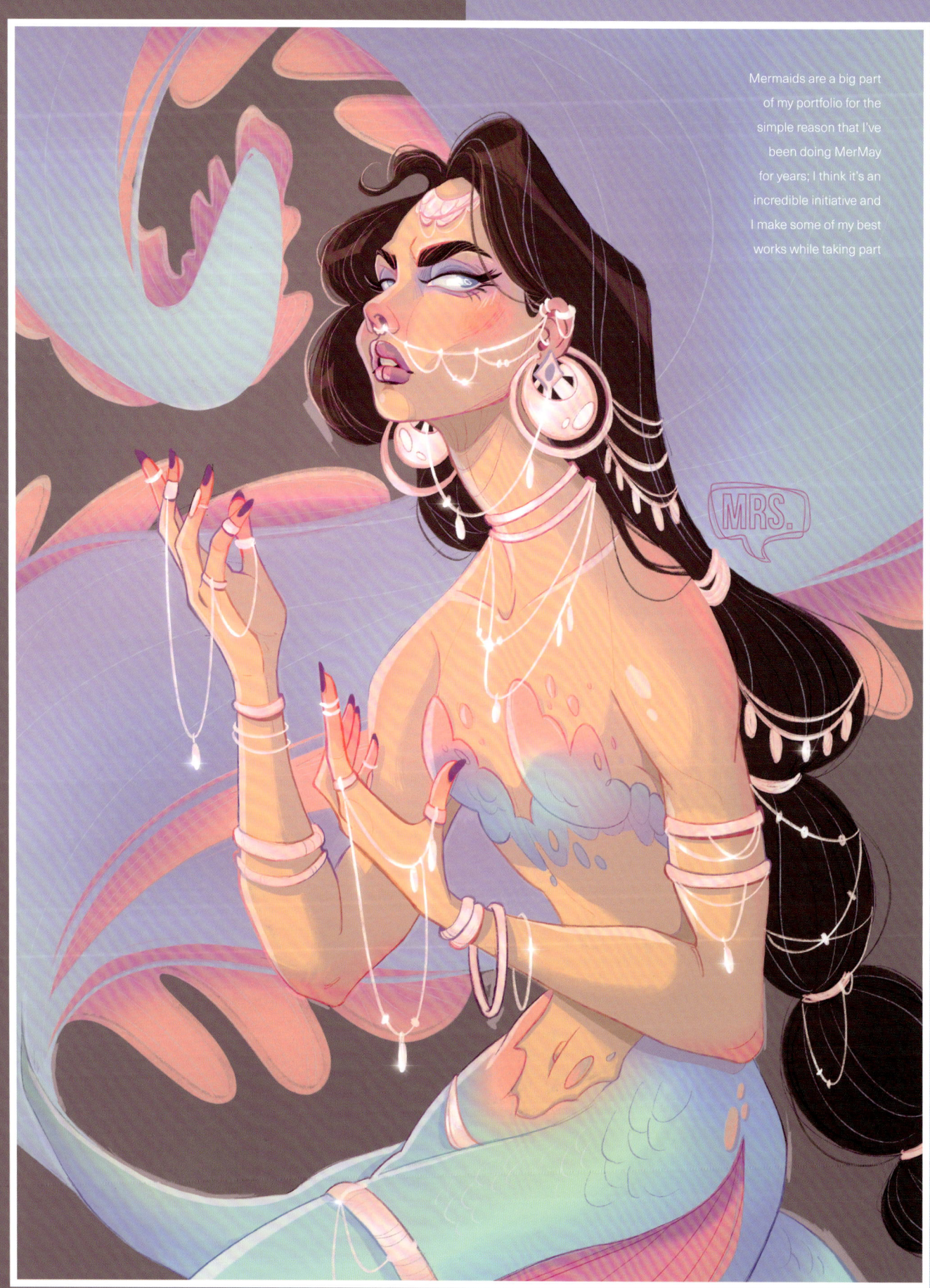

Mermaids are a big part of my portfolio for the simple reason that I've been doing MerMay for years; I think it's an incredible initiative and I make some of my best works while taking part

Do you have any advice for our readers who are looking to break into the industry?

Perhaps stating the obvious, but make sure you have a great portfolio. Some will tell you to specialize in one skill and do it really well, but I would suggest making sure you show recruiters you're flexible and can handle different tasks and styles. Show them a complete design pack for one of your original characters, including turnarounds, colours, and expression sheets, but also include some backgrounds. Show studios you can handle all kinds of design work. It's also important that you make your portfolio easily accessible. You don't want recruiters to have to click five times before they see your work. They have hundreds of portfolios to check and if they can't quickly see what you're capable of then you may miss your chance.

What would you be your dream project to work on?

I think everyone who works in the animation business at the moment is incredibly impressed by *Arcane* – what Fortiche have done with the *League of Legends* IP is just mind-blowing. I collect the artbooks of animation films because, more often than not, I like the painterly concept art even more than the final look of the film itself. Not only Fortiche, but Sony with *Spider-Man: Into the Spider-Verse* did an incredible job of blending that painterly style and a more finished look into one. The concept artists who work behind the scenes get pushed more into the foreground and I think that's just awesome. I will keep admiring these artists and work hard to match their skills, and who knows what dreams will become reality in the future!

Thank you for chatting to us Anne! Are there any upcoming projects we should be looking out for?

At the moment I'm working on something that I would love to go back in time and tell the child version of me about – I wouldn't believe it! I can't say much more about it yet, but keep an eye on my socials if you want to find out. Thank you so much for having me *CDQ*! You've been my favourite magazine since day one and I'm always looking forward to the next edition.

This is my ode to the Netherlands: I took two very Dutch objects – *The Milkmaid* by Vermeer and Delftware pottery – and combined them into something new

BEST OF ENEMIES

Annie Mation shows us her process for designing new characters

As of late, I have an interest in the character designs of 'ladies of a certain age'. I'm thinking of characters like the Disney villains Cruella, Ursula, and Yzma, and Zeniba and Yubaba, the sister witches from *Spirited Away*. Their age gives these characters personality, and I wanted to discover if I could create my own version of them.

To create this artwork I'm using my trusty iPad Pro and Procreate. I don't use any fancy brushes, just the standard Procreate Shale and Soft Brush.

To warm up, I start sketching different types of older women based on references I can find. Some of the sketches kickstart my imagination and I decide to draw a couple of ladies with very different body types.

> Your first idea may not always be your best, so keep sketching to see what you discover, even if you're happy with your first design. For example, I tried different hairstyles for my characters to see which would work best.

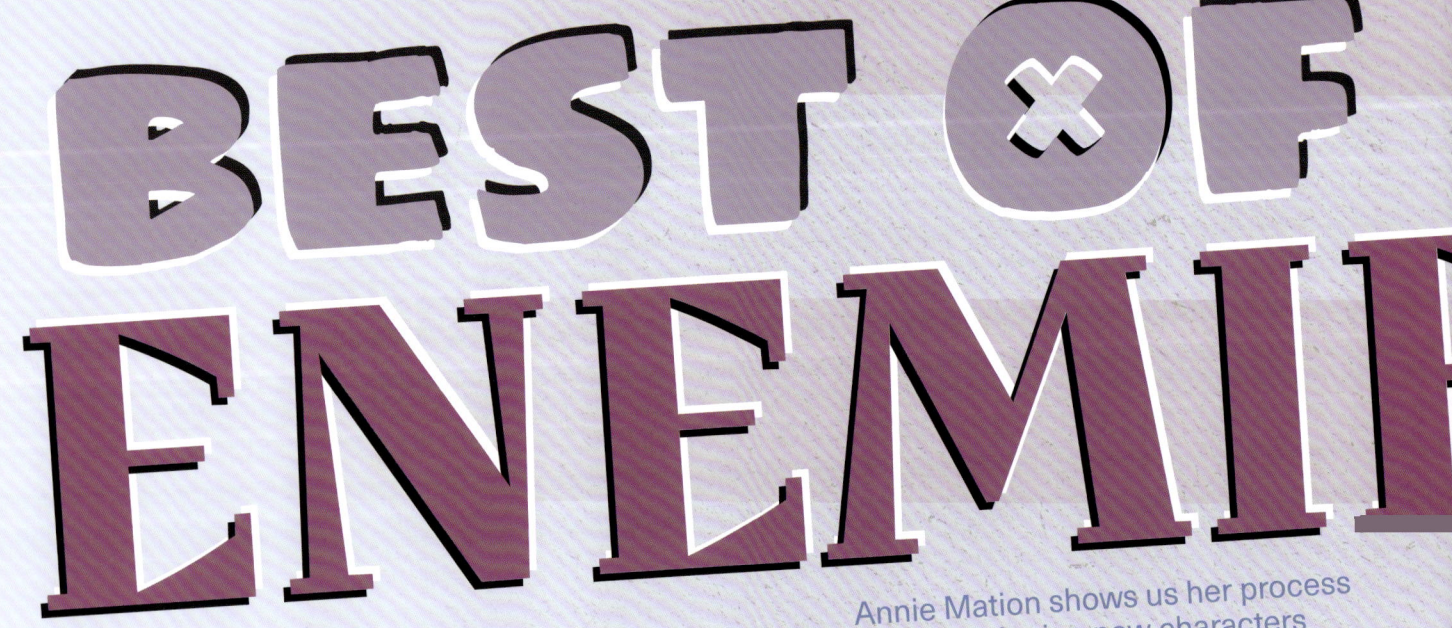

I refine the shapes on a new layer. Through trial and error I add more details to the characters to discover what works for each of them.

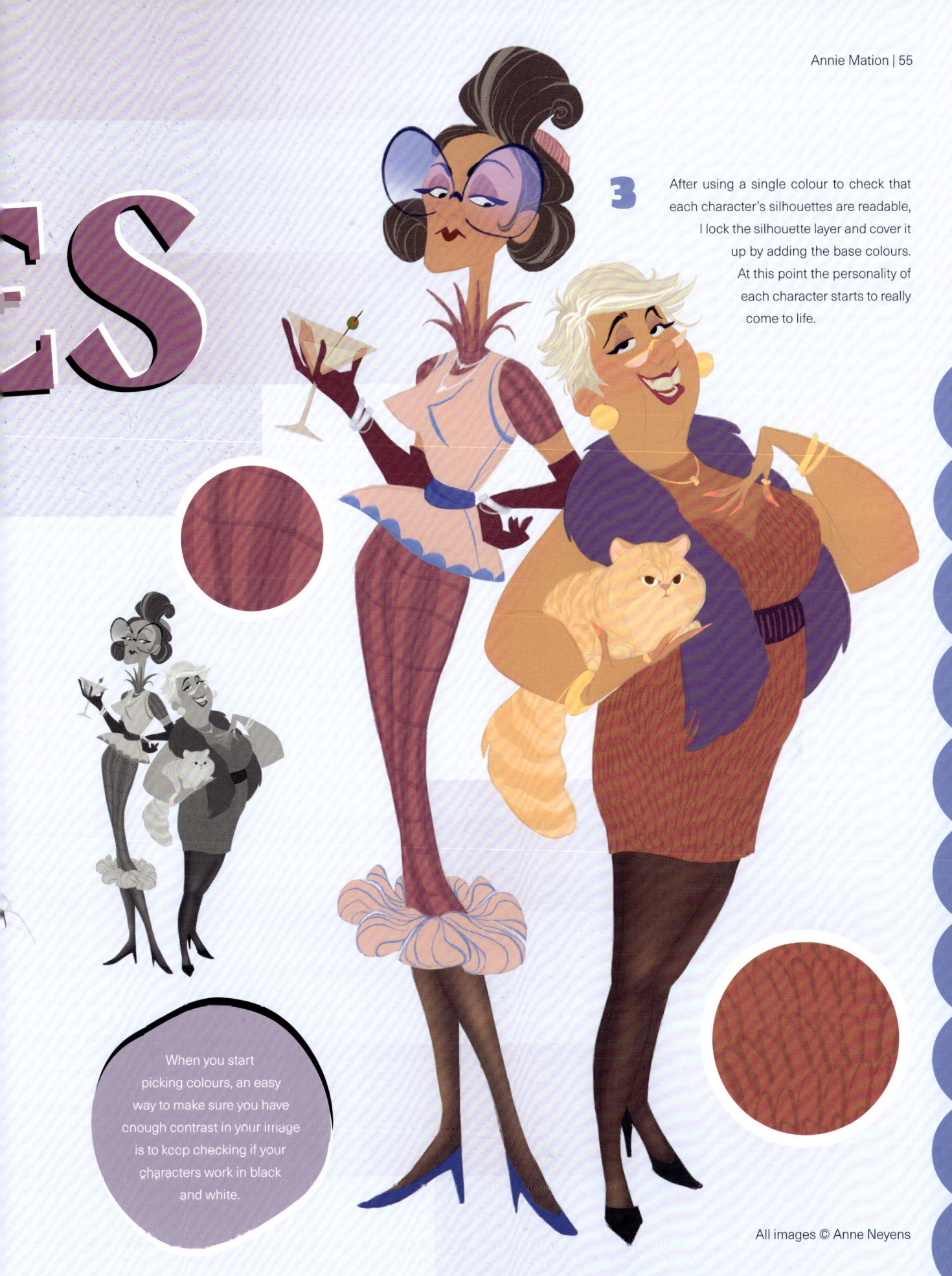

3 After using a single colour to check that each character's silhouettes are readable, I lock the silhouette layer and cover it up by adding the base colours. At this point the personality of each character starts to really come to life.

When you start picking colours, an easy way to make sure you have enough contrast in your image is to keep checking if your characters work in black and white.

All images © Anne Neyens

4

I paint the shadows on a new layer, constantly keeping in mind where my light source is. I add shading to every different shape within my characters' designs. I do the same with a vivid yellow for the highlights.

5

In the previous step, I was working rather roughly – I don't want to spend too much time on things that perhaps don't work. When I feel the characters are lit well, I start to go over the artwork with a sharper brush and gradually paint in more details.

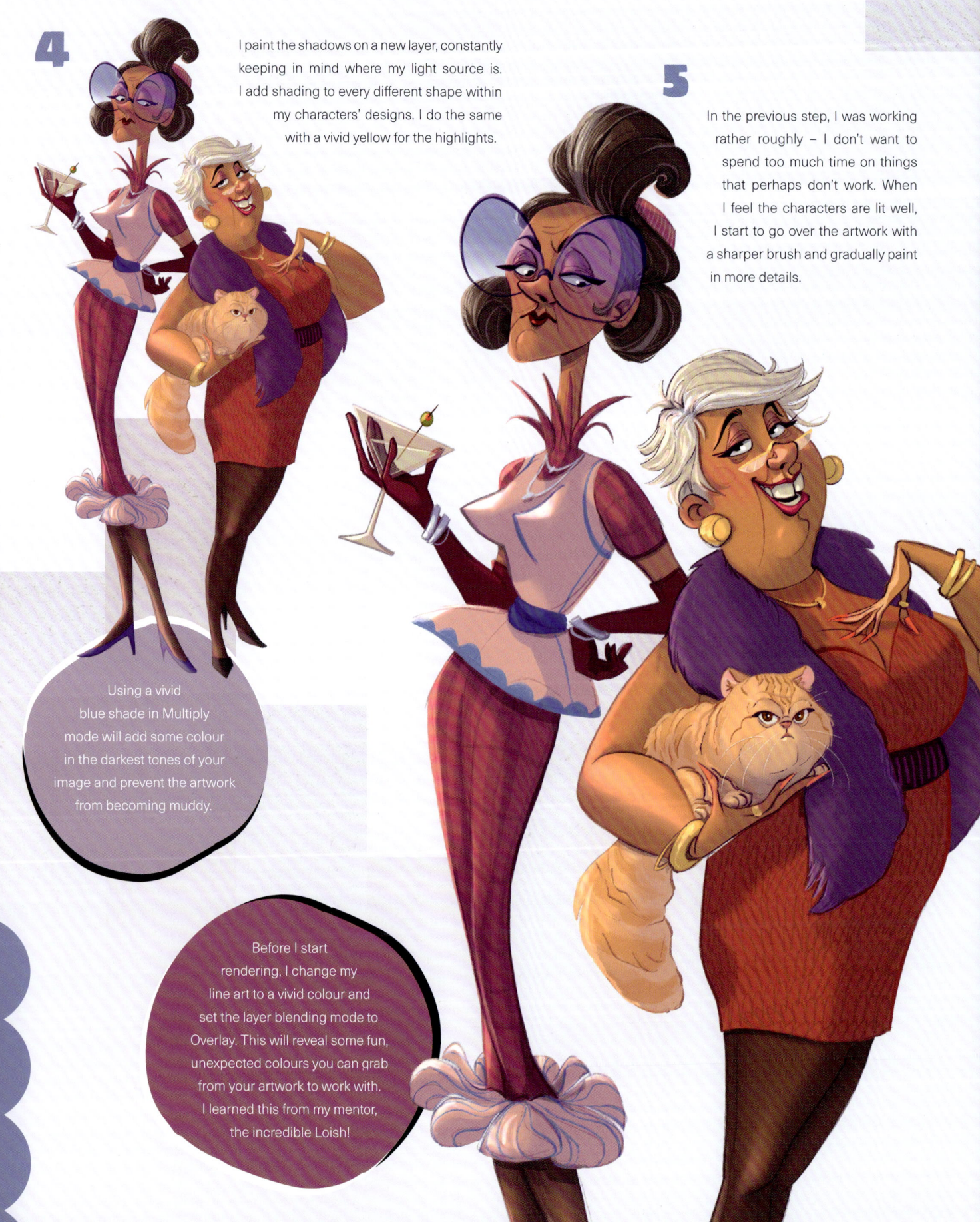

Using a vivid blue shade in Multiply mode will add some colour in the darkest tones of your image and prevent the artwork from becoming muddy.

Before I start rendering, I change my line art to a vivid colour and set the layer blending mode to Overlay. This will reveal some fun, unexpected colours you can grab from your artwork to work with. I learned this from my mentor, the incredible Loish!

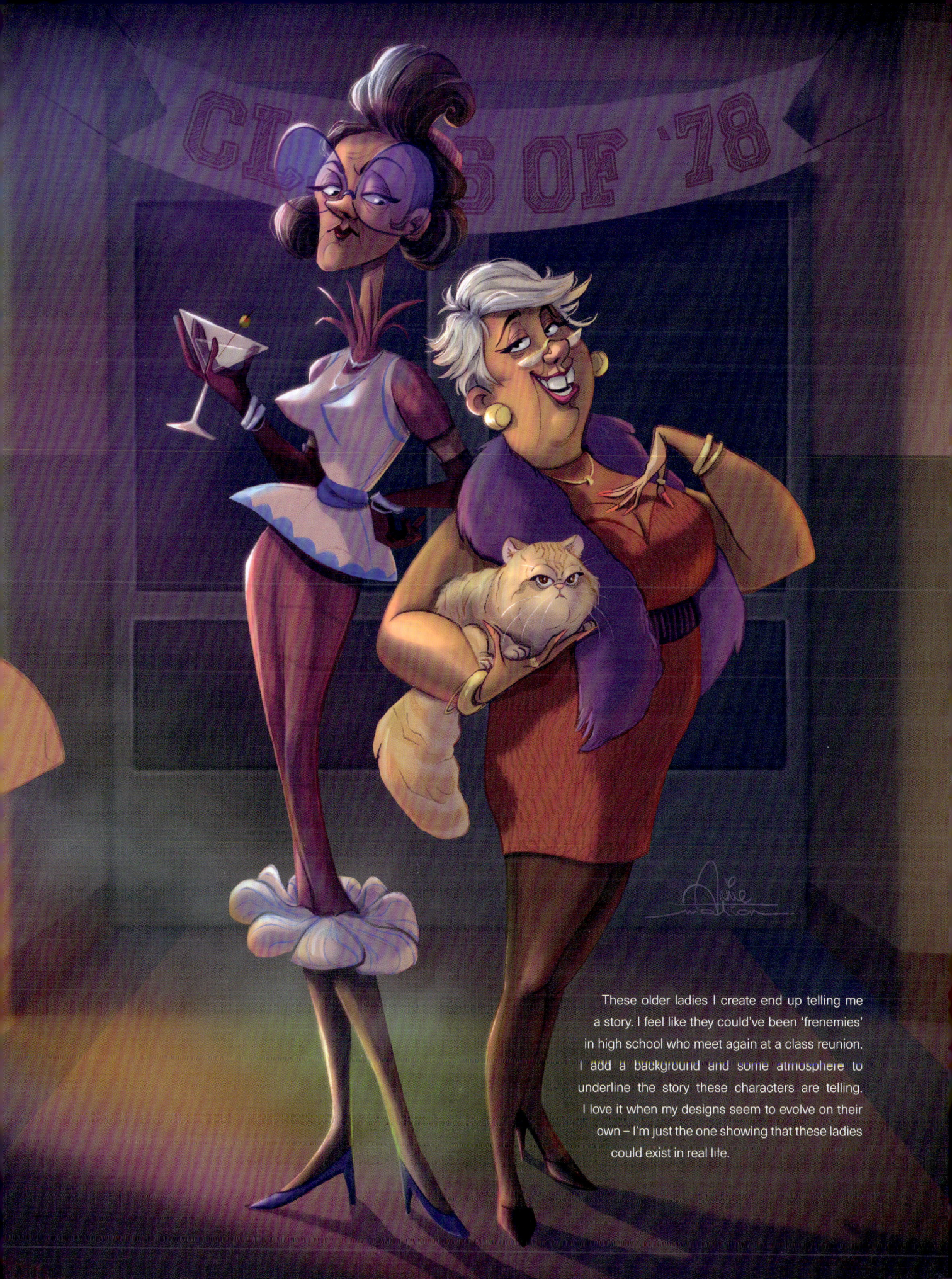

CLASS OF '78

These older ladies I create end up telling me a story. I feel like they could've been 'frenemies' in high school who meet again at a class reunion. I add a background and some atmosphere to underline the story these characters are telling. I love it when my designs seem to evolve on their own – I'm just the one showing that these ladies could exist in real life.

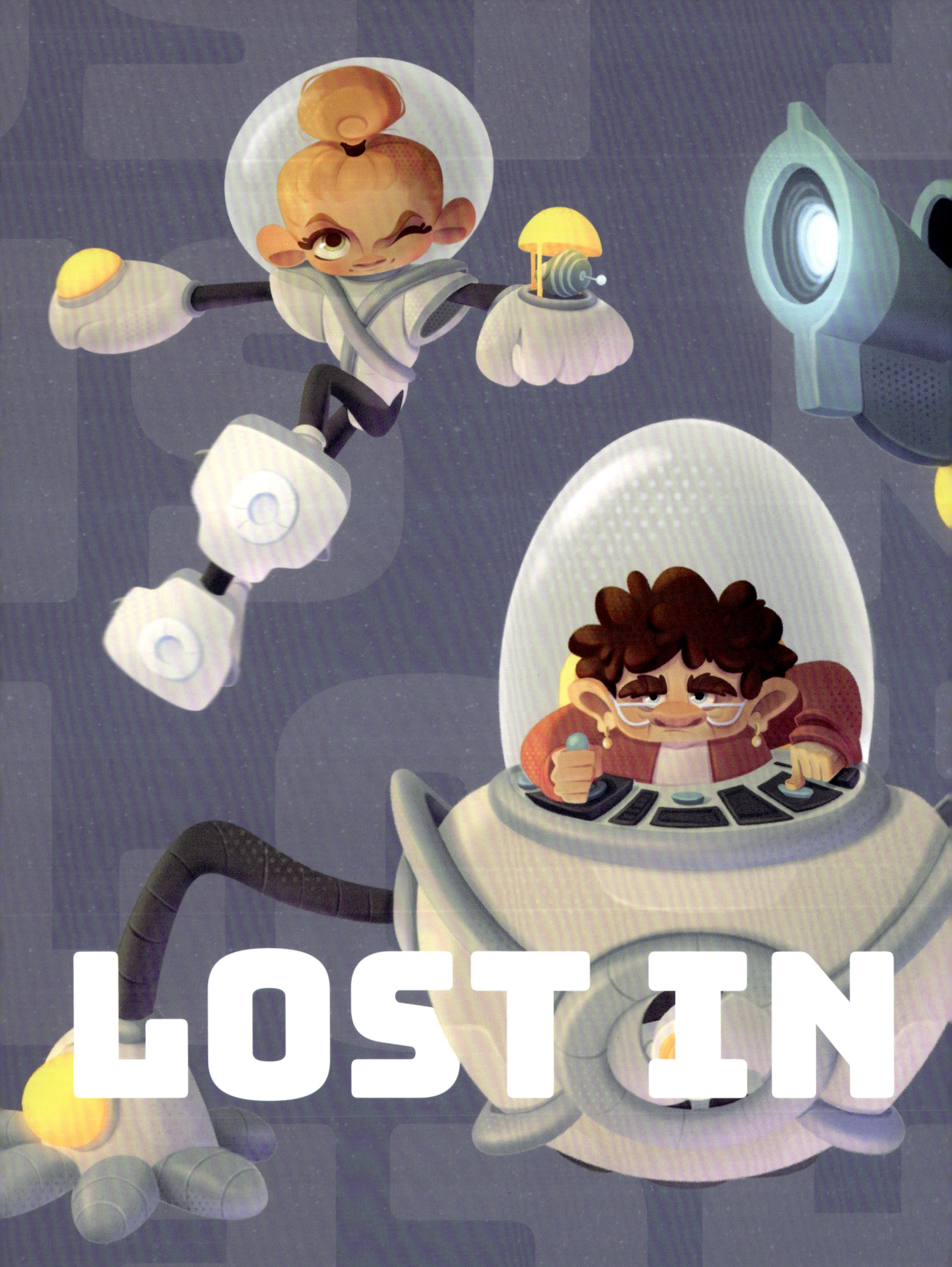

LOST IN

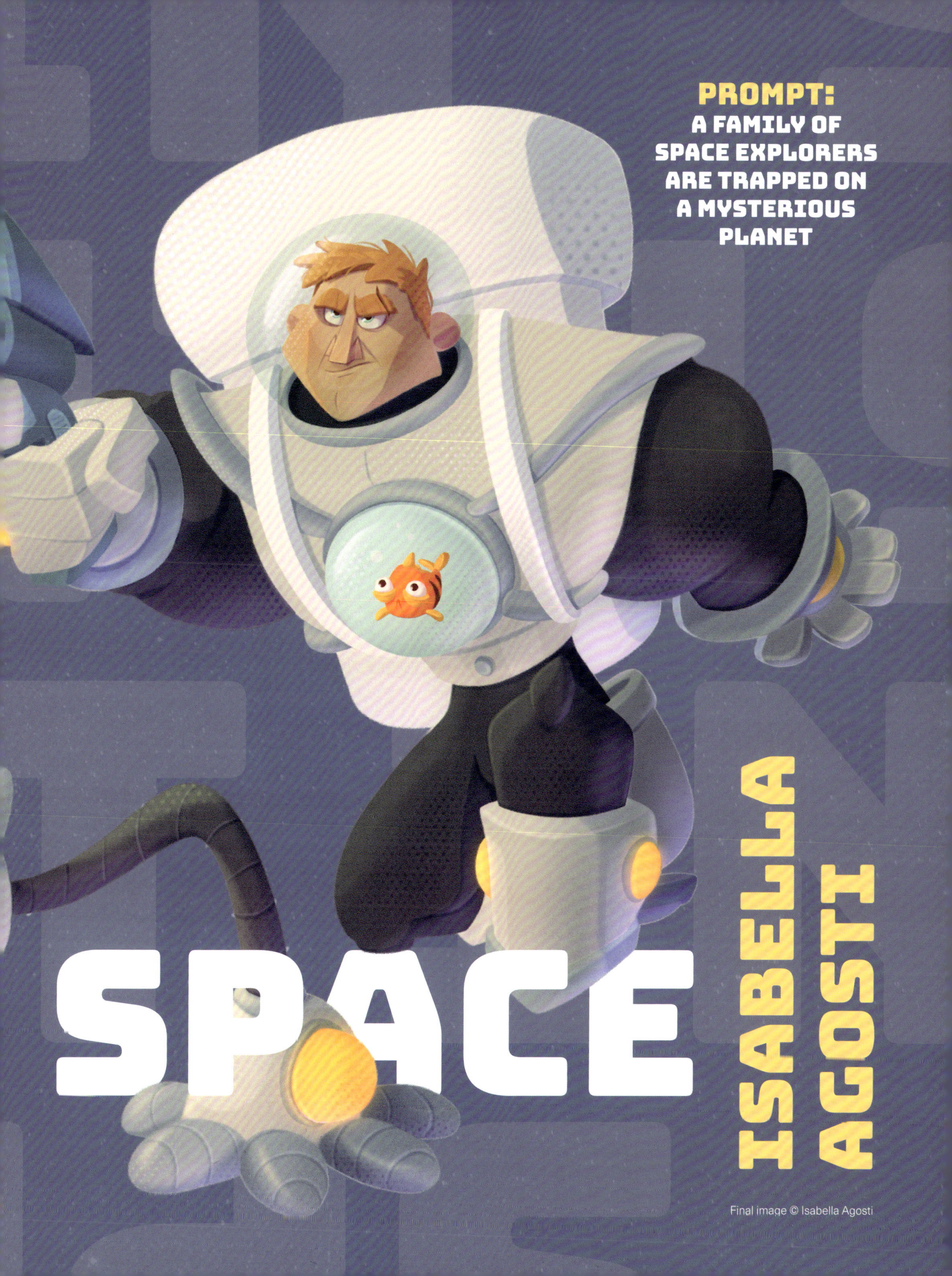

PROMPT:
A FAMILY OF SPACE EXPLORERS ARE TRAPPED ON A MYSTERIOUS PLANET

SPACE

ISABELLA AGOSTI

In this tutorial we'll be creating a family of space explorers. Start by thinking about your prompt, writing down everything that comes to mind. Organize your thoughts into a coherent structure to form a more comprehensive overview of the characters and better develop their attributes. In my case, 'family' is a key part of the brief, so first I make a mind map of ideas about how the family could be composed, and then further develop each member of the family by giving them different attributes.. My three characters will be an astronaut, his daughter, and her grandma.

Analysing each part of the prompt individually can prevent you from feeling overwhelmed with information, and thus help you come up with more interesting concepts. Let your ideas branch out naturally and don't discard anything, even if you're unsure whether it'll make it into the final design. Initial ideas don't need to be perfect. Character design is an evolving process, so be patient and let your ideas grow as you progress through the development.

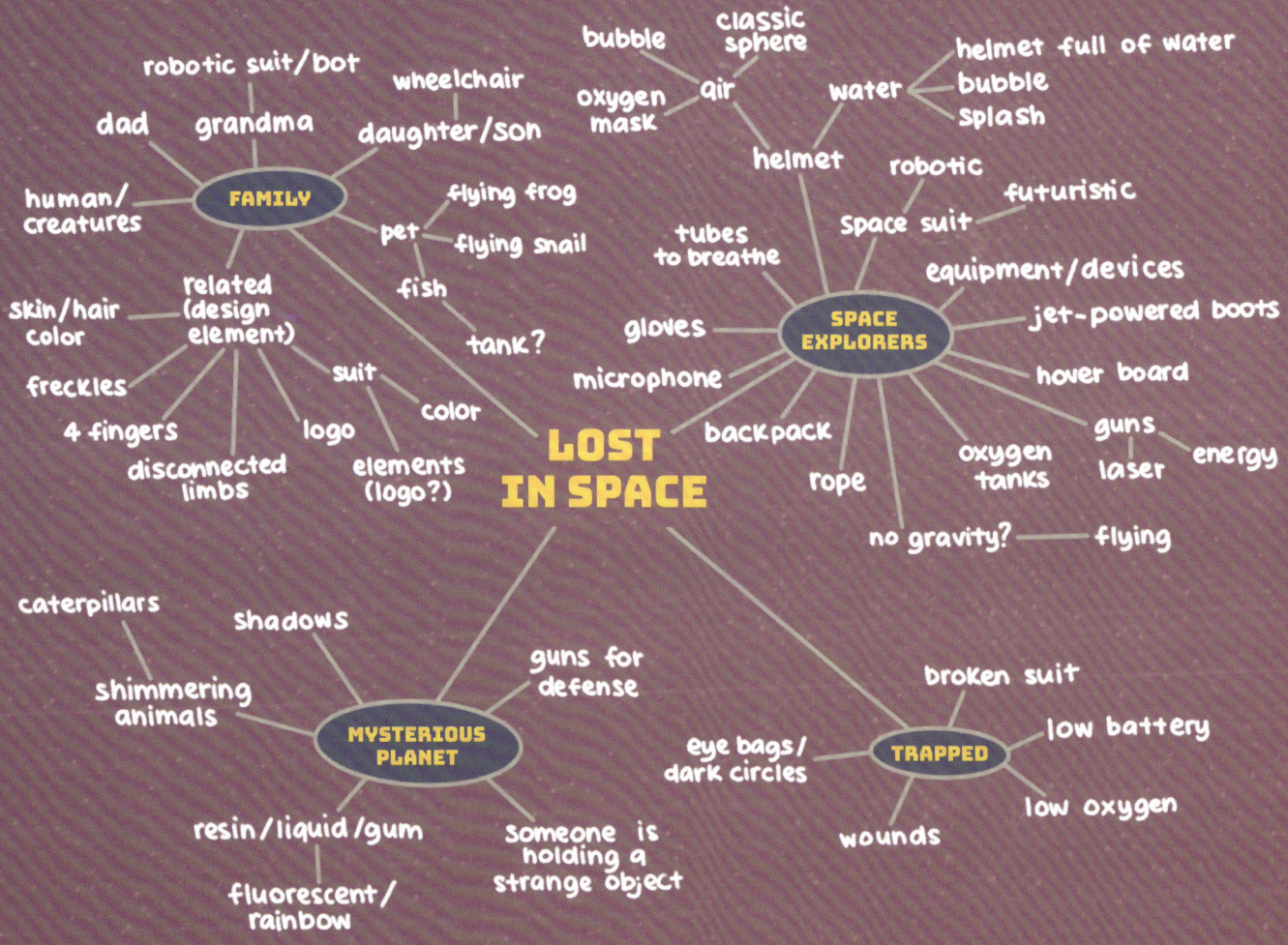

Jot down any ideas that come to mind when thinking about the prompts

'USING SIMPLE SHAPES AT THIS STAGE CAN HELP GENERATE IDEAS QUICKLY'

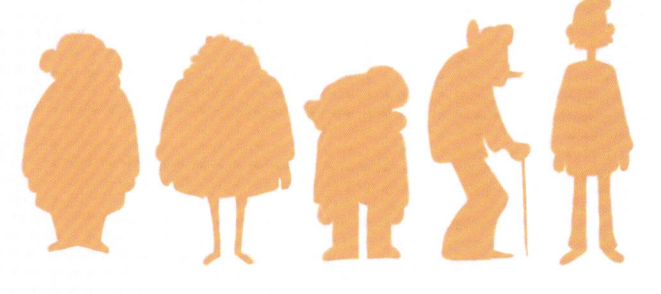

I explore different shape designs for my three characters

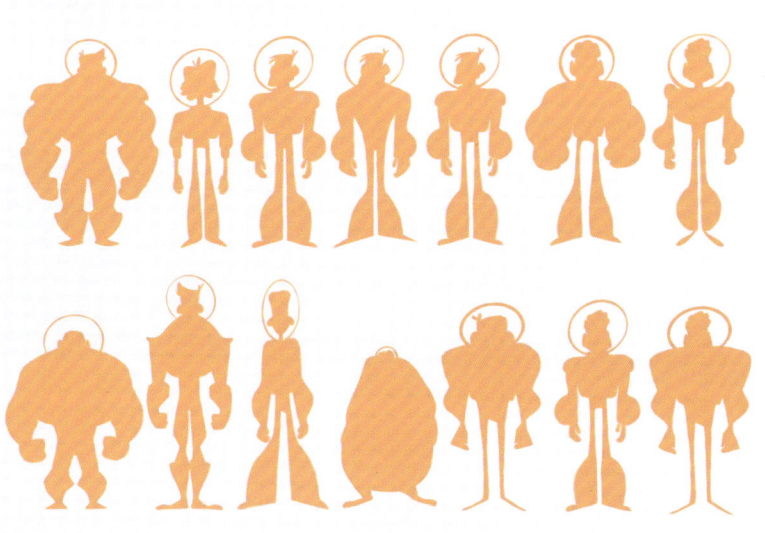

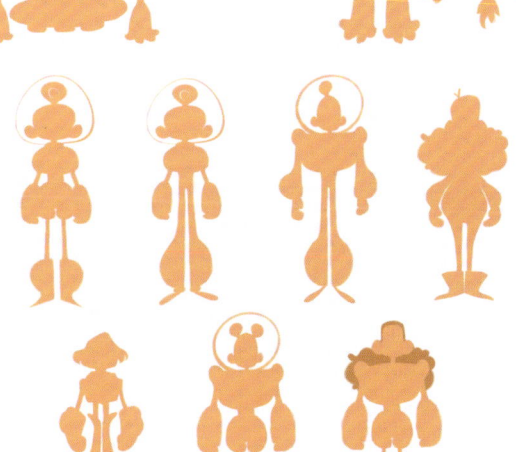

Have fun playing with silhouettes to create different visual concepts for the characters, inspired by your prompts and mind map. Using simple shapes at this stage can help generate ideas quickly and make tackling the blank canvas less daunting. Focus on creating clear and readable silhouettes that make the characters recognizable even in simple forms. Don't feel pressured to make each silhouette entirely different; if you like one but want to explore a slightly different version, duplicate it and tweak even just one detail. If there are props playing an important role in the story – like the bot my grandma is driving – it might be helpful to explore silhouettes for those as well.

At this point, you can decide to move onto the next step with all your silhouettes, or pick the ones that speak to you the most and that you feel are worth exploring. My dad character has a *lot* of silhouettes – I discard the ones that are too similar to the daughter's for the sake of character variation.

THINK BEYOND YOUR FIRST IDEAS

It's important to recognize when an idea isn't working and have the confidence to let it go. For instance, at the mind-map stage I considered giving the child a wheelchair. However, after deciding to pair the grandma with a bot due to her inability to walk, I realized the two concepts were too similar.

WHEN INSPIRATION FALTERS

If you find yourself stuck during the design process, try drawing inspiration from people you know. Personal connections can provide a fresh perspective and make the characters more relatable. For example, when designing the grandma, I drew inspiration from my own grandmother, incorporating elements of her personality and appearance into the design. This not only made the character more authentic, but also helped me break through creative blocks.

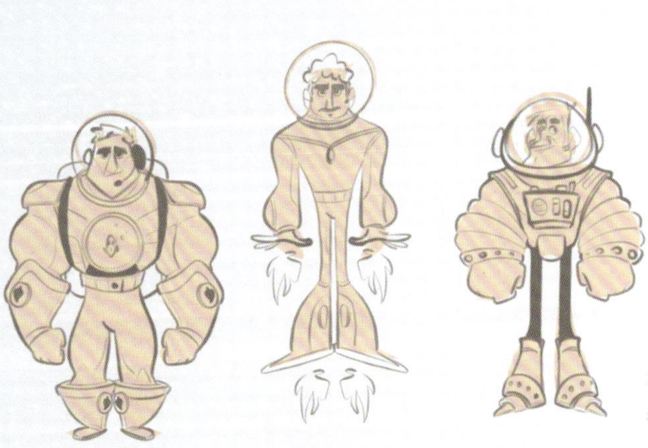

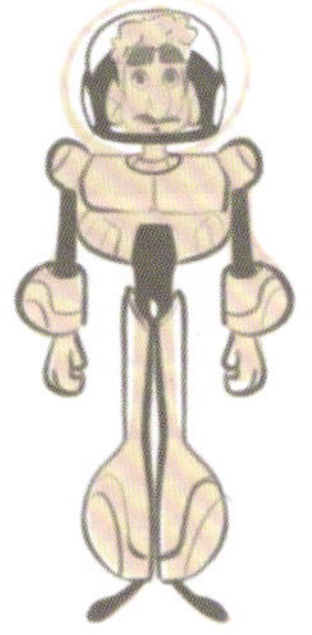

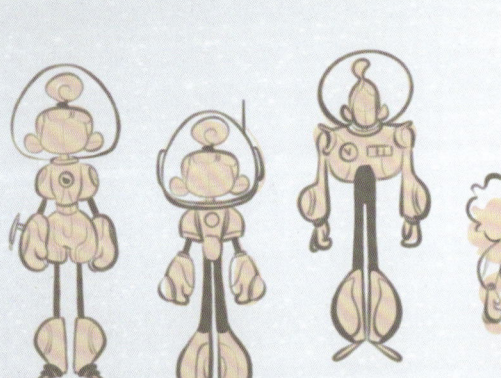

Loosen up and start sketching to explore different variations for your characters

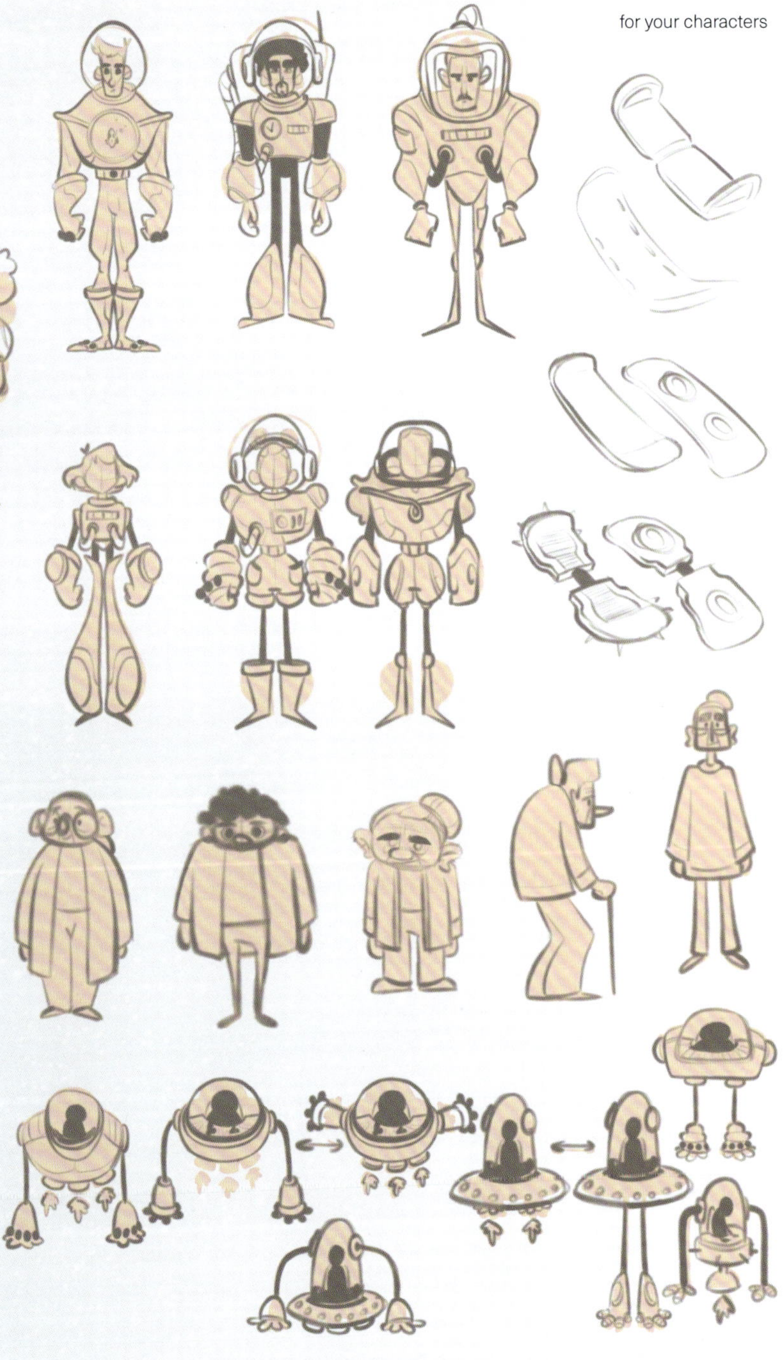

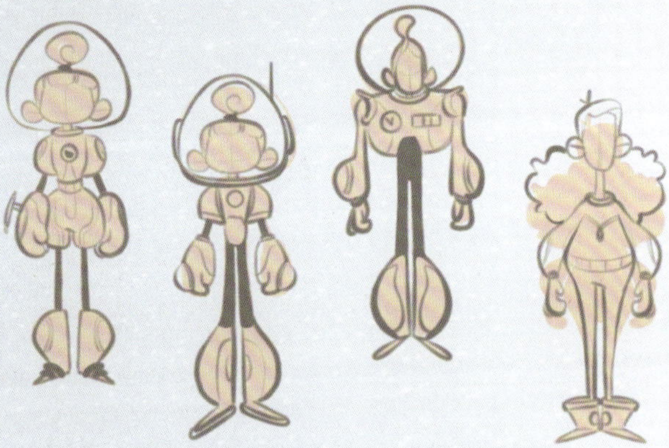

Sketch over your silhouettes and explore details, costumes, and variations for your characters. Approach this stage with energy and looseness, quickly transferring ideas from your mind to the page. Perfection isn't the goal here – focus on exploring possibilities and making wise design decisions, such as determining how specific features of your characters are uniquely theirs. At the same time, I repeat similar designs for the gloves and boots for dad, daughter, and bot, to link them all together. I add slight variations so that they fit the respective character's proportions and type. Once you feel like you've made enough explorations for the different designs, take your time to analyse them and select your favourite elements from each of them before moving onto the next step.

Keeping all of your favourite elements from your initial concepts in mind, take your time to mix and match them to create new, enhanced designs. Focus once more on character variation. This process will help you move in a clear and specific direction, ensuring the characters evolve into cohesive and compelling concepts. For the daughter character, I settle on a design with a thin body and legs, so I pick a muscular look for the dad, and a rounder shape for the grandma and bot. Never lose sight of the prompt, especially during these early stages. Each step brings changes to the design itself, so always make sure to stay aligned with the requirements before committing to a choice and moving onto the next stage.

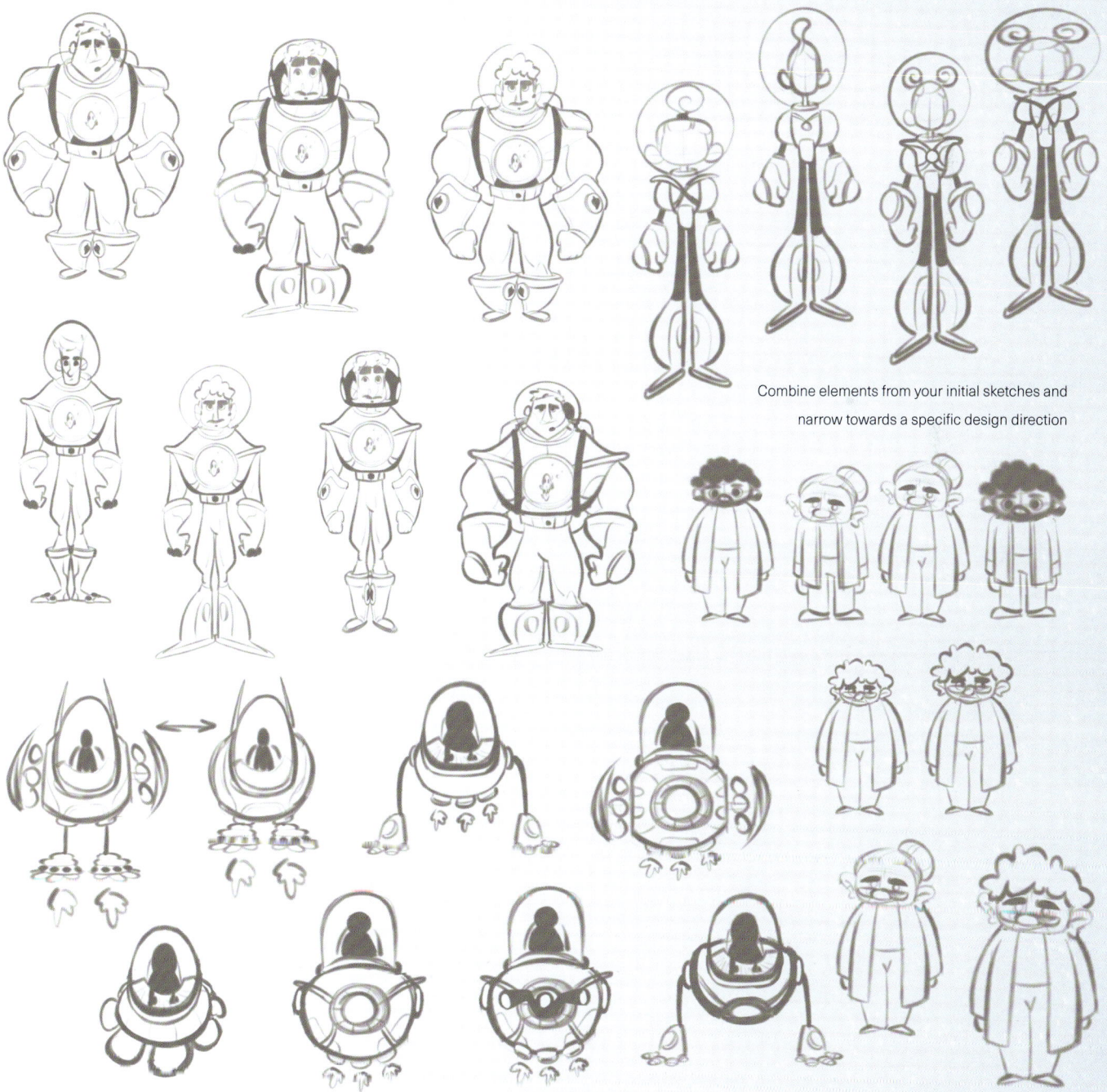

Combine elements from your initial sketches and narrow towards a specific design direction

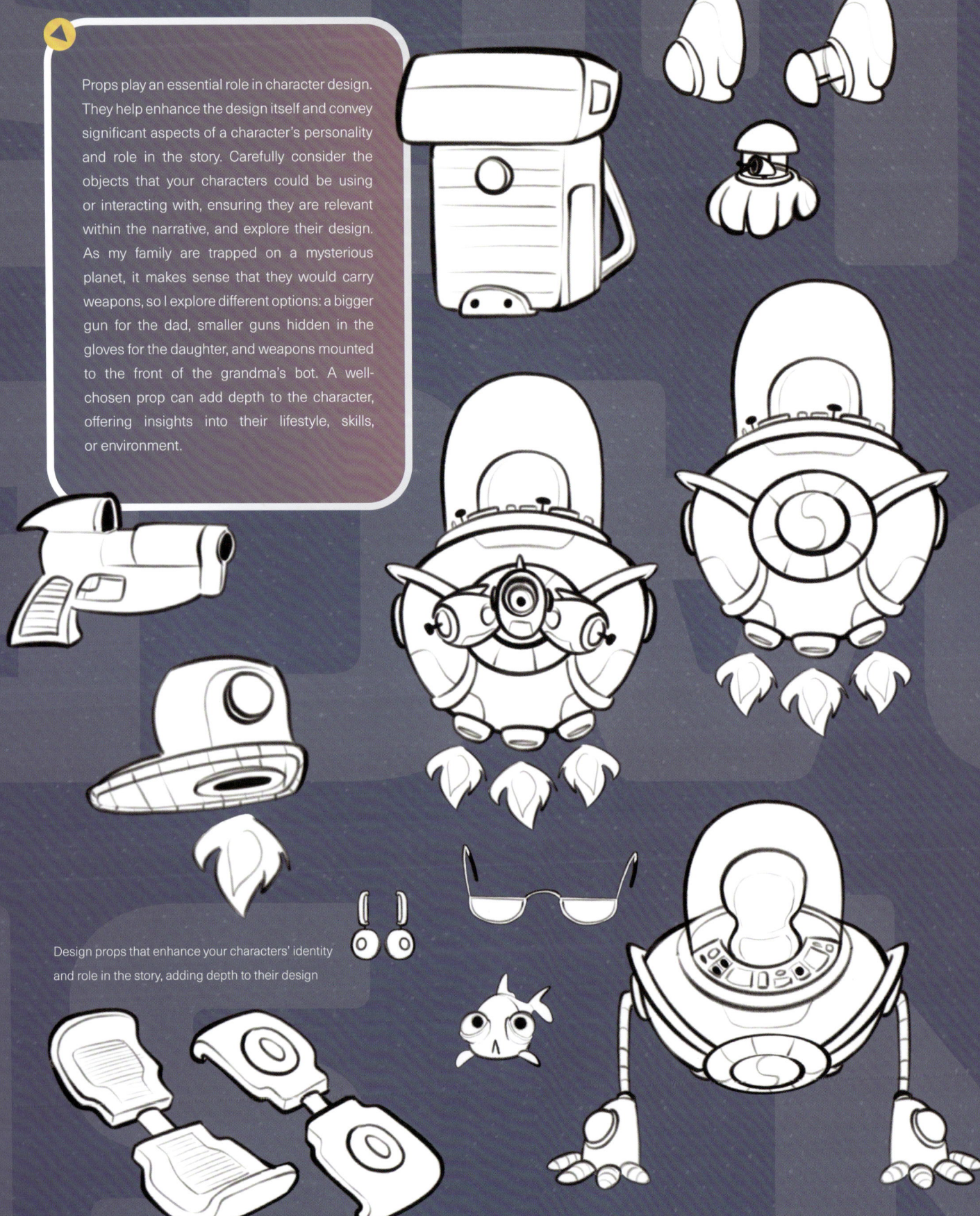

Props play an essential role in character design. They help enhance the design itself and convey significant aspects of a character's personality and role in the story. Carefully consider the objects that your characters could be using or interacting with, ensuring they are relevant within the narrative, and explore their design. As my family are trapped on a mysterious planet, it makes sense that they would carry weapons, so I explore different options: a bigger gun for the dad, smaller guns hidden in the gloves for the daughter, and weapons mounted to the front of the grandma's bot. A well-chosen prop can add depth to the character, offering insights into their lifestyle, skills, or environment.

Design props that enhance your characters' identity and role in the story, adding depth to their design

KEEPING UNITY IN MIND

When coming up with characters that belong to the same group, it's crucial to gradually design them together as a whole, rather than considering each one in isolation. Don't finalize one character and then move on to the next, but instead jump from one character to another at every stage, making decisions based on how they will look together. This approach ensures that their styles, proportions, colours, and overall aesthetics align, creating a cohesive and interconnected group.

Finalize your character designs by refining details while keeping the overall silhouette in mind

After choosing your preferred design for each character, and selecting and assigning all the appropriate props, it's time to assemble everything into a polished final design. Place props to aid the narrative. For instance, it makes sense that the dad is carrying the backpack, since he's the more robust character, and the bot would have a hard time handling it. Focus on adding more details while ensuring the characters remain clear and readable.

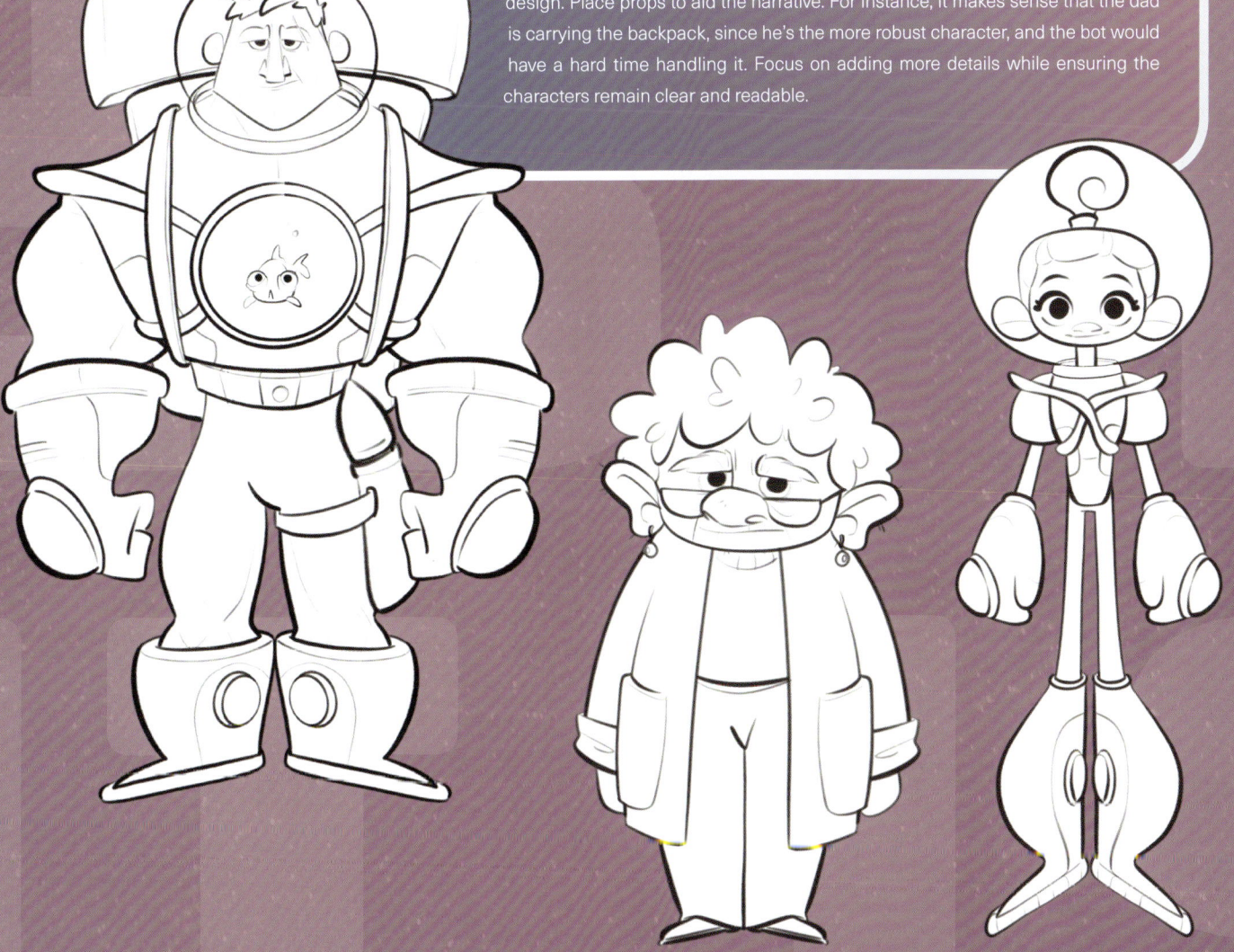

With the final designs locked in, explore different colour palettes to enhance their visual impact. Experiment with a variety of combinations to find the one that best reflects the characters' personalities, environment, and role in the story. Consider creating contrast through colour to make the palette more appealing. I use combinations of dark and light tones, cool and warm hues, complementary colours, and varying saturation. Refer back to your reference images to guide your decisions and find inspiration for colour choices, ensuring that the palettes you create complement the characters' designs and convey the right mood.

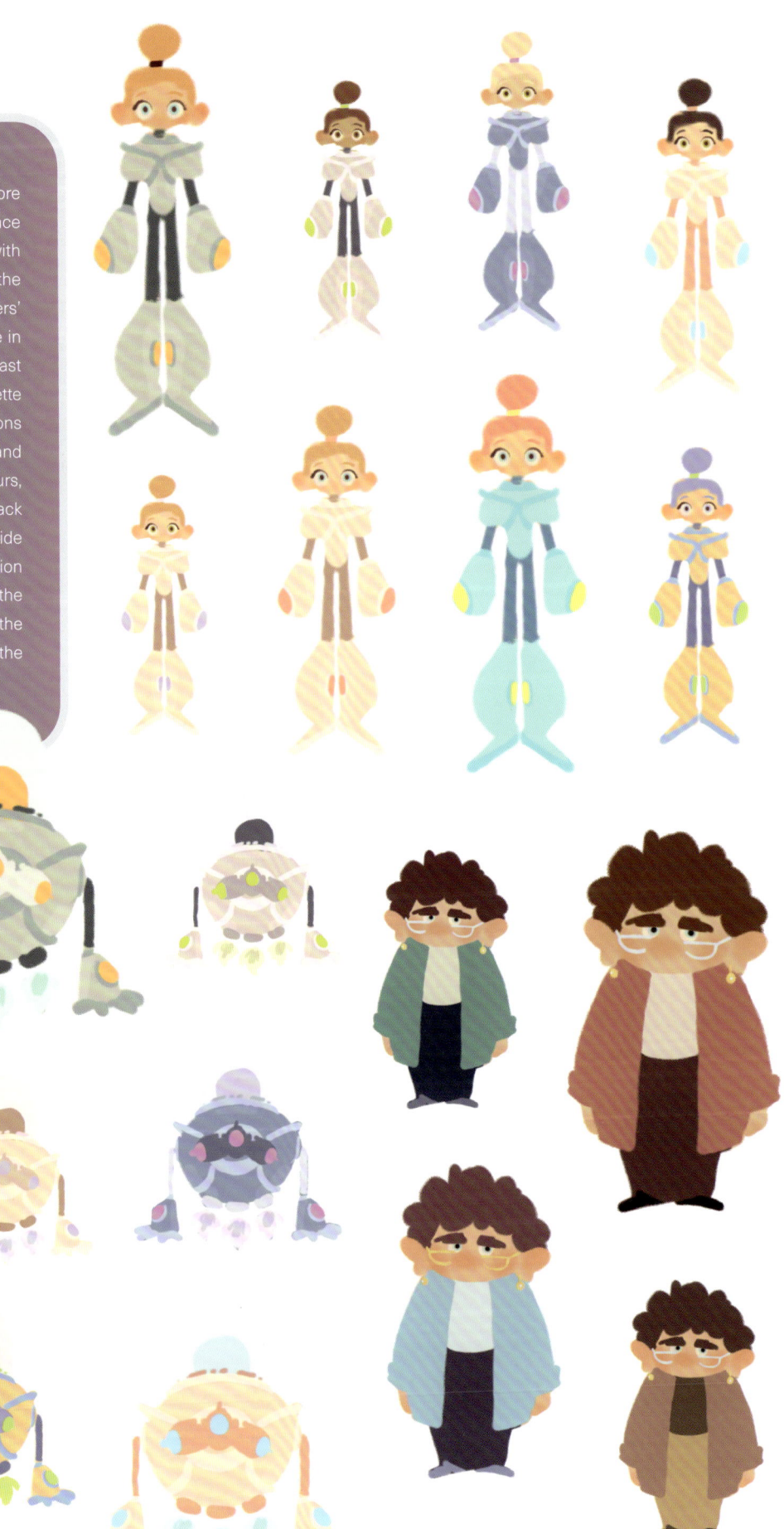

Find colour combinations that not only work for individual characters, but help enhance the group

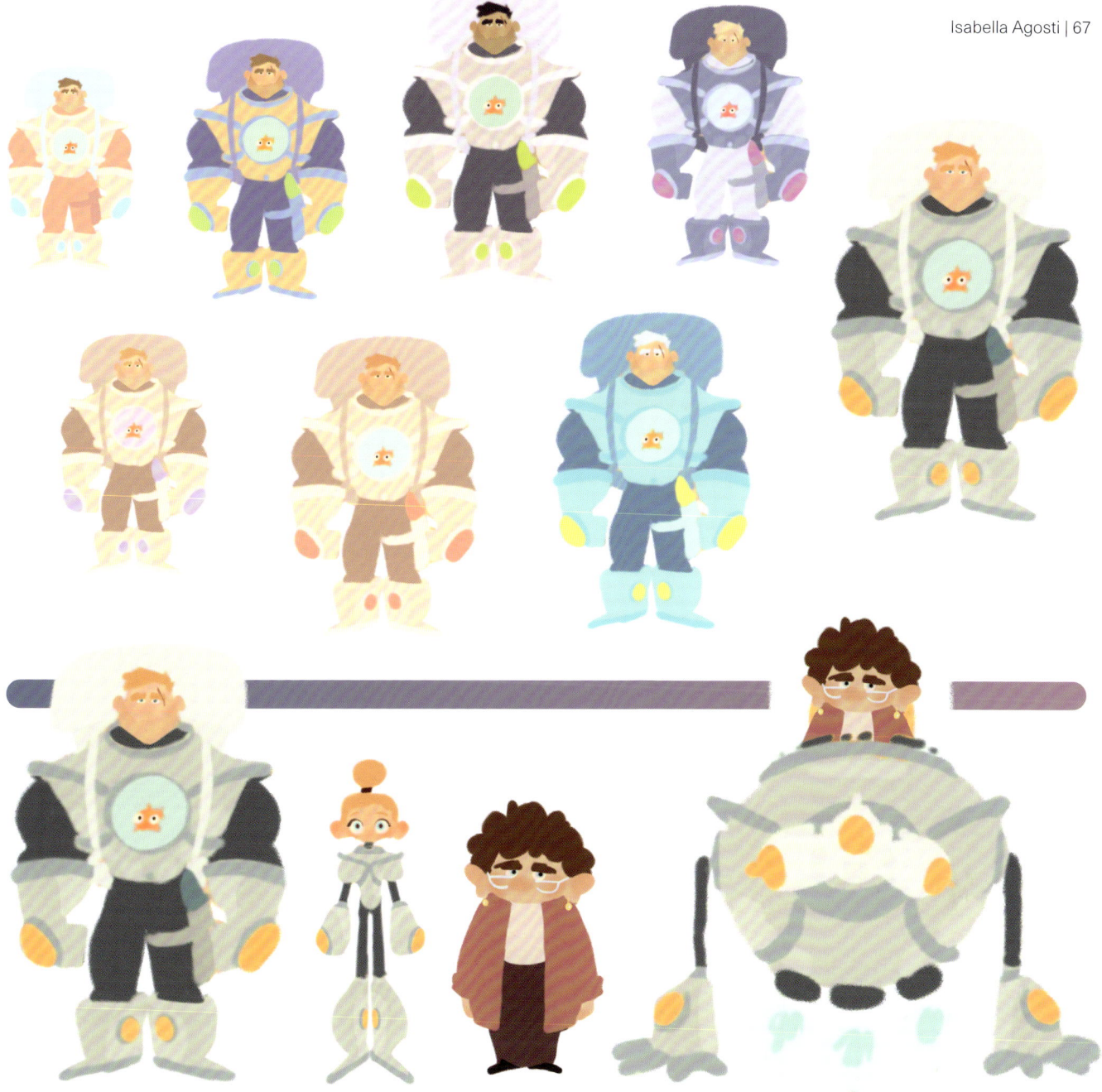

Place all the final colour palettes together and make sure they feel connected and cohesive

After testing several colour options, choose the palettes that feel most fitting and cohesive for your characters, and bring them all together on the same canvas. When designing multiple characters that belong to the same group, it's essential to ensure the colours work together as a whole. For the grandma, for example, I choose a red palette, as my blue and green version would disappear alongside the greys and blues of the bot, and the brown version doesn't create enough contrast.

DESIGN FIRST, POSE LATER

When working on character design, it's important to separate pose and expression from the core design itself. The character should be recognizable and communicate its concept even from a simple and static front pose. Finalizing the character design first, before focusing on pose and expression, ensures that design choices – such as shape, silhouette, and detail – are strong enough to convey the character's personality and story without relying on external factors like movement or facial expression.

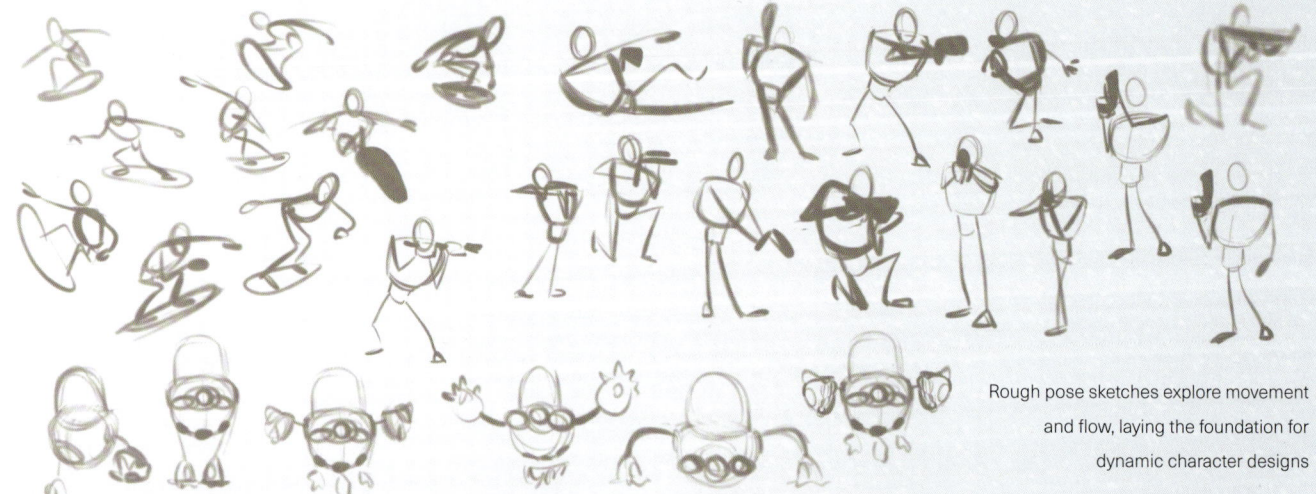

Rough pose sketches explore movement
and flow, laying the foundation for
dynamic character designs

Once your character designs are finalized, explore a variety of poses to bring them to life. Sketch the characters from multiple angles, focusing on movement and energy while making sure to maintain consistent proportions. Details are not important at this stage – simple stick figures and basic shapes guided by a clear line of action, often following the character's spine, are sufficient to capture the essence of each pose. Always address all the prompts, even one at a time, and experiment with different ways to convey the same idea. I want the dad to hold his weapon in his hand, but I explore different poses in which he could be doing that (standing, kneeling, the gun pointing forwards or upwards). Working through this process for each character helps ensure they feel alive, versatile, and true to their role in the story.

Select the most promising rough poses from the previous step and develop them further, adding details and making thoughtful adjustments to bring out the best in each idea. I want the dad to appear strong and powerful, the daughter fast and quick, and the grandma determined, so I pick poses that can help communicate that. Make sure to focus on the strongest sketches, enhancing each pose by emphasizing gesture and guiding the viewer's eye towards the focal point – in my case, the characters' faces. Pay close attention to how shapes communicate gravity, volume, and the direction of the character, ensuring the poses feel grounded and dynamic. Use this stage to clarify your design direction even more and create more polished and expressive poses.

Refined poses bring focus, volume,
and personality to the character

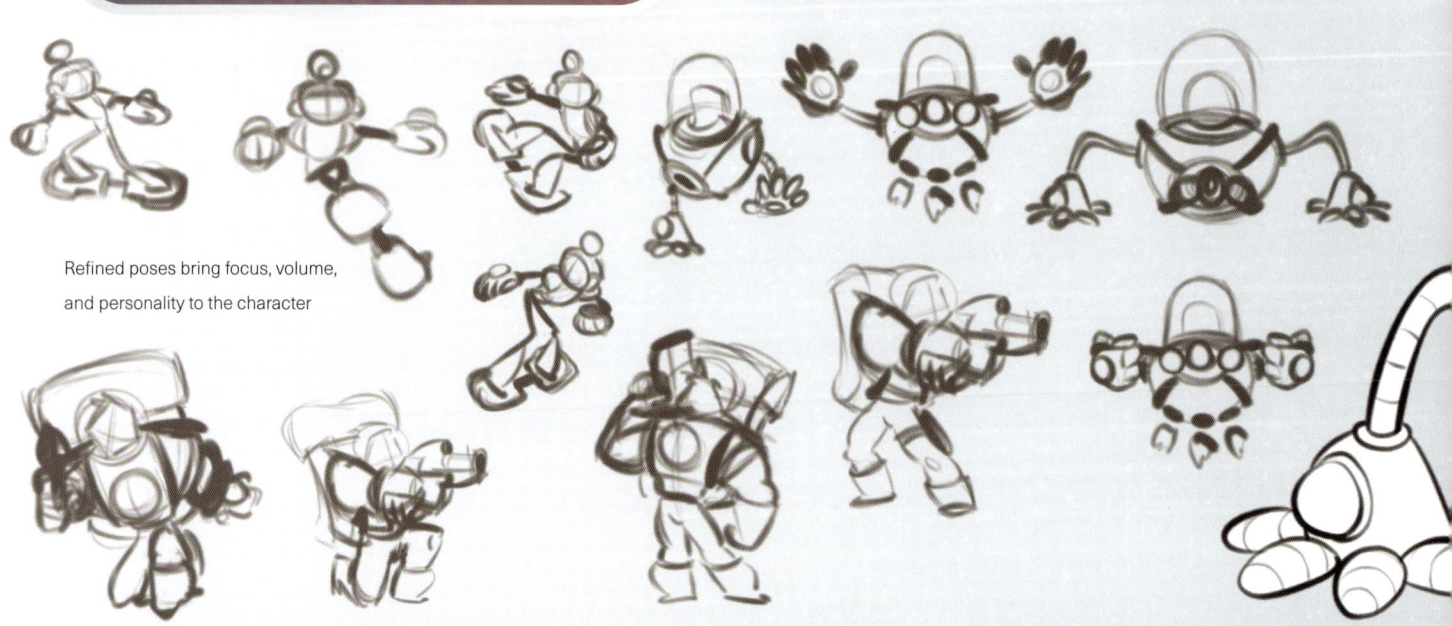

After refining your poses, select one for each character that best captures their personality and energy. I usually like my characters to be somehow directed towards the viewer because it makes the pose more engaging, but I also ensure that important elements of each character aren't hidden, like the fish in the dad's pose.

Arrange all the chosen poses on a new canvas, adjusting their sizes to define the scale and proportions of each character in relation to the others. Although it may not seem it at first, this step is crucial for ensuring your characters feel cohesive and believable as a group. By comparing the poses side by side, you can make final adjustments to maintain consistency while still emphasizing individuality.

Arranging the final poses together helps establish the characters' proportions and group cohesion

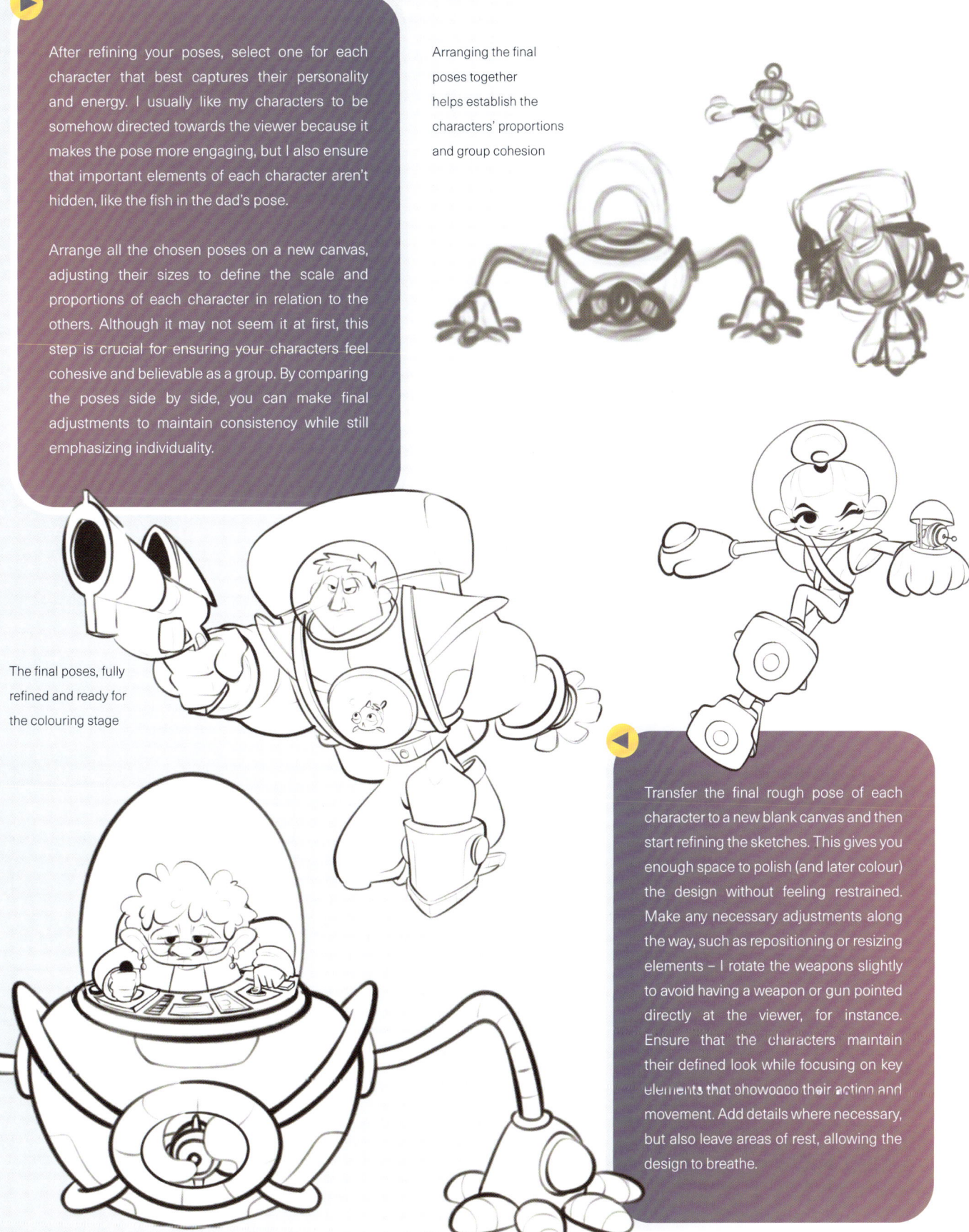

The final poses, fully refined and ready for the colouring stage

Transfer the final rough pose of each character to a new blank canvas and then start refining the sketches. This gives you enough space to polish (and later colour) the design without feeling restrained. Make any necessary adjustments along the way, such as repositioning or resizing elements – I rotate the weapons slightly to avoid having a weapon or gun pointed directly at the viewer, for instance. Ensure that the characters maintain their defined look while focusing on key elements that showcase their action and movement. Add details where necessary, but also leave areas of rest, allowing the design to breathe.

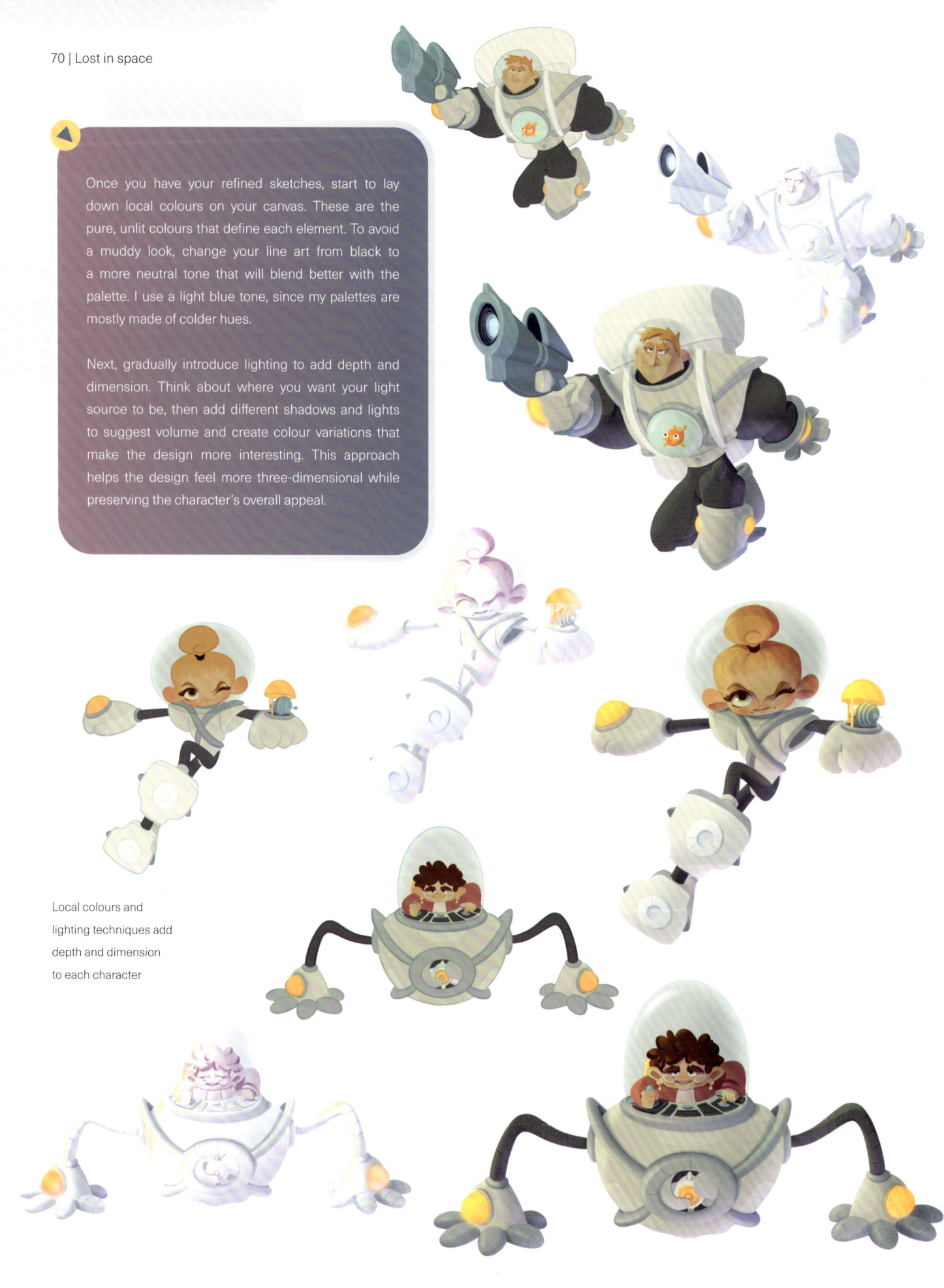

Once you have your refined sketches, start to lay down local colours on your canvas. These are the pure, unlit colours that define each element. To avoid a muddy look, change your line art from black to a more neutral tone that will blend better with the palette. I use a light blue tone, since my palettes are mostly made of colder hues.

Next, gradually introduce lighting to add depth and dimension. Think about where you want your light source to be, then add different shadows and lights to suggest volume and create colour variations that make the design more interesting. This approach helps the design feel more three-dimensional while preserving the character's overall appeal.

Local colours and lighting techniques add depth and dimension to each character

In this final phase, clean up the lines and refine your character designs, focusing on adding details and textures that bring the characters to life even more. Incorporate textures and patterns strategically to guide the viewer's eye and create visual contrast. I add high-frequency details in focal-point areas (like the dotted texture), paired with areas of rest or breaks in patterns to help maintain balance. These elements add depth and interest to the design, elevating it from a concept to a fully realized character, ready for presentation.

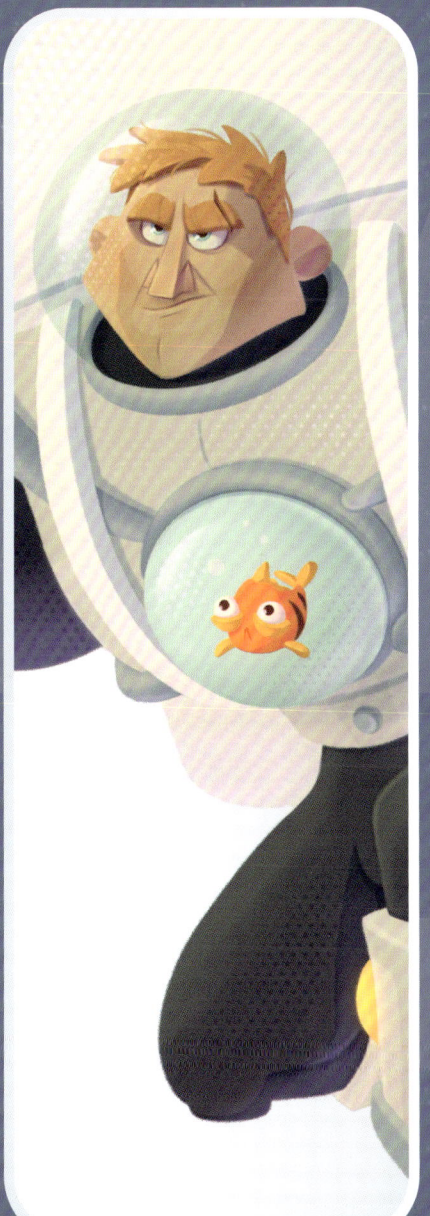
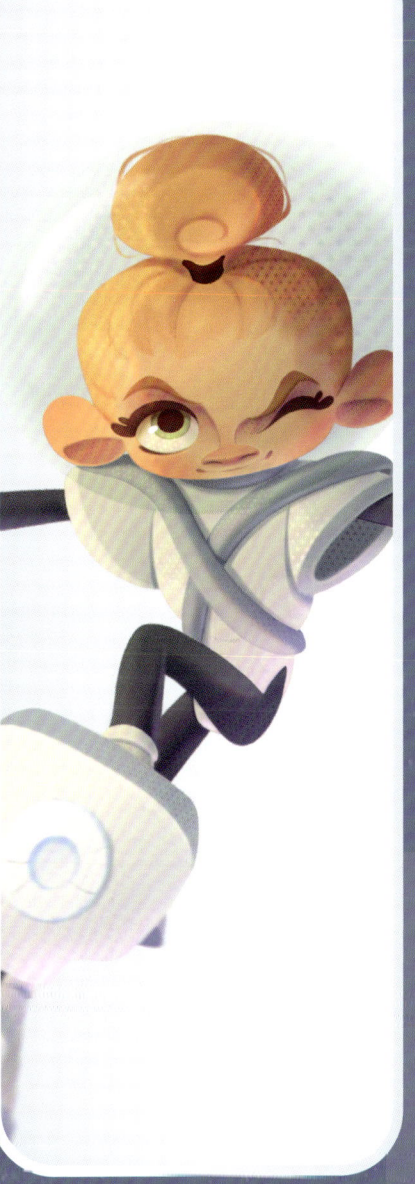
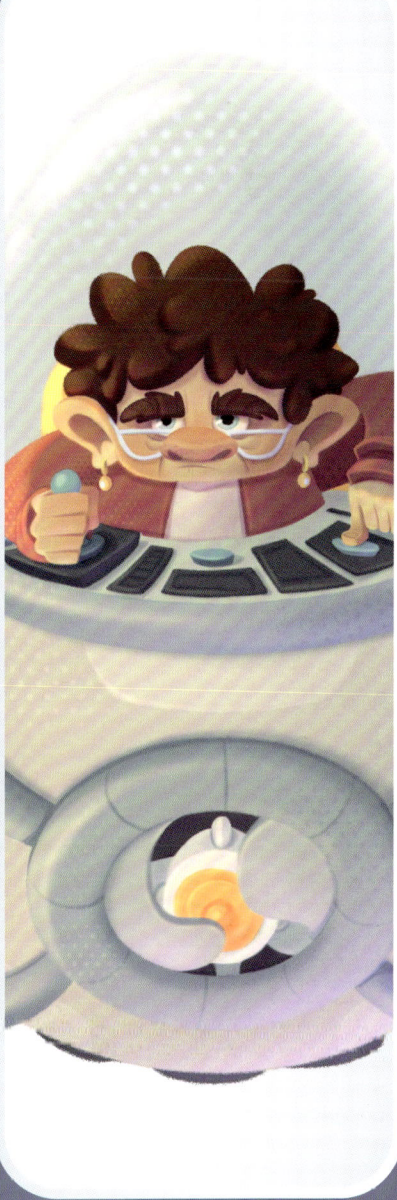

The final cleaned-up character designs, enriched with textures and refined details for a polished look

Once the characters are finalized, bring them back together on the same canvas – as they were in the posing stage – to evaluate how their sizes work in relation to one another. Set up the scene to feel dynamic, with a sense of movement and energy. Consider overlapping characters to add depth and visual interest. This creates a more engaging composition and helps strengthen the connection between the characters, ensuring they complement each other within the context of the scene.

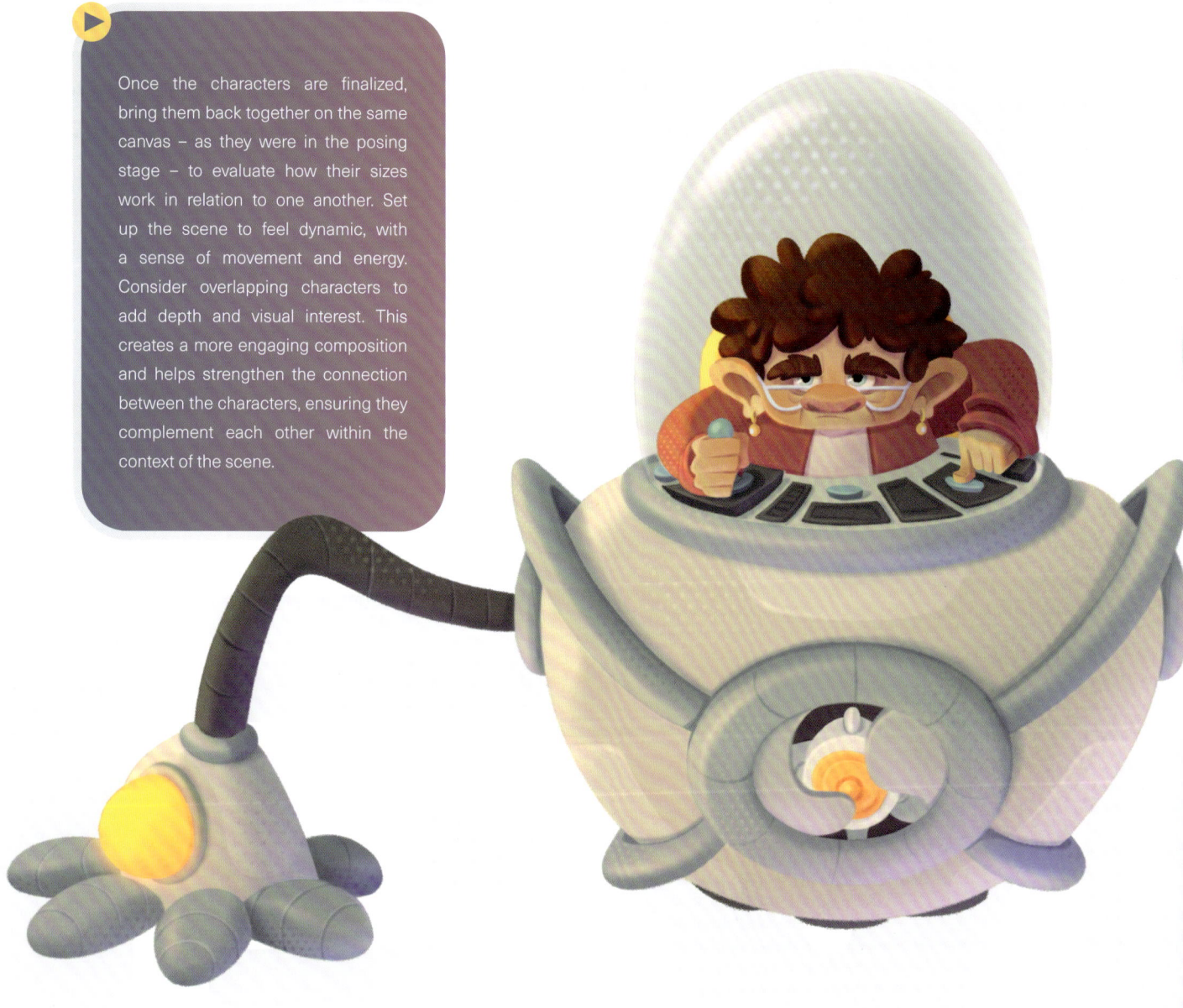

Final image © Isabella Agosti

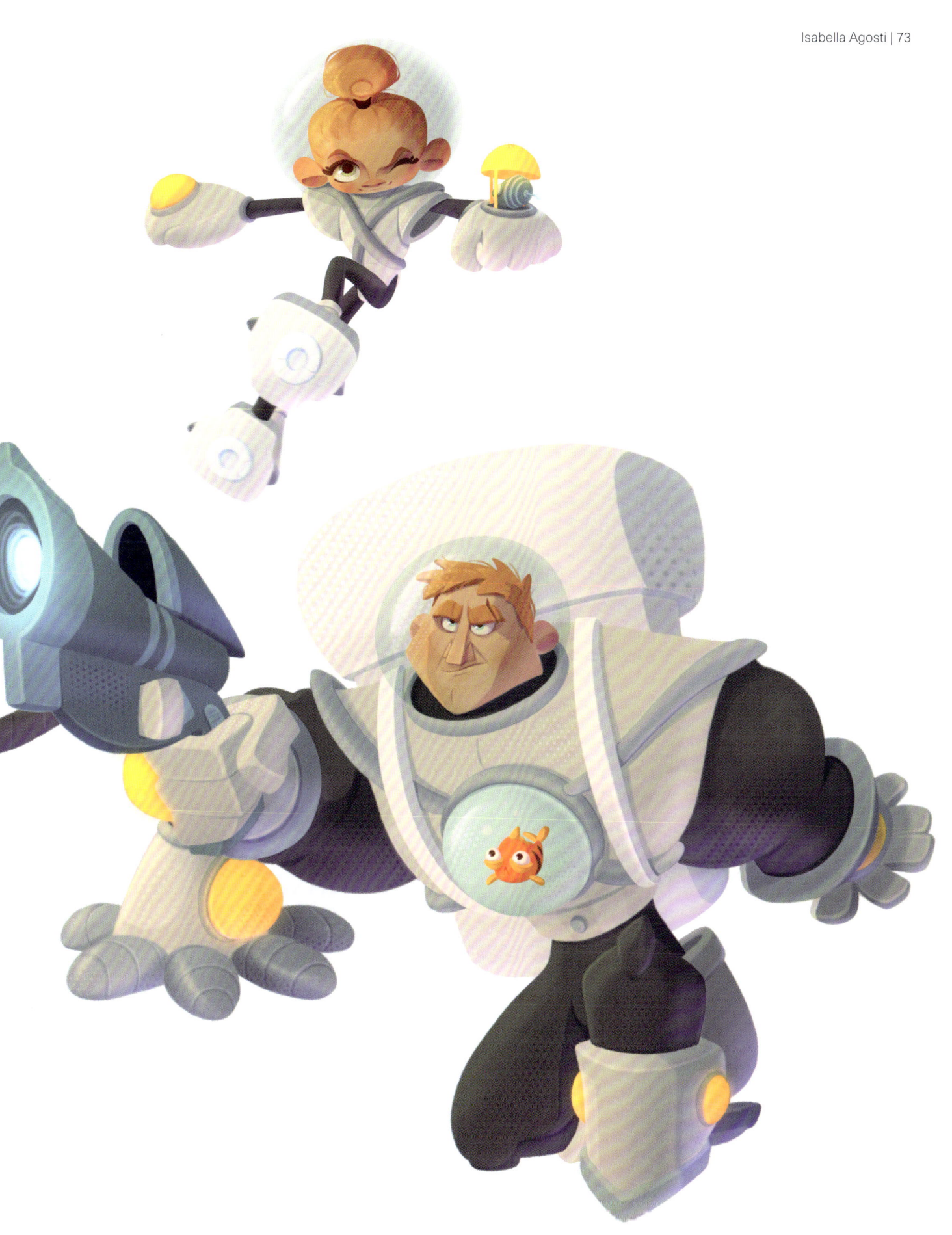

DEVELOPMENT GALLERY
SEDA KIR

My art style is colourful and full of magical elements. I focus on creating expressive characters, like princesses, extraordinary creatures, and other dramatic characters and scenes. Whether I'm working on a picture book, games or a personal piece, I want my art to connect emotionally and visually, leaving a lasting impression. I believe in the power of illustration to tell heartfelt stories without needing words.

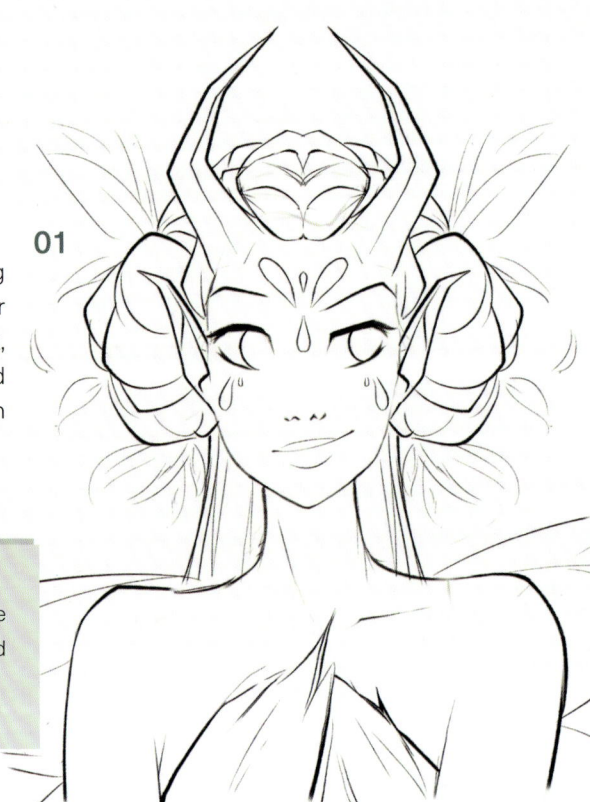

01

01. I sketched this character's portrait with almost completely clean line art. This way, I can better see where I will draw shadows, lines, and add details. I like to use the Symmetry tool in some parts of portrait drawings.

02

02. I added the base colours and facial details, and then the blushes and shadows on a different layer. I wanted to add details, while retaining the simple feel of the original sketch. I try to maintain a balance between these two competing forces.

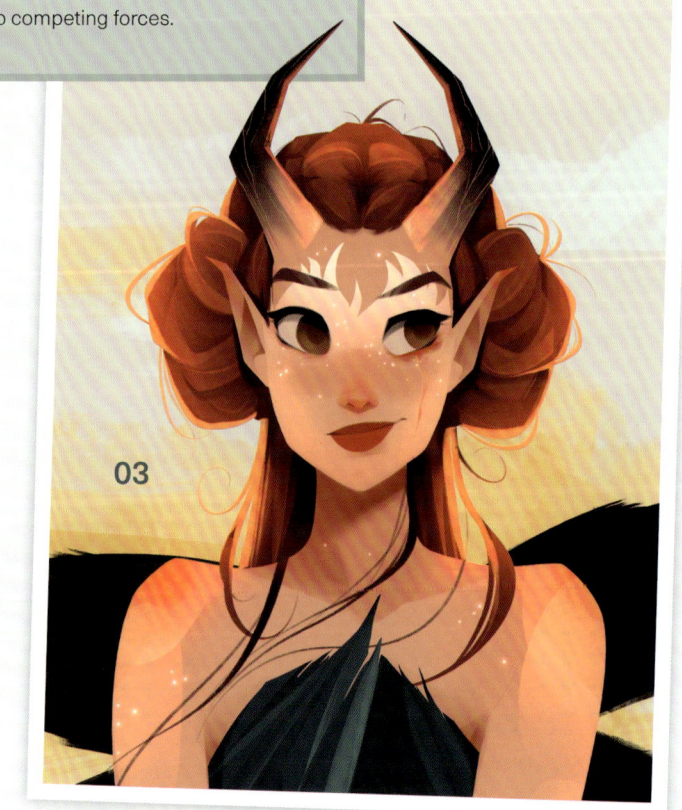

03

03. This character is a fantastical creature, so I wanted to add details which are unrealistic. I drew some sparkles, a gradient shape, and some scars on her face in separate layers. I added a weak red light to give her a slightly more epic look. Lastly, I added texture using simple brush strokes on the background.

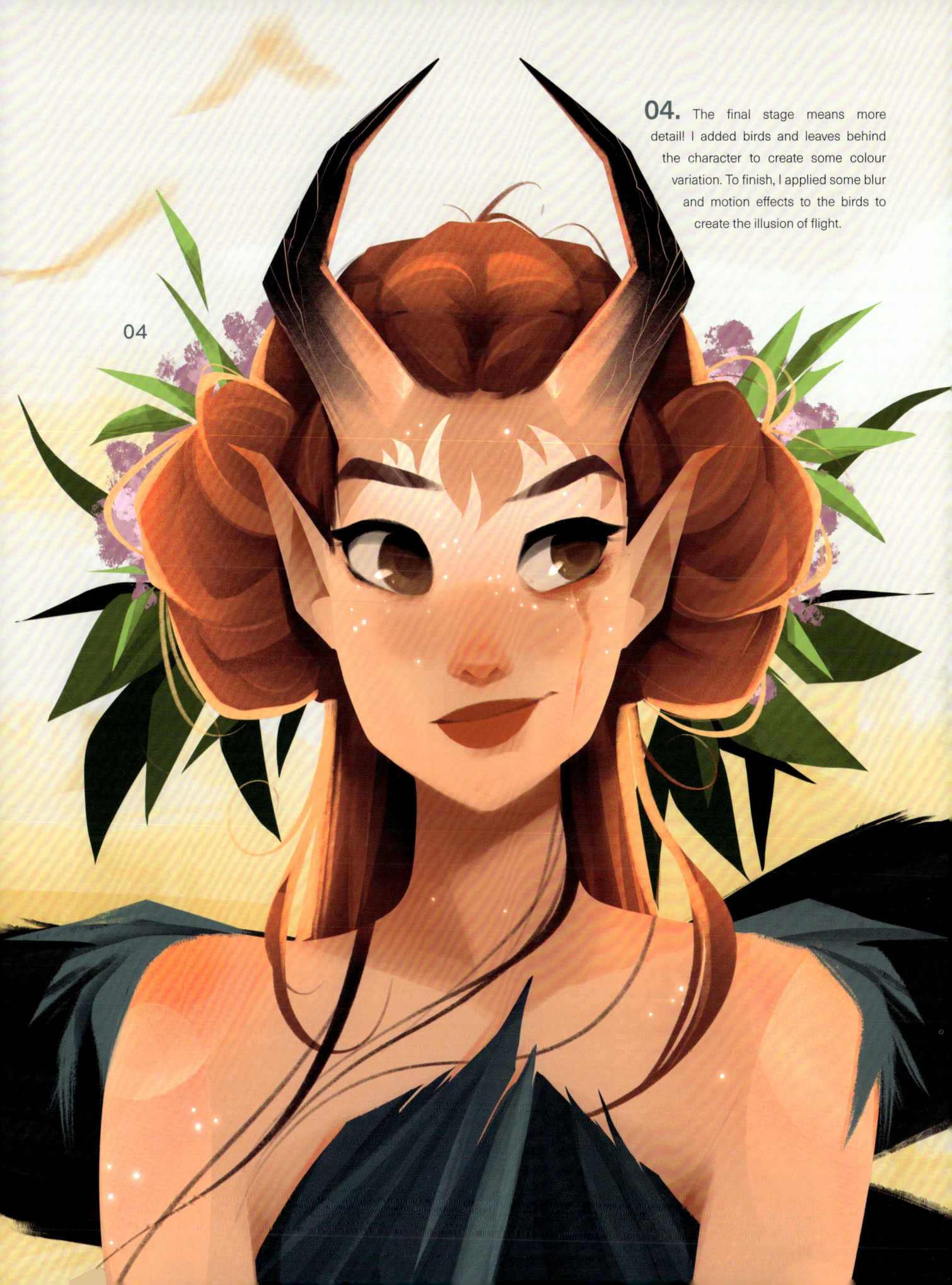

04. The final stage means more detail! I added birds and leaves behind the character to create some colour variation. To finish, I applied some blur and motion effects to the birds to create the illusion of flight.

04

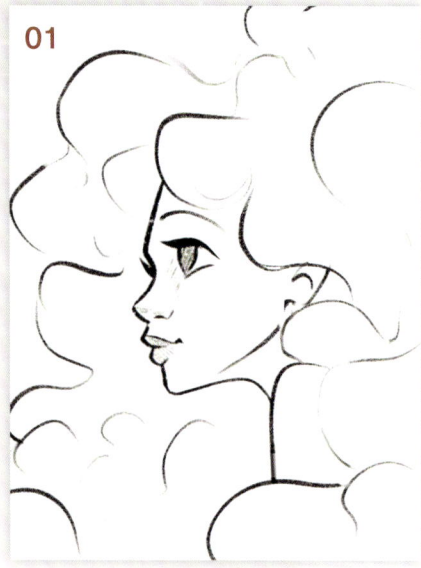

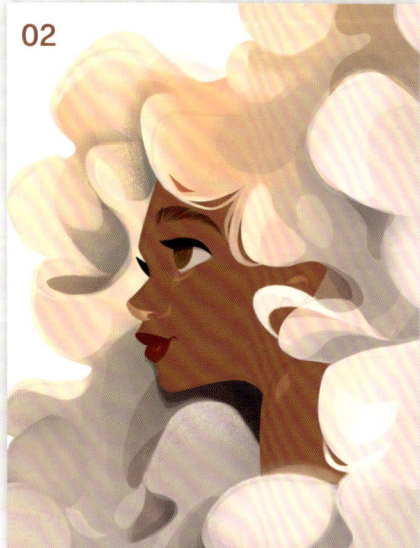

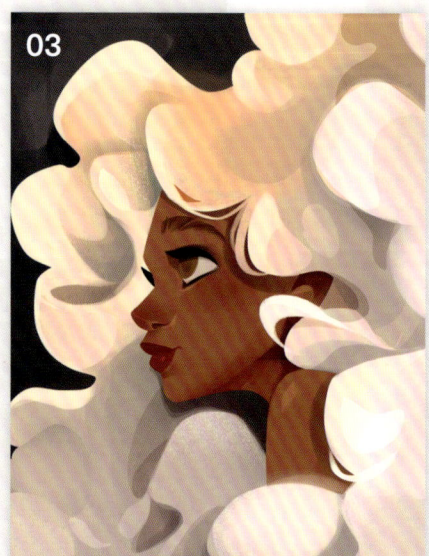

01. I started with a simple sketch here. I prefer not to make my sketches too messy, because I want to have a clear idea of what I'm working towards. I like to draw and erase as I go, and end up with everything on one layer in this phase.

02. I reduced the opacity of the sketch layer and started work on her hair. I added some texture and bubbly details to the upper area because I wanted the hair to evoke a cloud-like appearance.

03. Next, I added some blush and shadows to her skin. I use various brushes in my work, but never more than three on a single image – I want my style to come through in the design. I added textures lines, grainy brush strokes, and a smoother round brush to her face.

04. Adding finishing touches is my favourite part of the whole process. I drew light effects using a sharper brush and illustrated the background in one layer. I added stars and a holographic effect using my own brushes and Procreate's defaults.

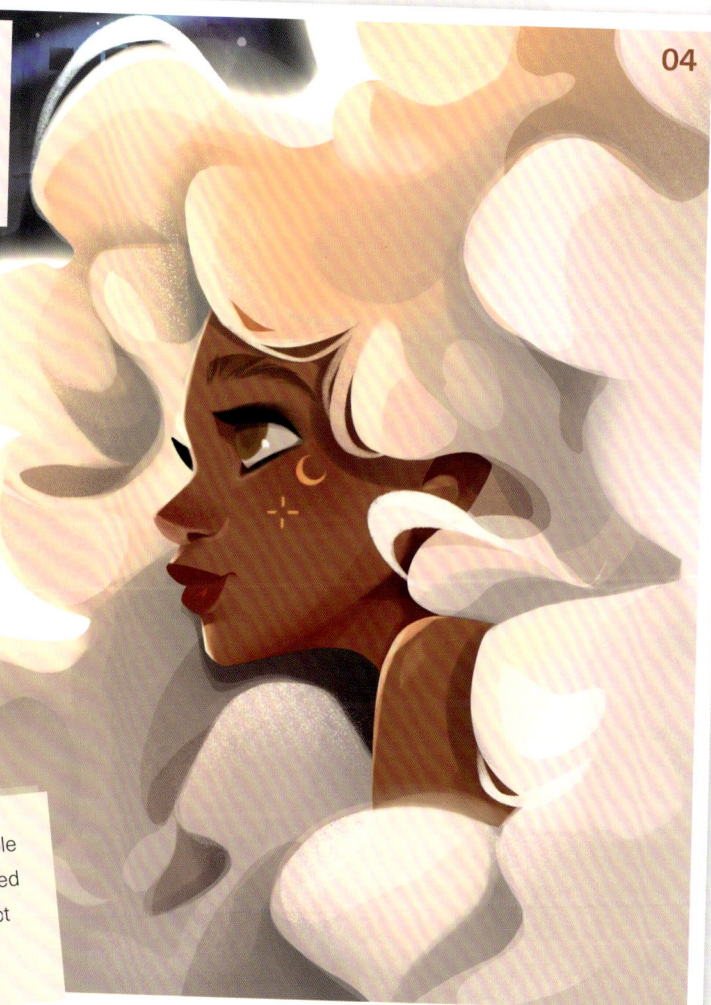

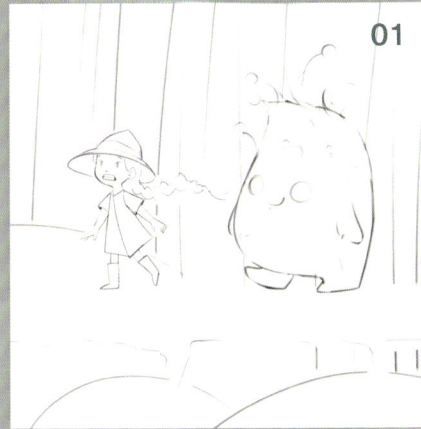

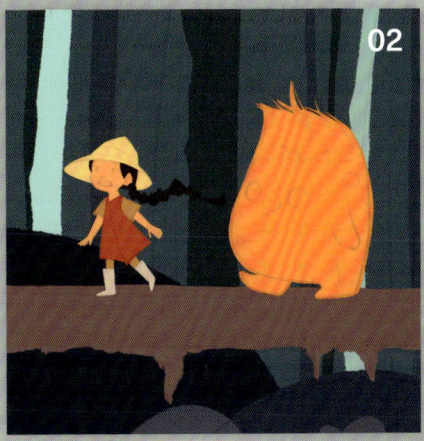

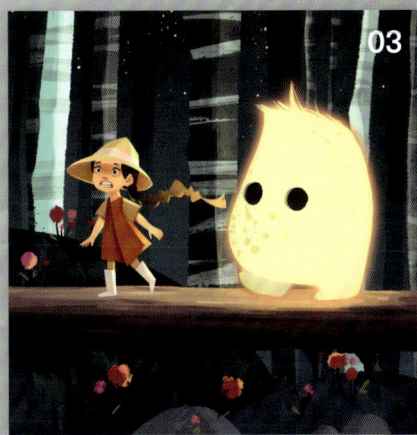

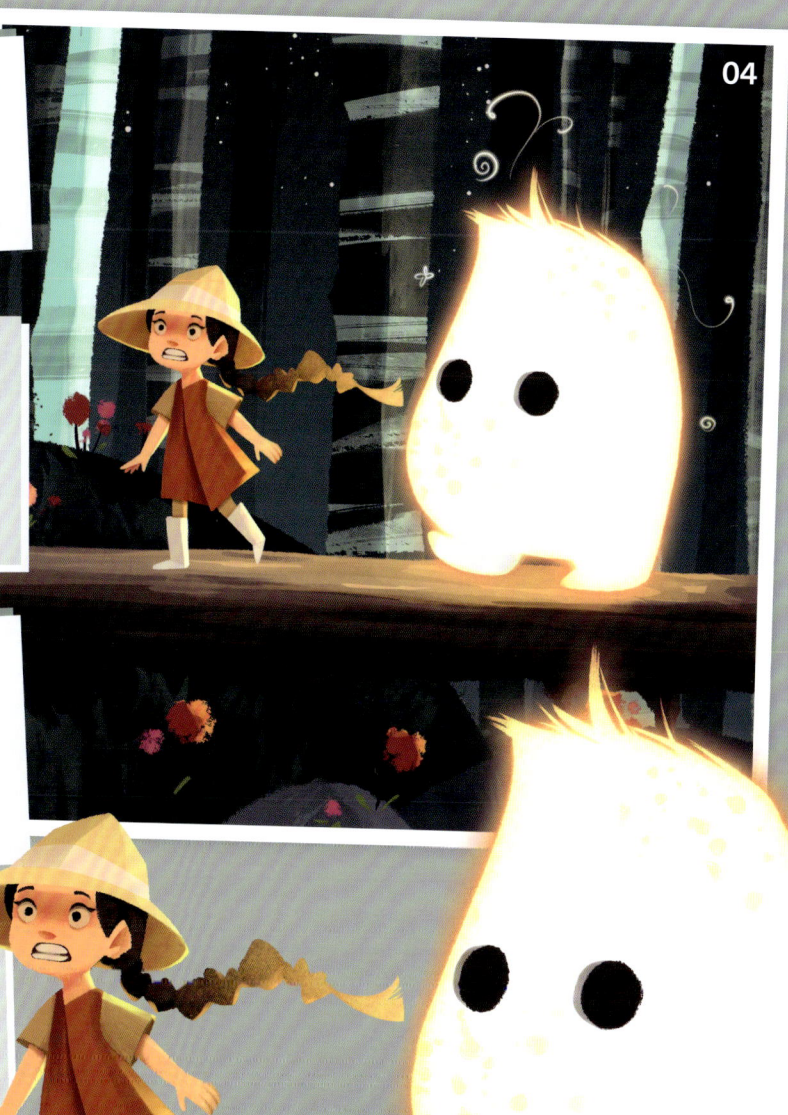

01. For this sketch of a cute kid I again tried not to make the draft too messy – this makes the next steps easier. I always keep in mind that I'm free to change the details later in the process.

02. I chose one of my favourite colour palettes for the base colours. I think this combination works especially well for kid-lit artwork. I used a textured brush for the external lines to add personality and make the characters appear more child-friendly.

03. I added the details on a separate layer, using lots of textured brush strokes. I decided the cute monster would be a light source that would influence its surroundings. The Bloom feature in Procreate was perfect to make this effect really pop.

04. I like to do one final check of my artwork at the end of the process to see if adding or changing any details will improve the illustration. In this case, I added some tiny details around the cute monster and changed its colour to emphasize how much it glows.

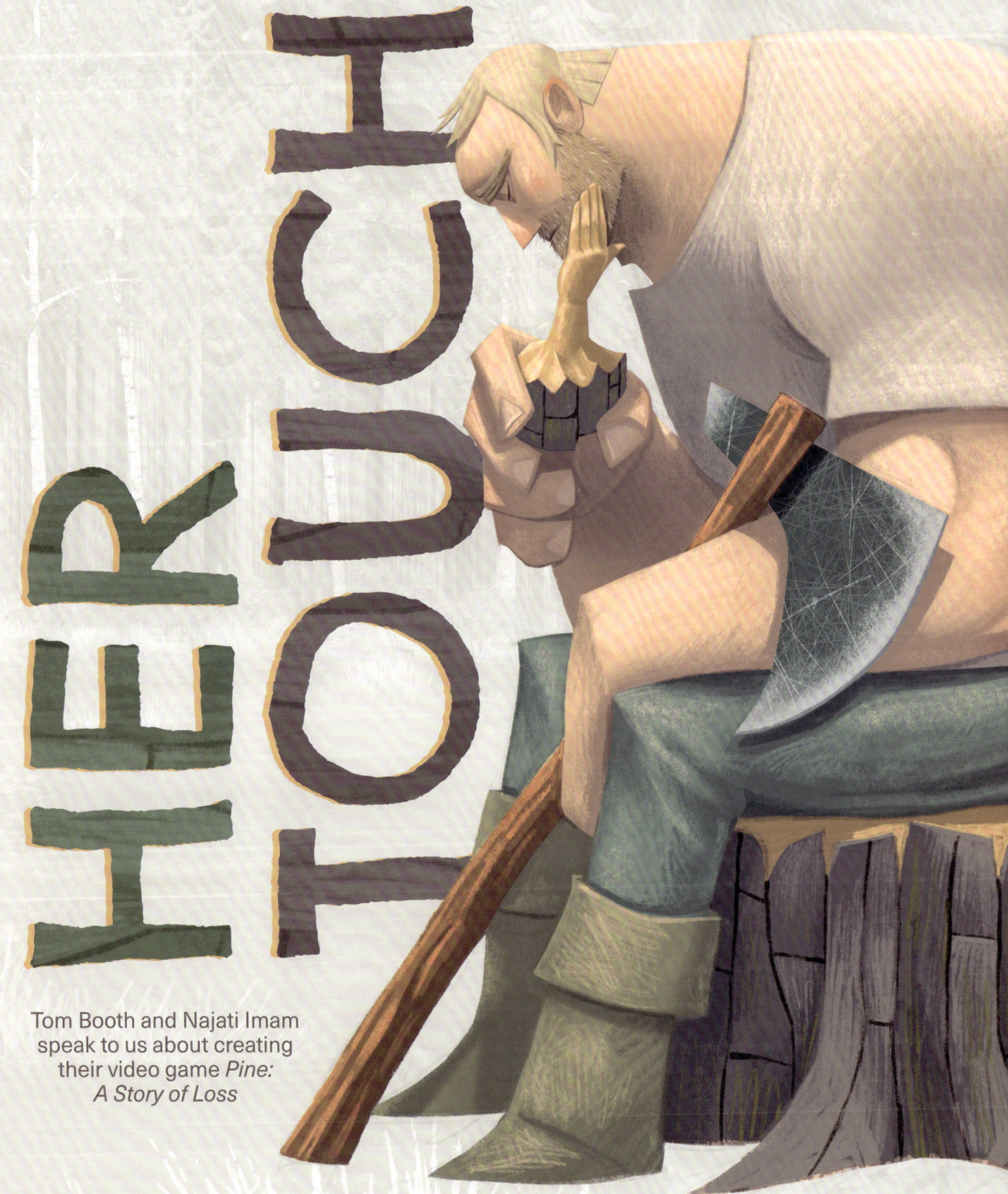

HER TOUCH

Tom Booth and Najati Imam speak to us about creating their video game *Pine: A Story of Loss*

Tom Booth **TB** | **NI** Najati Imam

While the couple is represented throughout the game, the focus remains on the woodworker

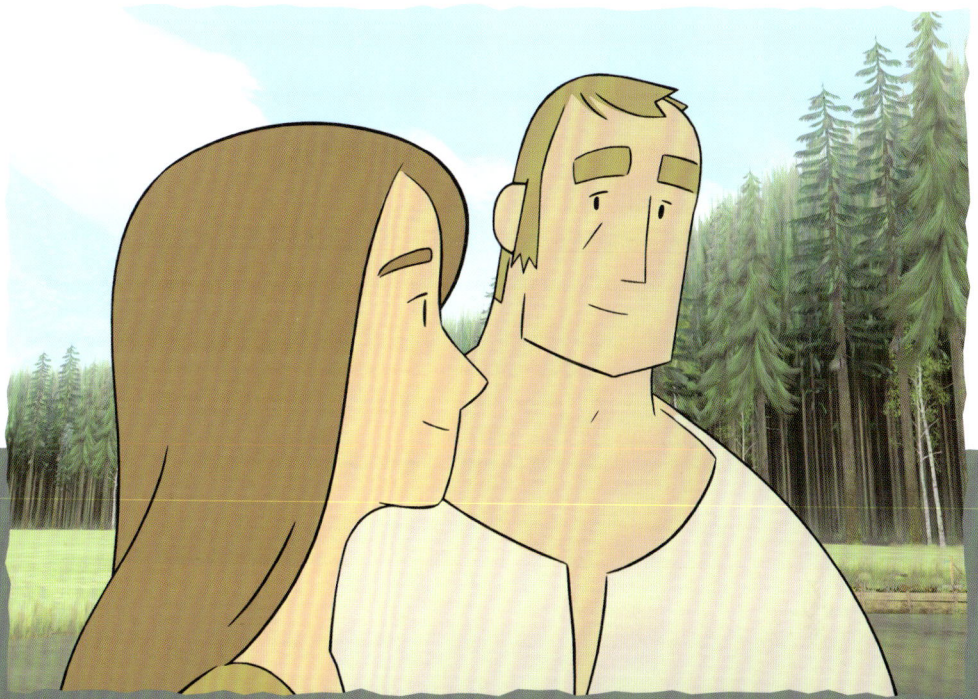

Hi both, welcome to *CDQ*! Can you start by telling us a bit about your working lives before *Pine*?

TB Thank you for having us! My background is primarily in illustration and occasionally writing children's books. I developed my drawing skills from an early age, finding inspiration in comics, books, movies, and video games, with some of the more influential examples being *Calvin & Hobbes*, *The Iron Giant*, and *Shadow of the Colossus*. After college, I worked for the children's book publisher Scholastic in New York City. A friend encouraged me to try Instagram, so I started sharing my illustrations and designs online, and found an audience. That led to freelance work – designing for animation and video games with a focus on character design.

NI I've been programming for quite a while – since I was a kid in fact, as I went to school to study it. After that I worked in the broader industry as a development consultant and engineering director. The only thing I've been doing as long as programming is playing games – teaming up with Tom and finally making one was long overdue!

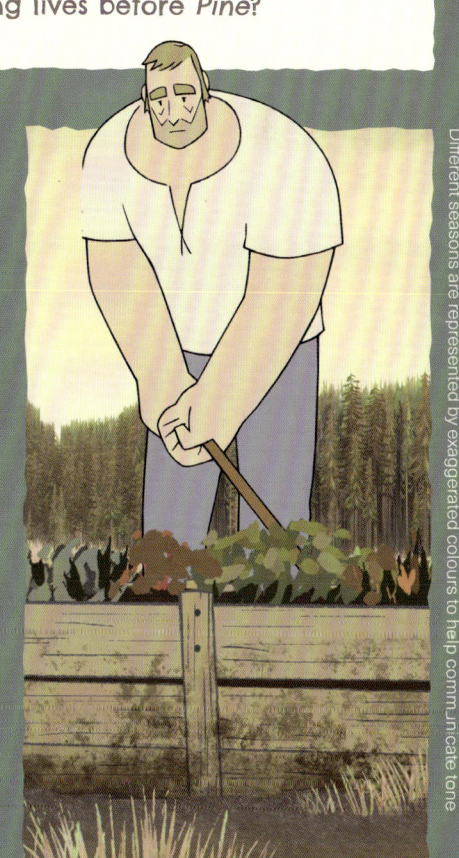

Different seasons are represented by exaggerated colours to help communicate tone

How did the project come about?

TB Before *Pine*, Najati and I developed a small project – a FreeCell game with a comic that players could unlock as they won hands – to cut our teeth a little before taking on more ambitious ideas. As that project was wrapping up, I experienced a pretty devastating loss. As part of working through that experience, I developed the concept of a grieving woodworker who used carvings to remember the person he lost. After considering telling the woodworker's story in a book or animated short, we saw the potential of making a game out of it. Compared to other mediums, a video game can be a less passive experience, and we thought the agency and engagement it provided would be invaluable while trying to connect with an audience about the process of grieving.

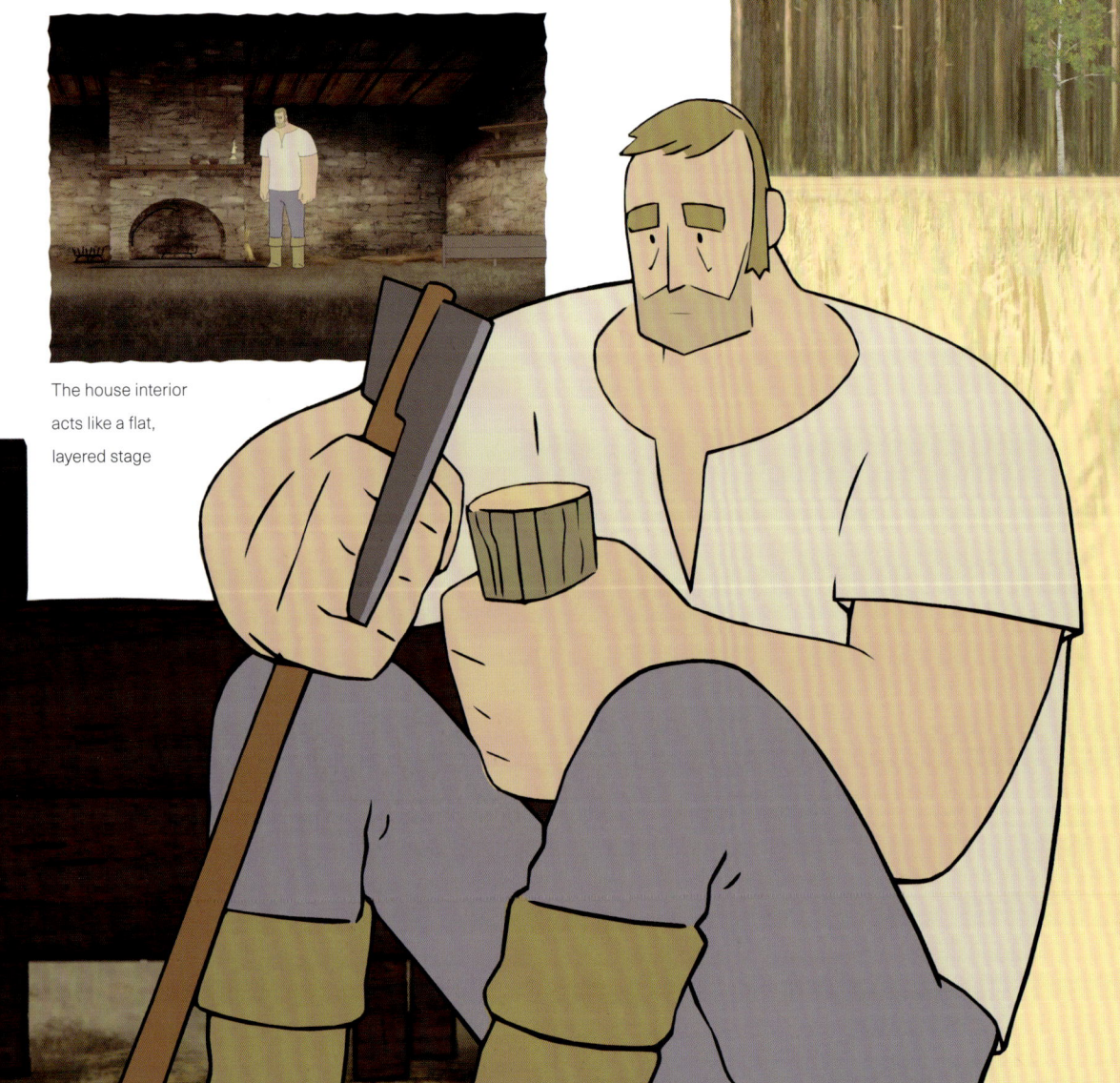

The house interior acts like a flat, layered stage

The game's compositions are often designed to make the woodworker feel small and alone

The world is rendered in 3D, skinned with digital paintings, and populated with 2D painted objects, like rocks, tufts of grass, and trees

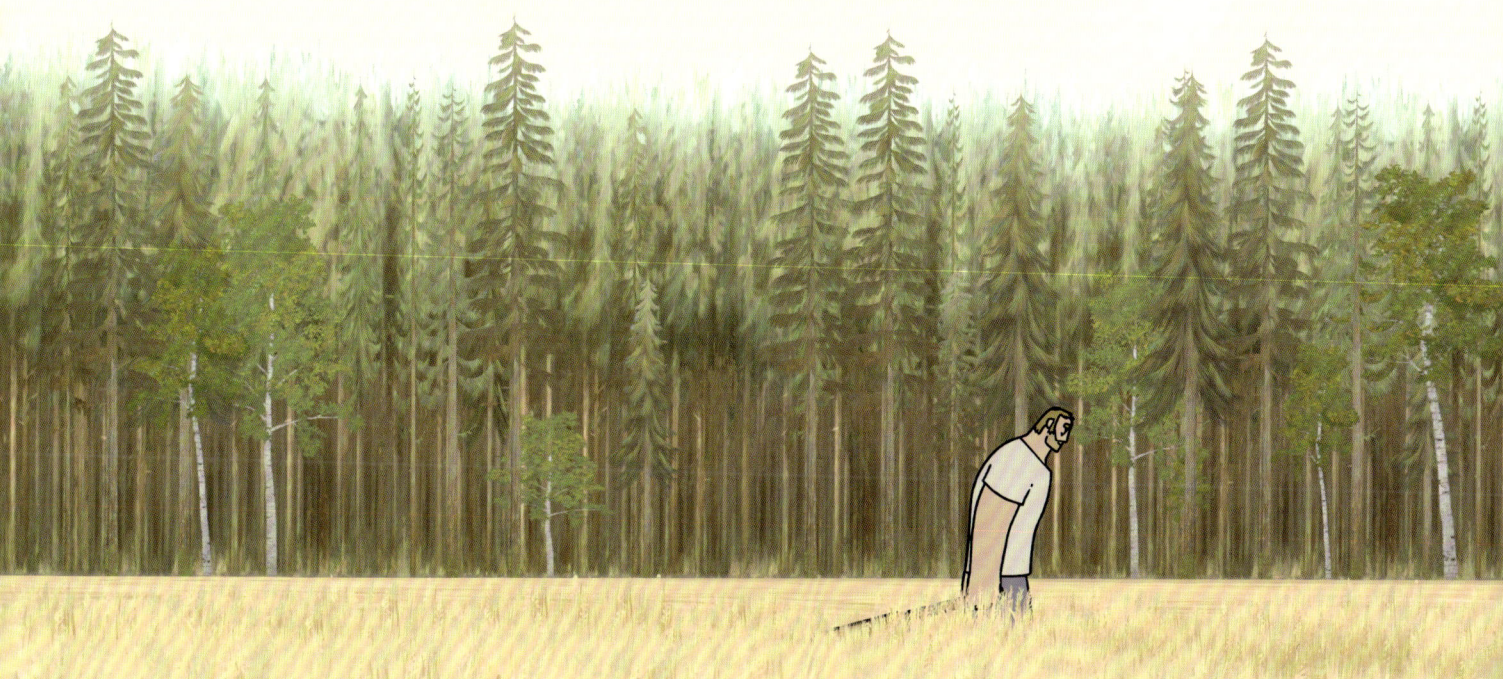

Pine started life as a successful Kickstarter project – how did you find this process?

TB Perhaps the biggest challenge for *Pine*'s campaign was bringing the backers along as the vision developed from the very rough concepts we had in the trailer into the final style of the game. While we were lucky to have a vision that inspired an audience to get behind our project, that vision was very rough, and as we got deeper into development we realized we needed to make some significant stylistic departures from how the trailer looked. Thankfully the backers were receptive to the style we developed.

NI That was a big challenge. There's also just the matter of how long things take. We were super lucky to be approached by Fellow Traveller who were interested in publishing the game; having some additional funding from them meant we could do more with the project. It also meant more time. This was very much a good problem to have, but it did mean asking our backers for even more patience.

Thankfully, our backers have been almost entirely supportive the whole way through. I think that's in part because we were pretty transparent with them about how things were going and when they weren't going well. Some backers don't understand the risk in backing a project, but most understand that they're along for the ride with us, through good and bad. It was great to have a community like our backers when developing a game.

All that said, being on the other side of this, it's easy to understand how so many Kickstarter projects fail. Many indie video-game Kickstarter campaigns do not reflect the true cost of development in the slightest; *Pine*'s goal on the platform was $80,000 – the budget needed to be more like $1 million if we wanted to be able to pay ourselves during development. So, while everyone, backers and developers, are acting with the best intentions, it's easy to overextend yourself and find yourself sorely lacking the resources needed to finish your project.

How have you found working as an indie developer on your first big project?

TB Making games is hard. Very hard. But at the same time, it's very rewarding. Seeing how players interpret our wordless story has been a fascinating experience. It's wonderful to see some players understand why we designed *Pine* the way that we did, as well as the reactions from players who maybe expected a more familiar, formulaic experience.

As an illustrator and character designer, I consider problem-solving to be part of my job, and there is more problem-solving in game development than in any other medium I've worked with. One big challenge was maintaining the structure of the narrative while still enabling a good amount of agency for the player.

NI As I mentioned before, another big challenge was the financial reality of indie-game development – it's only because we both have really supportive families that *Pine* was possible. The Kickstarter and publisher largely paid for the talented artists we were able to hire, but Tom and I didn't take any salary throughout development of the game, barring a little bit of the Kickstarter funds. By and large all that money went to our team, and our families supported us during most of the development. Perhaps a savvier business brain could have managed that differently, but given the niche experience that *Pine* is, it seems unlikely.

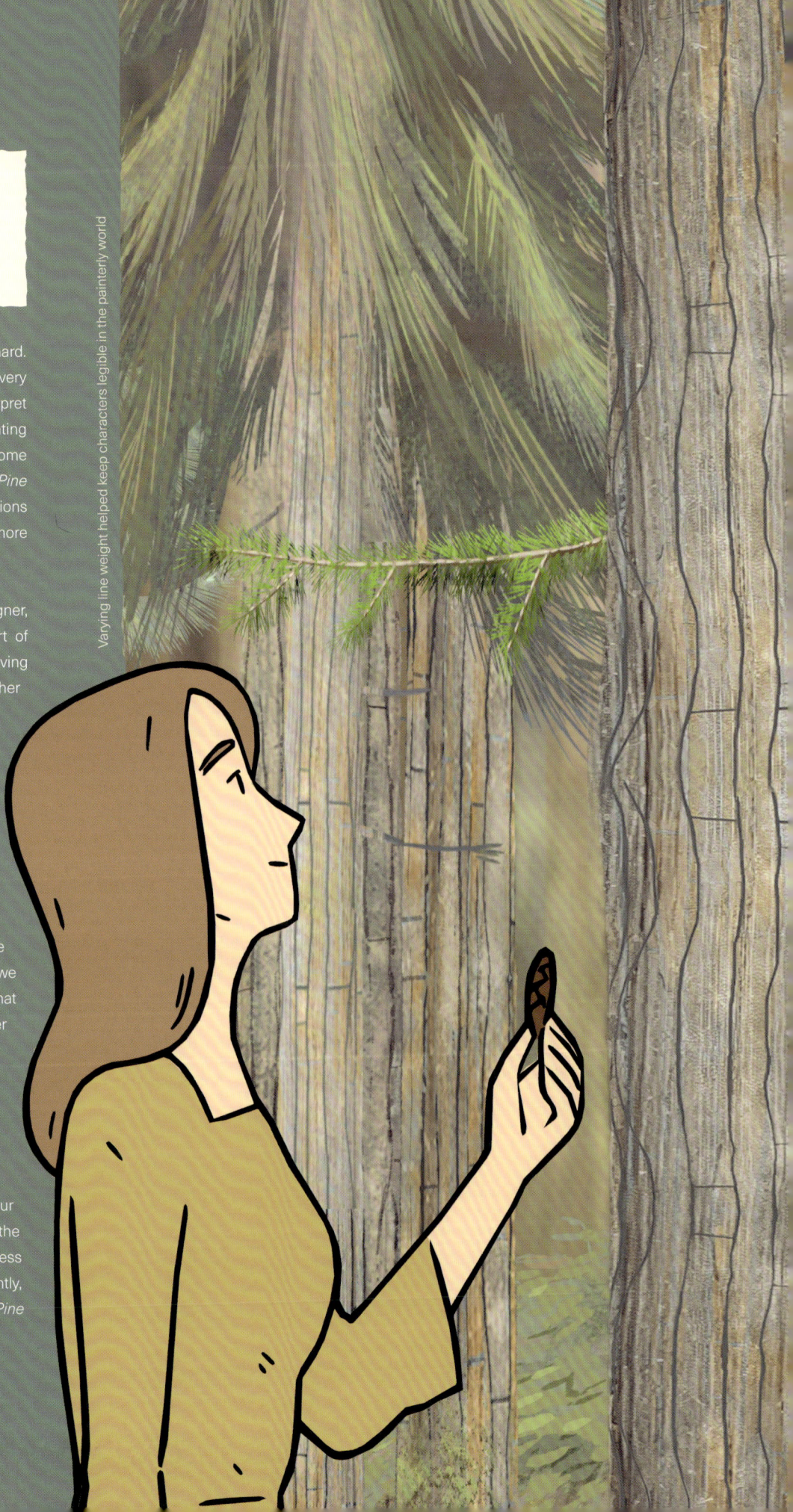

Varying line weight helped keep characters legible in the painterly world

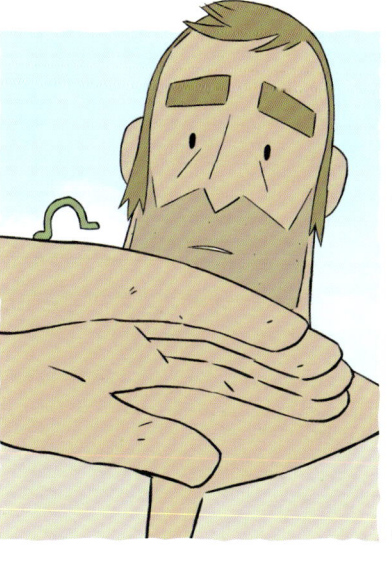

We reserved close-up shots for emotional moments in the story

What were the major influences behind *Pine*?

NI We drew our inspiration from a variety of media when it came to designing the look and mechanics of *Pine*. Indie games – like *Florence*, and *If Found...* – were evidence of compact teams creating small but ambitious projects with unusual themes.

TB We also drew inspiration from films like *Ernest & Celestine*, and comics like *The Adventures of Tintin*, when deciding on the look of both our world and our characters. Regionalist painter Andrew Wyeth, and his father, realist painter and illustrator N.C. Wyeth, have been influences on my work for as long as I can remember – their styles inspired the aesthetic of the woodworker's world, both past and present.

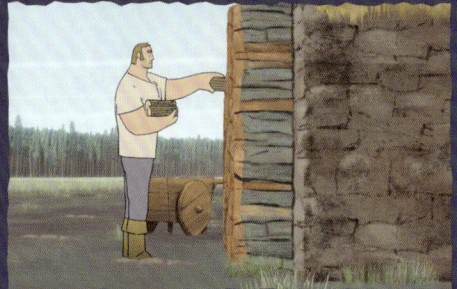

Chores are designed to feel mundane, often tedious

There's a simple elegance to the character designs and how they convey so much emotion with a few strokes of a pen. How did you come to these designs – was it immediate or a long process?

TB The simplicity of the characters was initially born out of a practical constraint. With a small team, we couldn't render our character designs and their animations more fully within the budget of the project. At first this seemed like a problem, considering that the woodworker's audience was used to seeing him in very rendered illustrations. However, when we embraced this limitation, we realized it came with some benefits: a simpler, flatter style made our characters more legible, especially in shots when they are farther from the camera. We also didn't want the characters to have unnecessary details that ultimately didn't say much about who they were, or what they were going through. The simpler designs let the focus be on their expressions and body language.

NI From the technical side, focusing on a simpler character style let us develop techniques that in turn allowed the game to load animations quicker and take up less space in memory, which improved performance and opened up the game to more devices. The animation frames in game are actually polygon meshes that are generated from the animation sprites, so they're vectorized, in a sense.

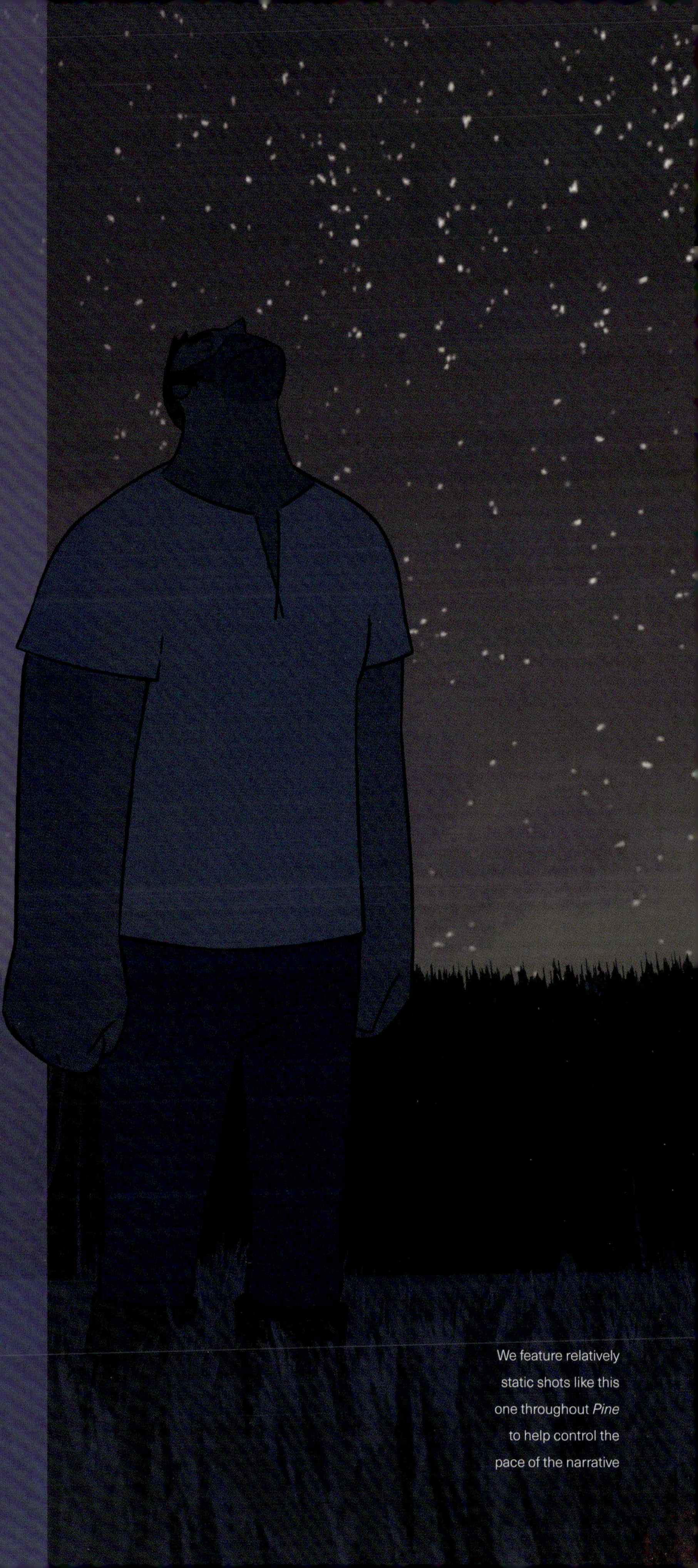

We feature relatively static shots like this one throughout *Pine* to help control the pace of the narrative

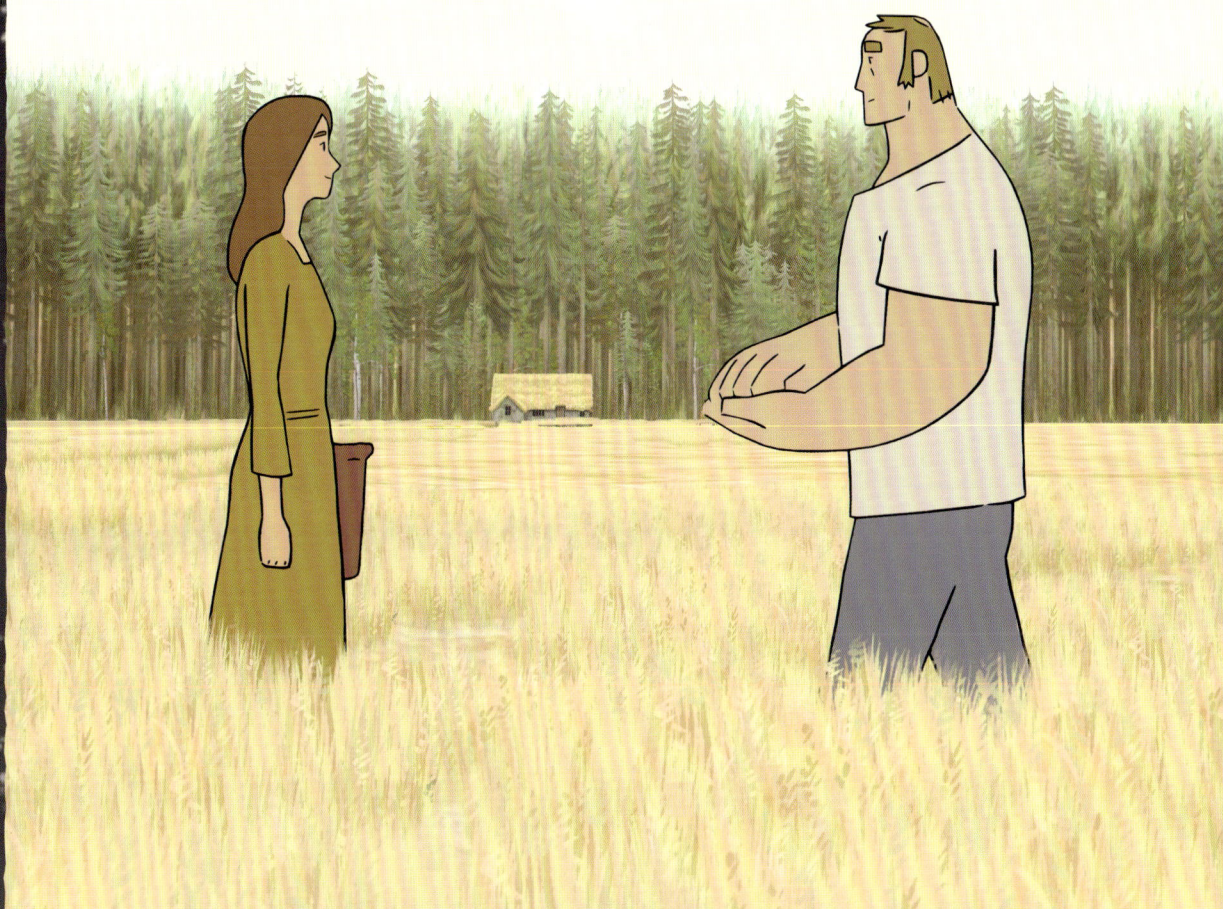

The 3D world helped maintain a sense of scale throughout the story

Can you talk about how the progression of the seasons works throughout the game?

TB On the visual side, the biggest challenge was making sure the seasons were visually distinct enough while also ensuring they conveyed the appropriate weather. We also needed to leave room for subtle variation between the present narrative and when we are seeing the woodworker's memories. In the later seasons, we used unnatural colours and textures to further indicate the woodworker's decline.

NI To make the setting up of scenes as easy as possible, the world is populated by avatars that each represent a different environmental asset, be it one of our trees, or a chunk of grass, a rock, or some dirt. Each one of those assets has a version for each season and the engine knows how to quickly switch between the different sets of assets, so each scene in the game can have its own season.

TB This flexibility allowed us to repurpose camera angles between seasons, adding some subtle storytelling to the monotony of the woodworker's routines. One subtle bit of storytelling is how the objects that make up the woodworker's home, like the garden beds, drying rack, and the water pump, change over the course of the story, mirroring the woodworker's emotional state.

TB From the beginning, we wanted to make a game that reflected the actual experience of grieving as much as possible. Grieving is a struggle, and often remains that way for a long period of time. Many other stories will treat grief like a speed bump that exists in a quick montage or a quick, cute epiphany. We wanted to capture a real sense of the time it takes to process a loss.

While we show the woodworker's fond memories of the woman, and his intricate carvings, the rest of the woodworker's experience – the quieter, intentionally tedious moments – is what we were trying to emphasize.

We also put a lot of effort into allowing the story to unfold in a predictable manner, independent of what order the player did the chores. This gives the players some agency over the woodworker's actions and choices in a way that's intended to bring them closer to his experience.

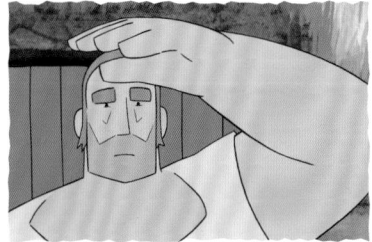

Character designs were kept simple, with enough detail to capture expression and emotion

NI Given the mix of reviews and responses, I think we ended up about where we wanted to be. In making a game that someone grieving might identify with, we definitely alienated a lot of players, but I don't think we could have so clearly made the point that grieving is hard without doing so. As such a small, unestablished studio, that was certainly a risk, and while *Pine* has its flaws, we're happy to have taken the approach we did.

What advice would you have for artists and developers looking to get into indie development?

TB Making a game requires conviction, a great deal of hard work, patience, and perhaps skills you don't have... yet. Don't be afraid to ask for help when you need it, especially when it will help you maintain your momentum. Be prepared to compromise, as the players will ultimately determine how your story is told and interpreted. Lastly, surround yourself with people who inspire you. Small teams with the tools of today are capable of extraordinary things, but only if you are able to support each other over the course of what might be a lengthy development period.

NI Without meaning to sound pessimistic, balance your ambitions of becoming an indie dev with the realities of the world around you. Don't quit your day job, don't give up on sleep, and remember to exercise. Maintain (reasonably) healthy habits and finances, and gradually work towards your goals. We're super fortunate to have been able to get *Pine* published, but we sacrificed a lot, both financially and personally, to be able to release the game. This isn't the only version of success. Like people that paint or play guitar just for the joy of it, making games is rewarding in and of itself. If you're making games, you're a game developer – whether you get paid for it, or published, or not.

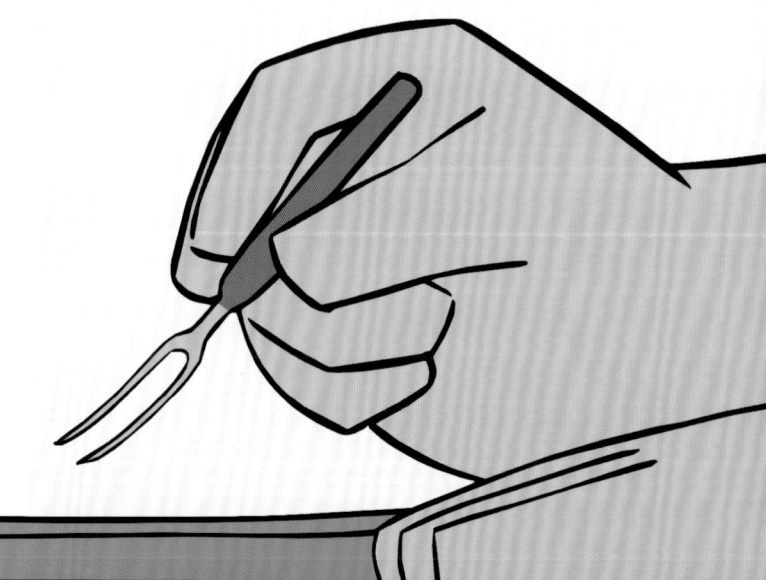

Thanks for talking to us! What's next for both of you?

TB Thanks for the chat! It turns out making and releasing a game can be pretty exhausting, so we're taking some time to recover with our families and to pay some bills. That said, we do have another big project we're eager to start developing. It's too early to tell what shape it will take, but we'll be drawing on inspiration from some of the games that helped make us lifelong gamers.

NI Yeah, the next game is the one we founded the studio to make – we had no idea *Pine* would delay that plan by five years! We're excited to get started on it after taking care of some other life stuff first.

Flat, simple compositions help capture the woodworker's quiet existence

Pine: A Story of Loss is available now on PC, Switch, iOS, and Android.

PINE
A STORY OF LOSS

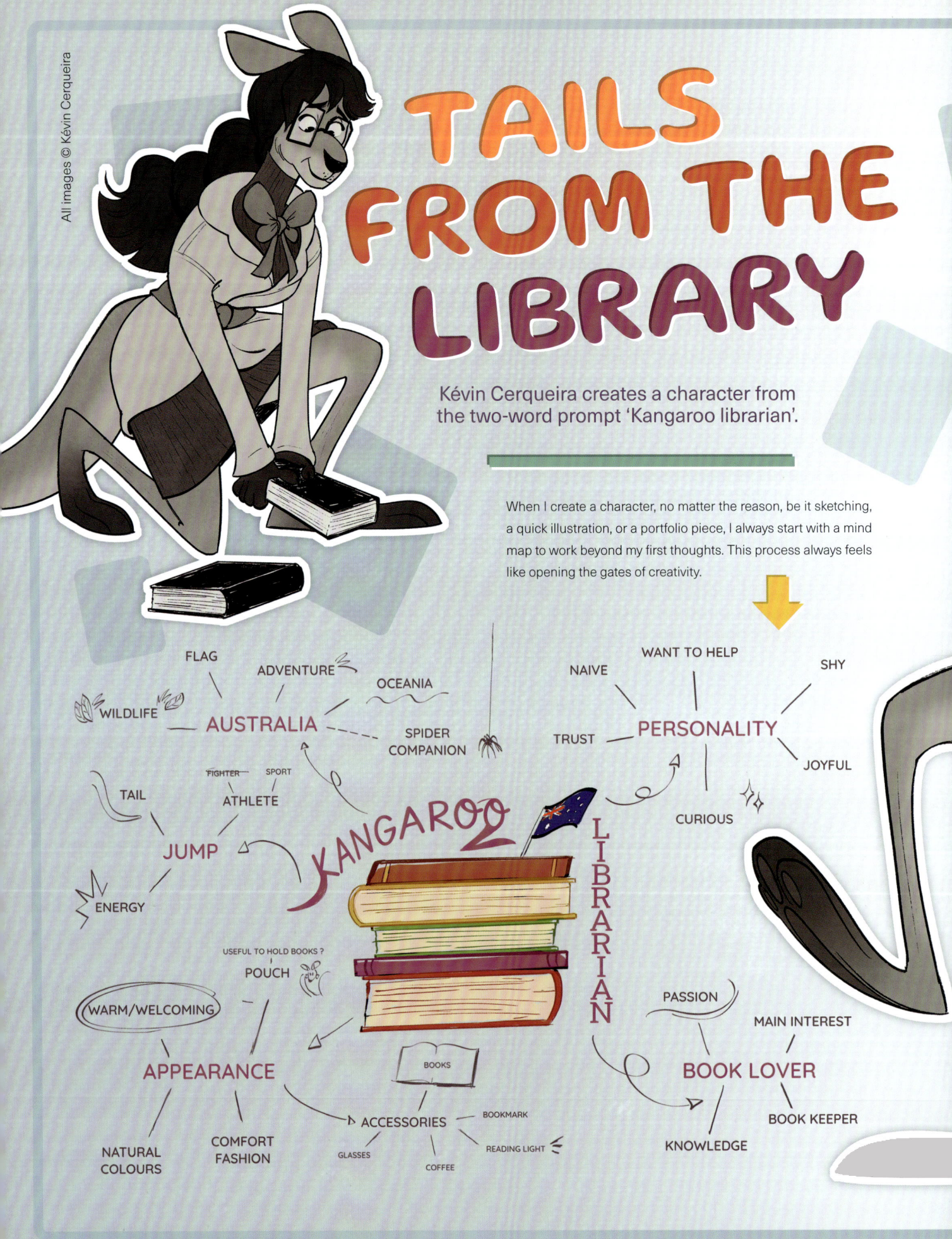

TAILS FROM THE LIBRARY

Kévin Cerqueira creates a character from the two-word prompt 'Kangaroo librarian'.

When I create a character, no matter the reason, be it sketching, a quick illustration, or a portfolio piece, I always start with a mind map to work beyond my first thoughts. This process always feels like opening the gates of creativity.

FLAG

ADVENTURE

OCEANIA

WILDLIFE

AUSTRALIA

SPIDER COMPANION

NAIVE

WANT TO HELP

SHY

PERSONALITY

TRUST

JOYFUL

CURIOUS

FIGHTER SPORT

TAIL

ATHLETE

JUMP

KANGAROO

LIBRARIAN

ENERGY

USEFUL TO HOLD BOOKS ?

POUCH

WARM/WELCOMING

PASSION

MAIN INTEREST

APPEARANCE

BOOKS

BOOK LOVER

NATURAL COLOURS

COMFORT FASHION

ACCESSORIES

BOOKMARK

BOOK KEEPER

GLASSES

READING LIGHT

KNOWLEDGE

COFFEE

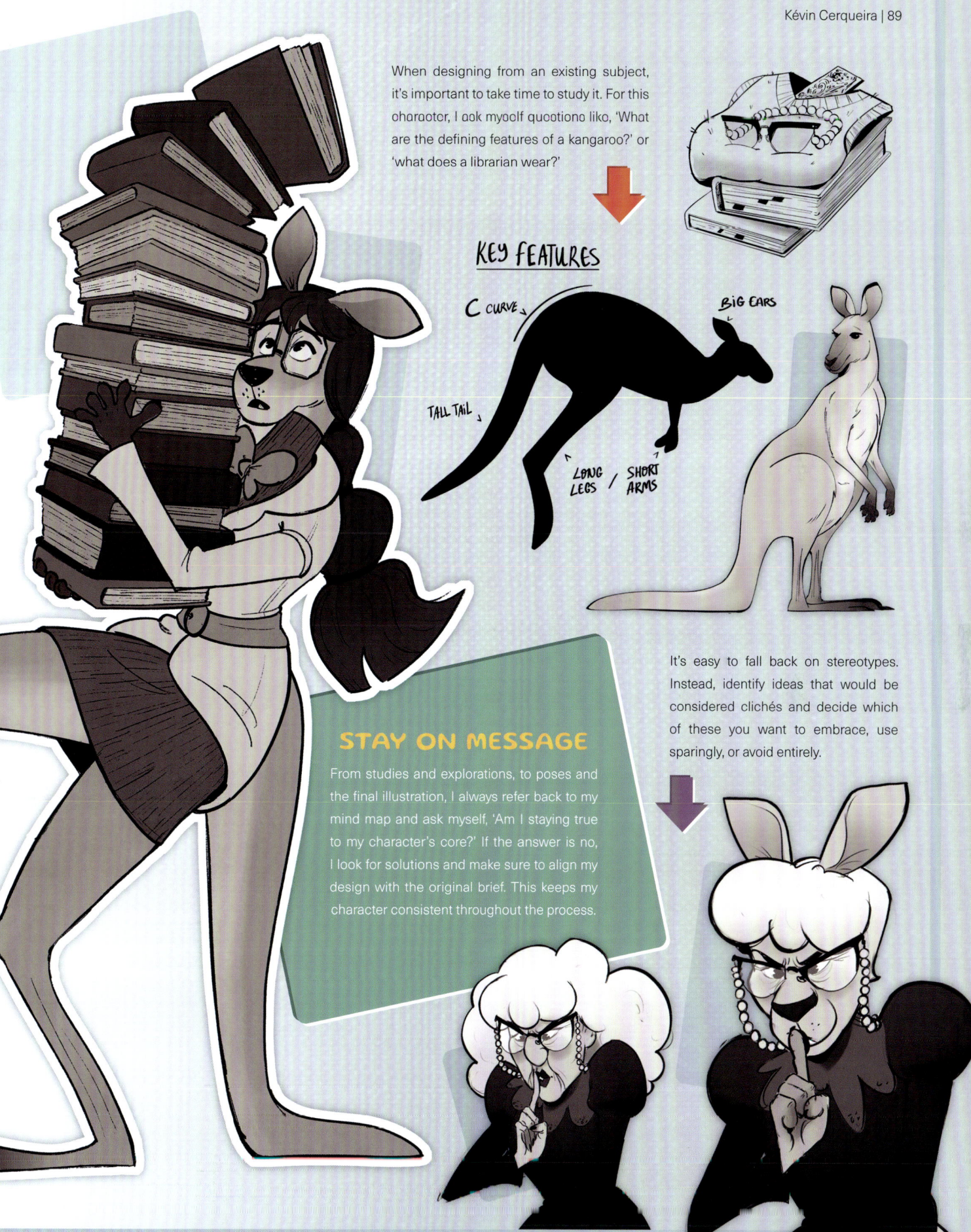

When designing from an existing subject, it's important to take time to study it. For this character, I ask myself questions like, 'What are the defining features of a kangaroo?' or 'what does a librarian wear?'

KEY FEATURES

C CURVE

BIG EARS

TALL TAIL

LONG LEGS / SHORT ARMS

It's easy to fall back on stereotypes. Instead, identify ideas that would be considered clichés and decide which of these you want to embrace, use sparingly, or avoid entirely.

STAY ON MESSAGE

From studies and explorations, to poses and the final illustration, I always refer back to my mind map and ask myself, 'Am I staying true to my character's core?' If the answer is no, I look for solutions and make sure to align my design with the original brief. This keeps my character consistent throughout the process.

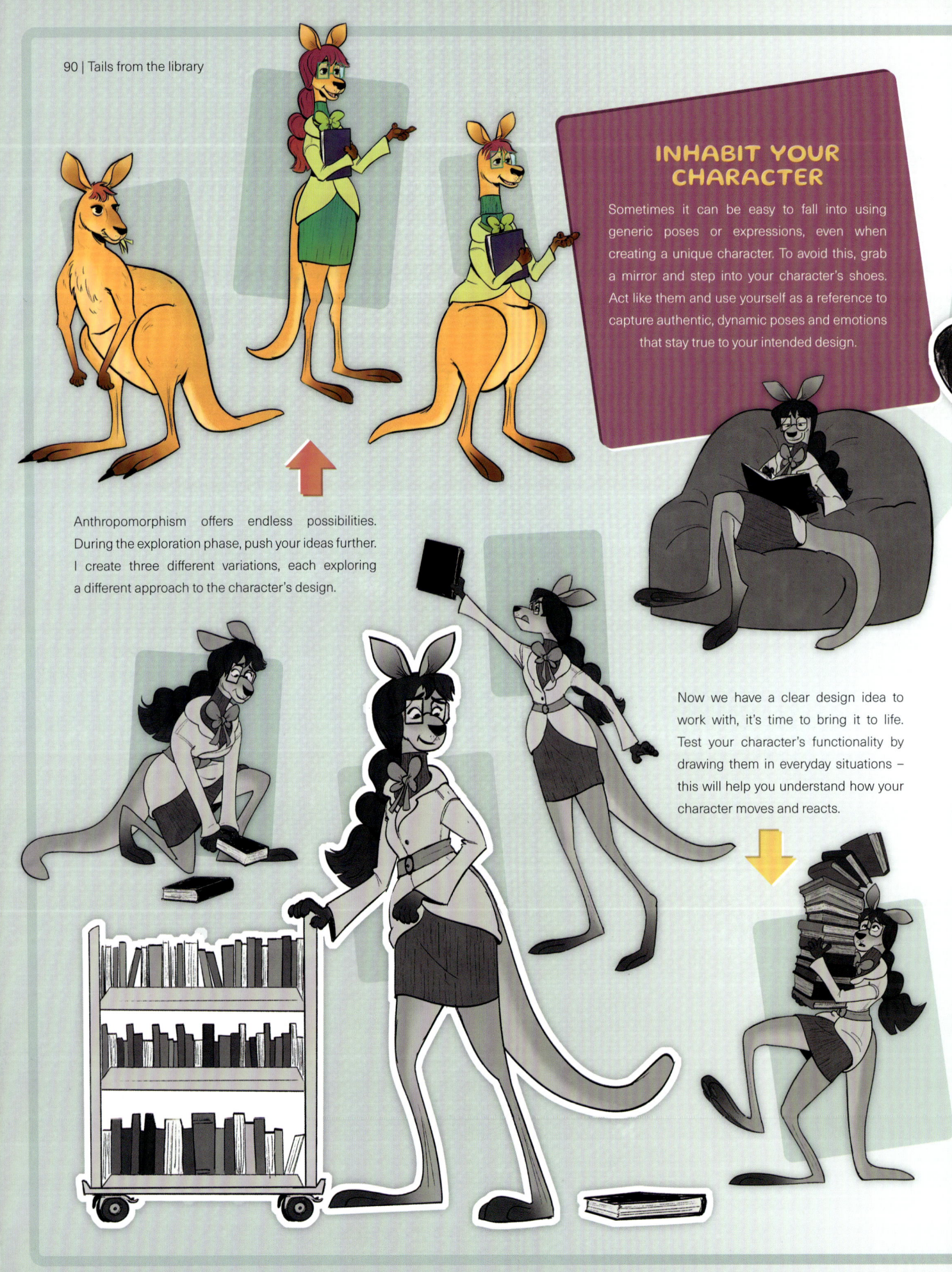

INHABIT YOUR CHARACTER

Sometimes it can be easy to fall into using generic poses or expressions, even when creating a unique character. To avoid this, grab a mirror and step into your character's shoes. Act like them and use yourself as a reference to capture authentic, dynamic poses and emotions that stay true to your intended design.

Anthropomorphism offers endless possibilities. During the exploration phase, push your ideas further. I create three different variations, each exploring a different approach to the character's design.

Now we have a clear design idea to work with, it's time to bring it to life. Test your character's functionality by drawing them in everyday situations – this will help you understand how your character moves and reacts.

Another way to enhance your design is by drawing expressions. Imagine a situation for each and decide how your character reacts. Focus on how they uniquely convey emotion.

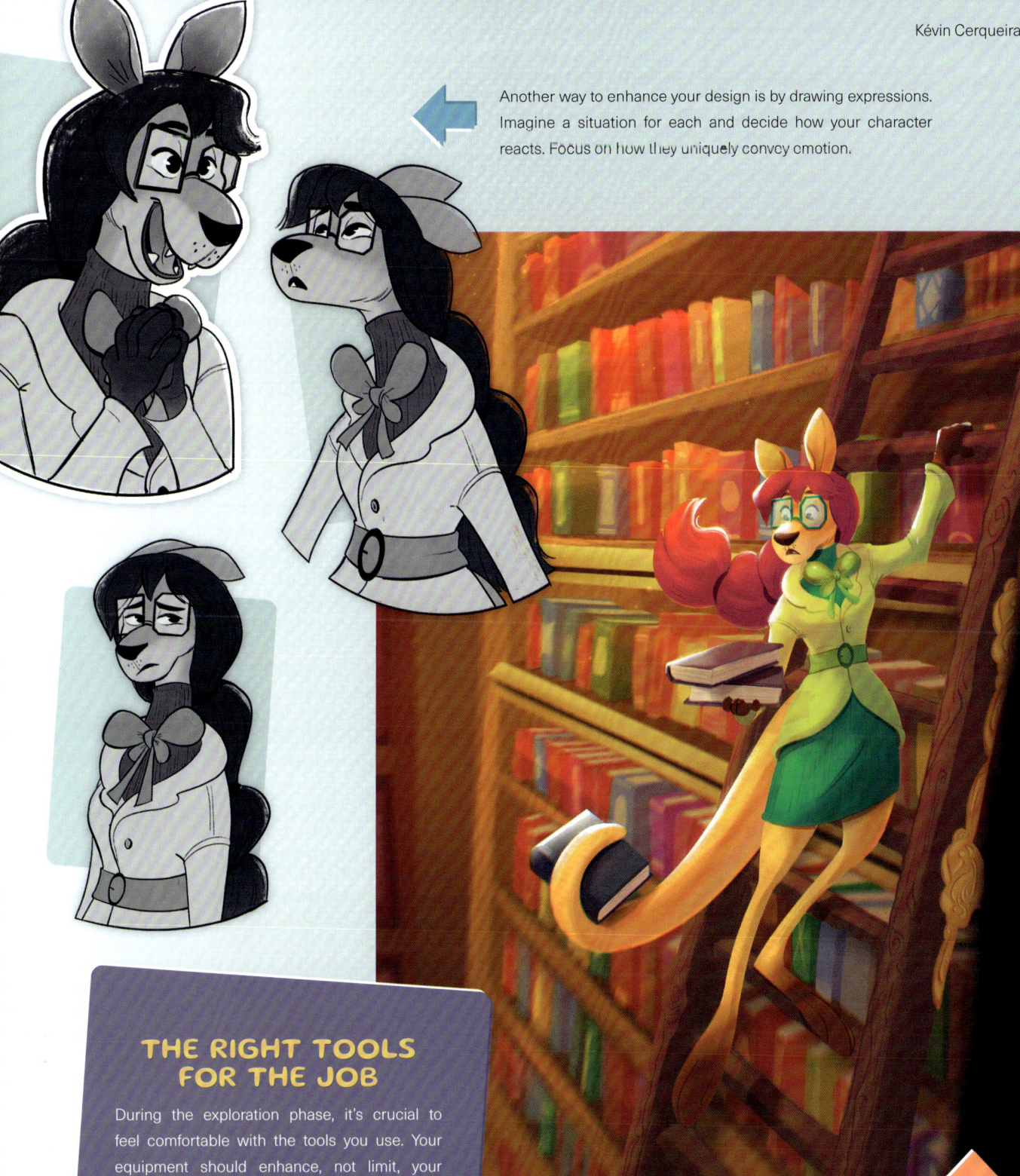

THE RIGHT TOOLS FOR THE JOB

During the exploration phase, it's crucial to feel comfortable with the tools you use. Your equipment should enhance, not limit, your creativity. Pick up your favourite pen or brush and let your ideas flow freely. Draw whatever comes to mind without overthinking it – this is where true creative freedom begins.

Now I'm satisfied with my character, I place them in an environment. A great way to do this is to imagine a specific situation in which you would find your character – in this case, of course I choose a library! Now it's your turn – think of a two-word prompt and start creating your own unique character design.

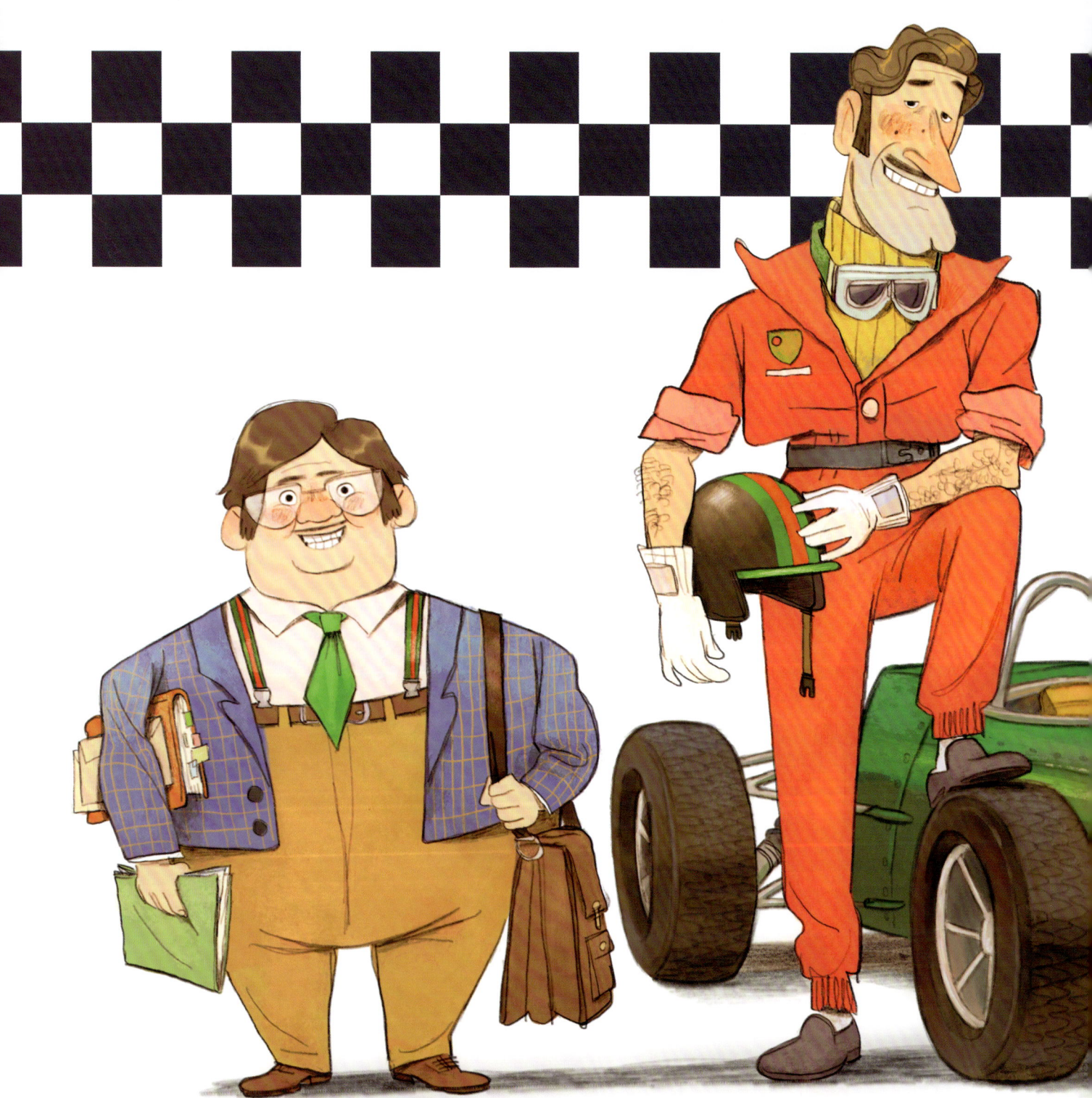

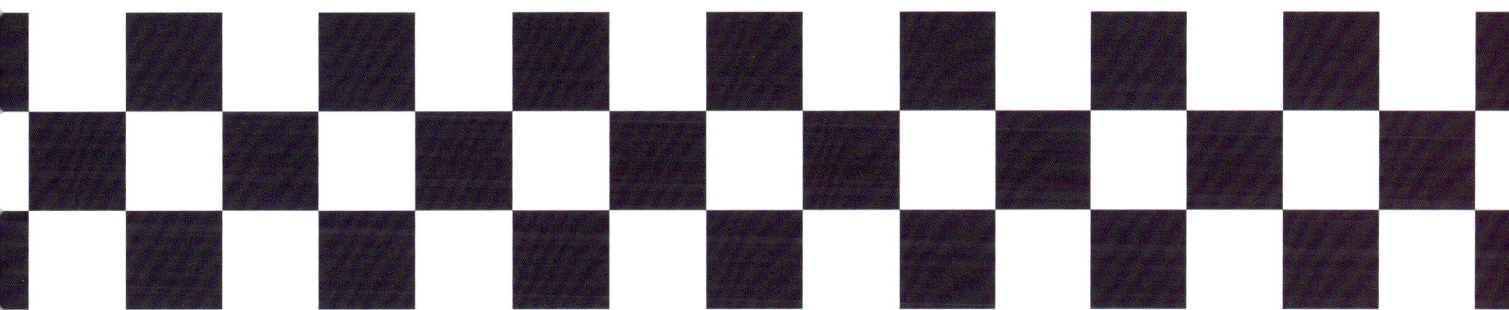

RIGHT-HAND
WHEELMAN

Meet the world's greatest driver (and his manager)
in this tutorial by Alberto Exposito

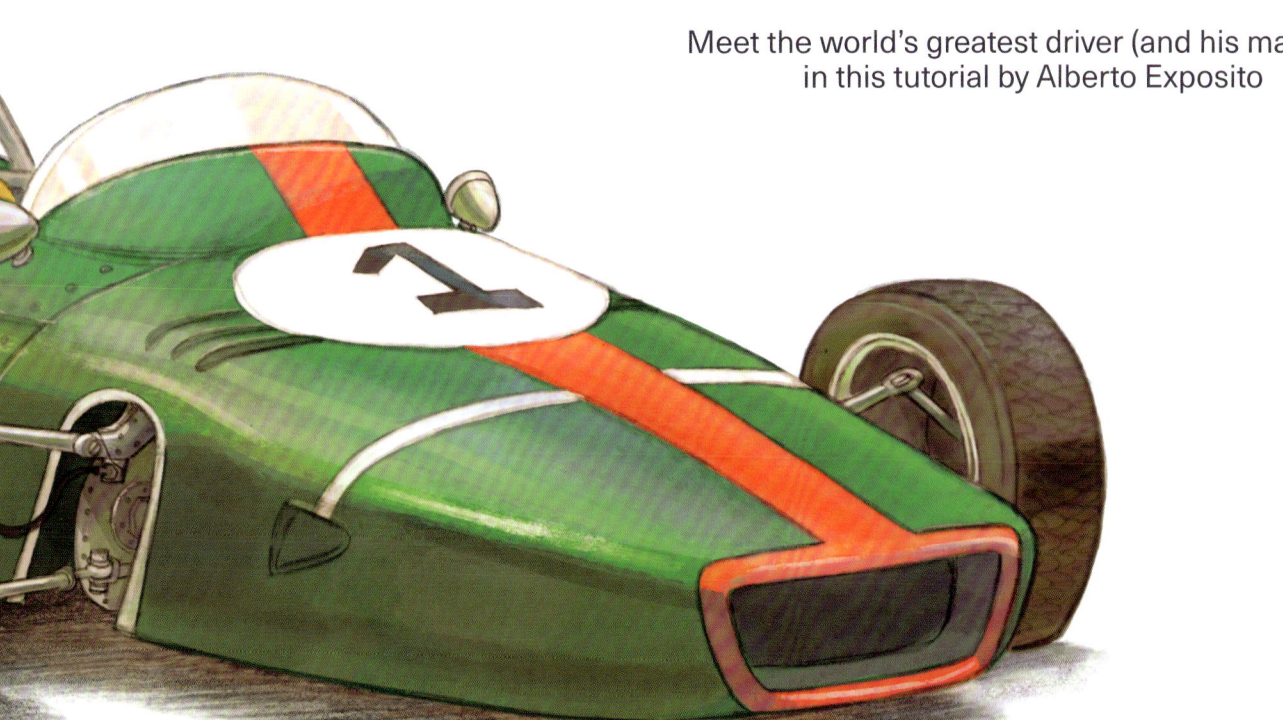

1 Sidekicks are a wonderful way to get to know our main characters. They are often the most sympathetic character, and through their relationship with the protagonist, who can sometimes seem mysterious and distant, you come to know them better. How can Sherlock Holmes not be a great man if Watson, that lovable character we adore, admires him so deeply?

In this tutorial, I will develop a famous racing driver and his friend and manager, who keeps his feet on the ground and makes sure everything works.

Start by collecting some references that remind you of the characters you want to design, to help you put the story in context. At this stage, any image is useful, from faces to clothing, objects, settings, and more. Once this is done, organize them into a large mood board that you can easily refer to at any time.

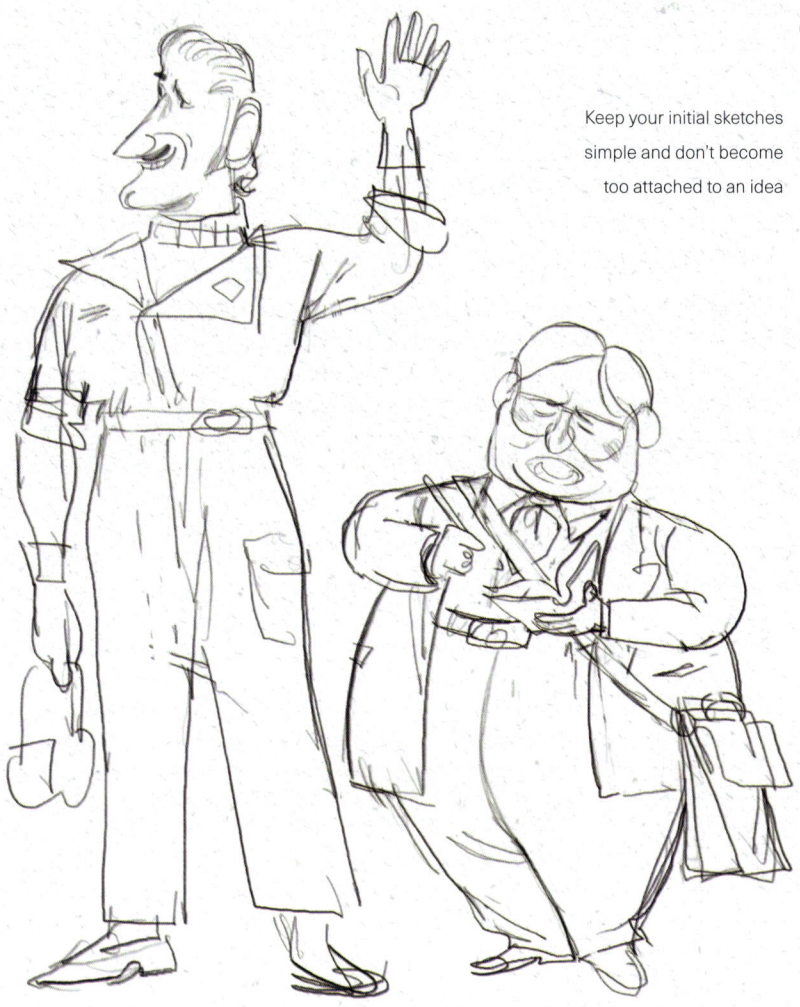

Keep your initial sketches simple and don't become too attached to an idea

QUESTION YOUR CHARACTER

Before you start drawing your characters, ask yourself some important questions about their relationship, such as are your characters friends? How do they feel about each other? How long have they known one another? How do they act when they are together?

2 Develop very simple sketches that establish the attitude of the characters and the shapes of their designs without worrying too much about the quality of your drawing. As you can see, these sketches are very crude. The less time you spend on them at this stage, the better – the more you refine these early explorations, the harder it will be to discard them and start again. Don't fall in love with your first idea! Be creative and keep exploring.

In these initial drawings, you should clearly see the relationship between the two characters and their personalities start to develop, as well as the contrast of silhouettes and shapes in their designs. For this particular duo, I went with a classic shorter and chubbier sidekick, like Sancho Panza in Don Quixote.

3 Next, select the sketches you like best and draw over them again to clarify their designs. At this point, you are still free to change or adjust anything you think could be improved, but try to keep the characters' appeal and freshness. Sometimes, we change our drawings so much when we clean them up that we lose everything we liked in the sketch, so stay loose and always refer back to your original drawing.

A refined sketch, keeping what I like about each character intact

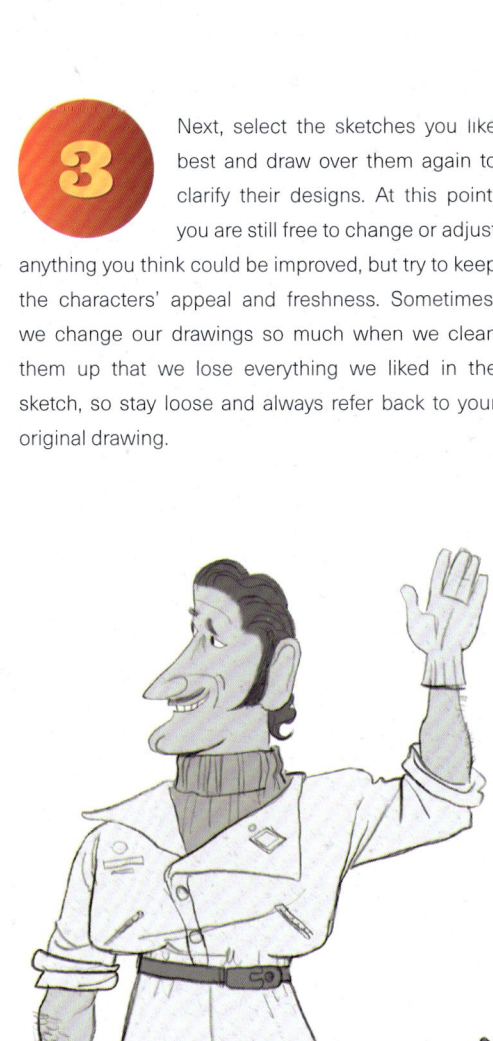

4 Use shades of grey to give more information about the clothing and appearance of your characters, as well as to create contrast between them. This step is not required, but when presenting your work online or to a client, it never hurts to put a little more effort and love into it.

Shading characters is a good way to quickly give them more depth

Details start
to bring the
characters
to life

5 Since my story is set in the 60s, I add noise to the image to take us even more directly to that era. Other details, such as the blush of their cheeks or the highlights in their hair, help us focus on their faces when we first look at the image, as our eyes tend to be drawn to detailed and contrasting areas.

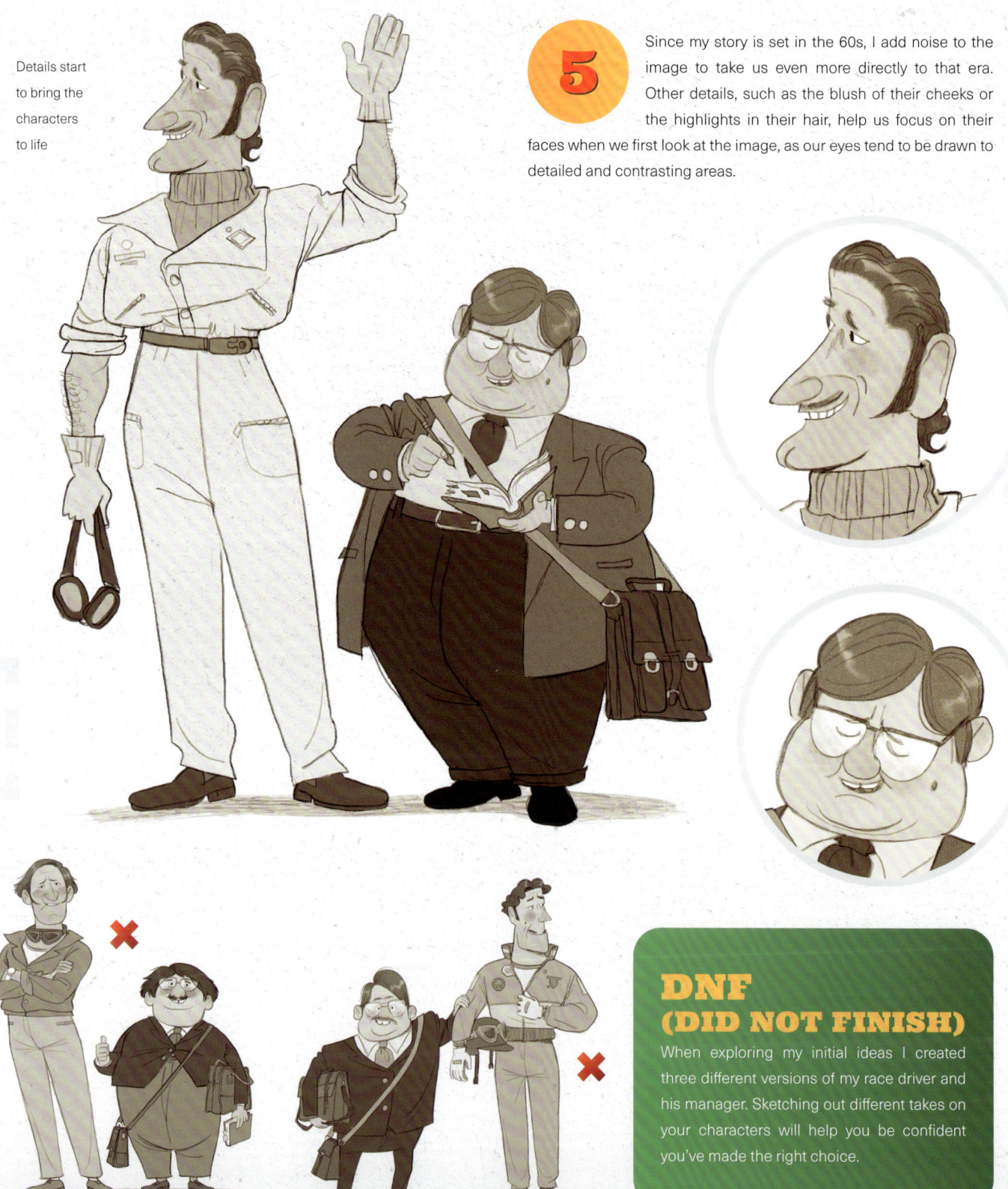

DNF (DID NOT FINISH)

When exploring my initial ideas I created three different versions of my race driver and his manager. Sketching out different takes on your characters will help you be confident you've made the right choice.

6 This first series of explorations may not always lead you to a design you truly love. Since the face is the most important feature of a character, if you are not satisfied with your options so far, you can make a series of exploratory drawings of your character's bust or face. Never stop thinking about their personality and always have fun with the proportions.

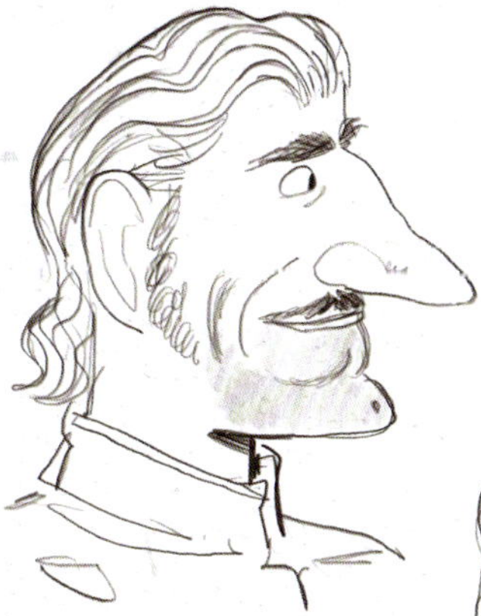

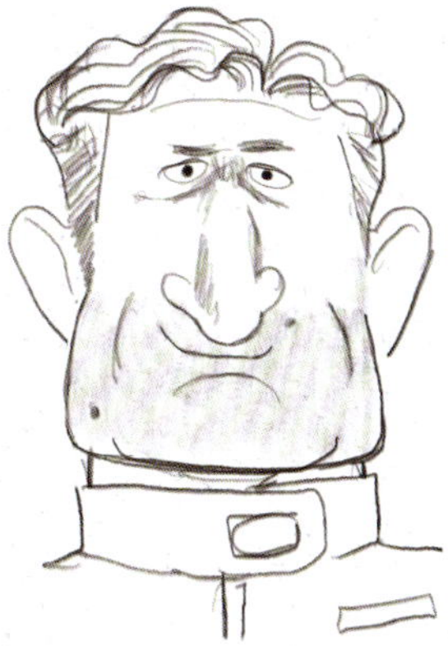

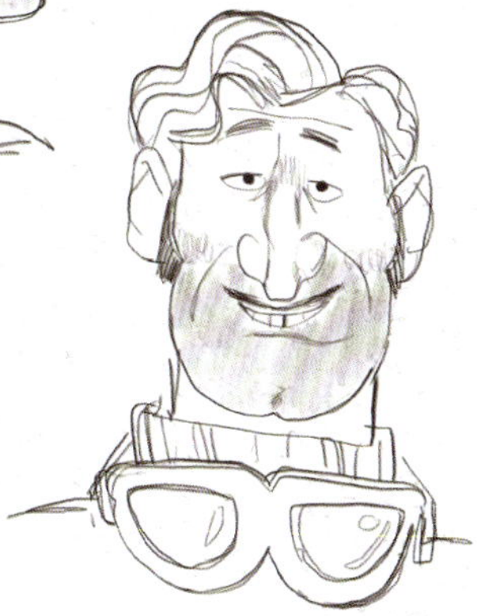

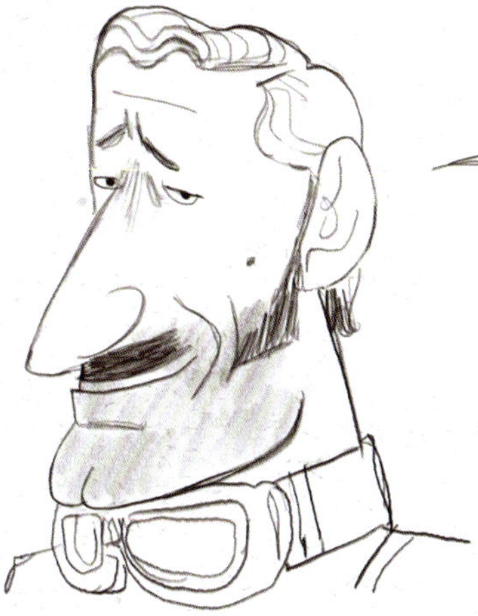

Exploring new options for the driver's face

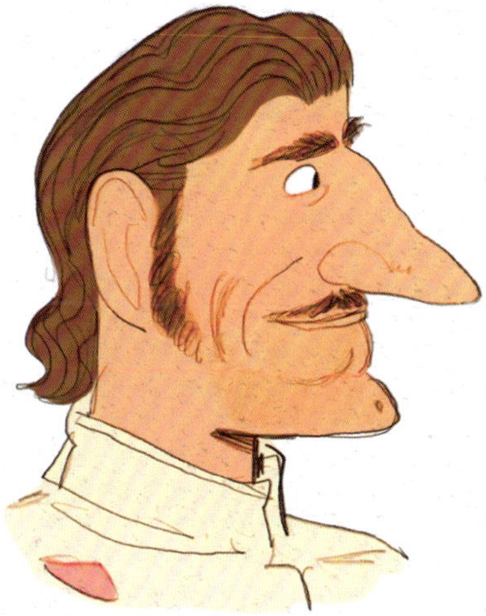

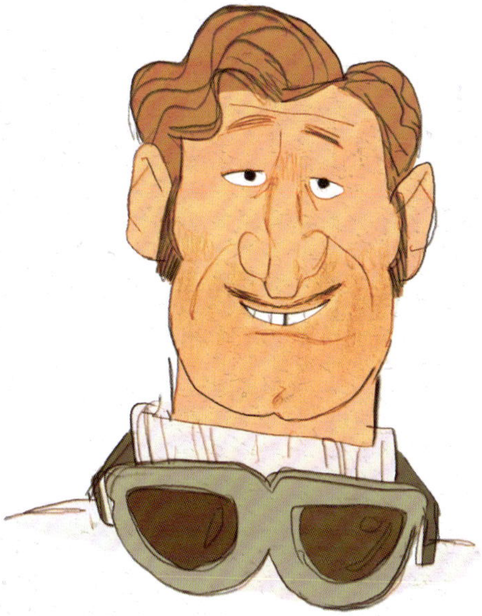

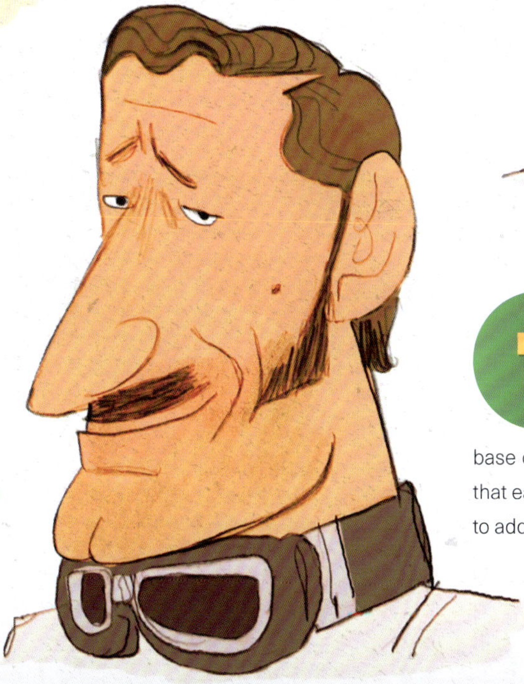

7 Colour is very important when designing your character as it makes your work more visually appealing and professional. I start by exploring different possibilities for the base colours. I like to use a brush with some colour jitter so that each stroke changes the hue slightly. This is a quick way to add some texture to your colour.

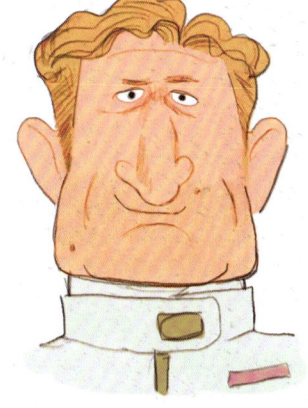

Colour jitter quickly adds texture to the base colours

8 I continue to explore my different ideas for the driver's face. For more striking and specific results, details such as rosier noses and cheeks, beard shadow, hair shine, or contact shadows make our designs stand out even more. But be careful not to get too carried away with the details. Keep your designs simple and fresh – if a design is too busy it can be distracting. Learn when to stop.

The driver's face is finished with blush and extra detail

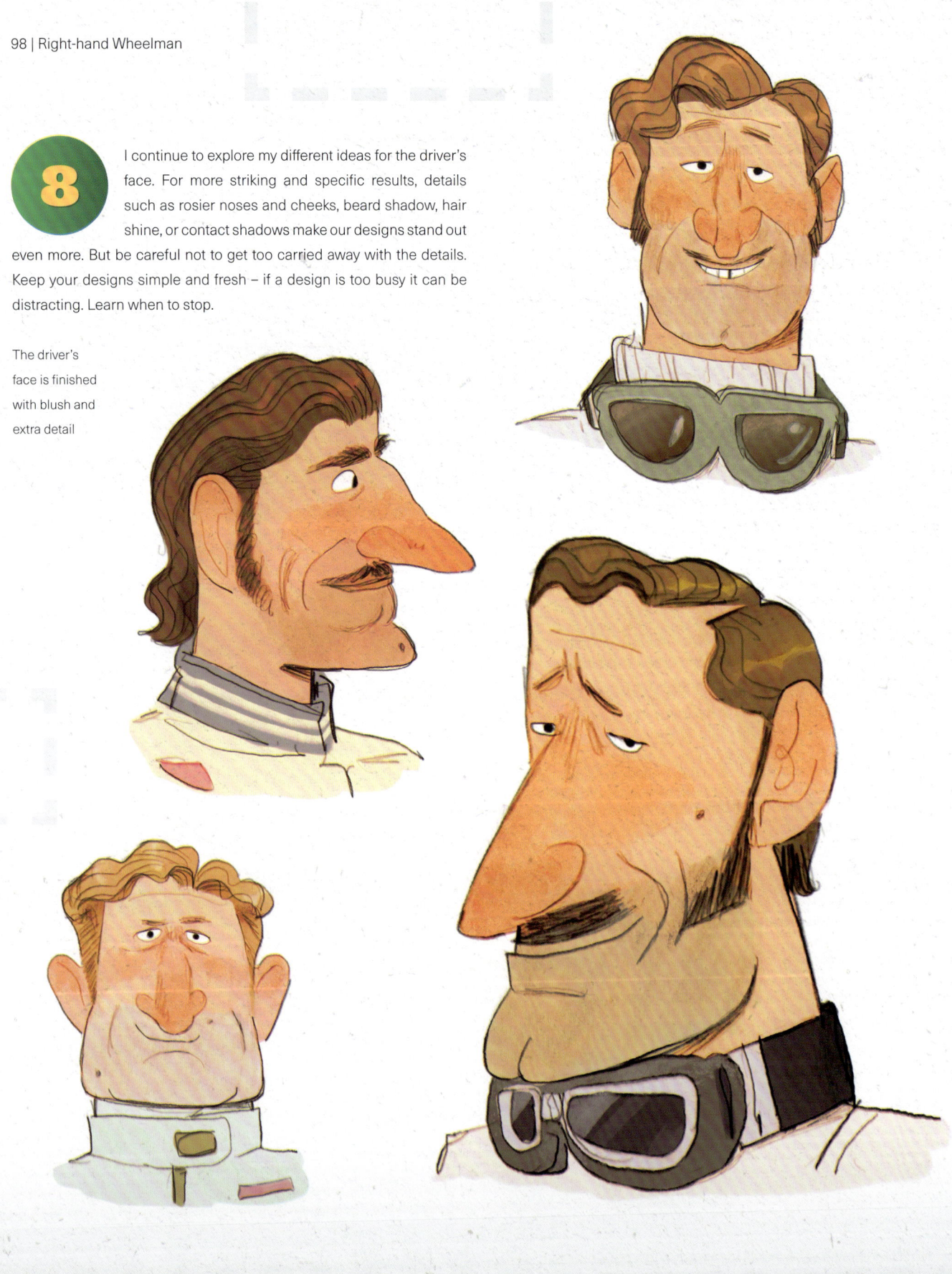

Placing characters in a scene immediately makes them feel more realistic

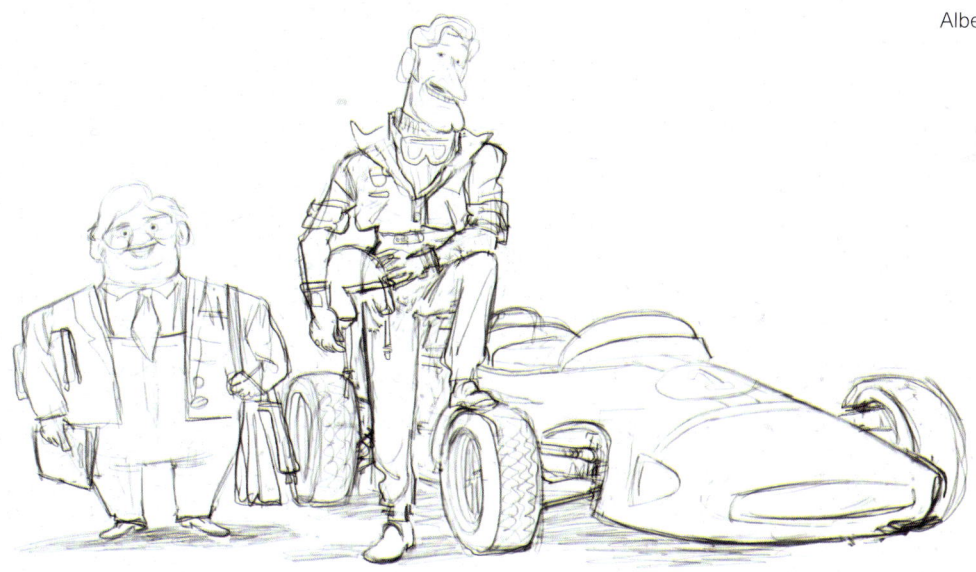

9 Create an illustration to show off the final designs of your characters. By placing your characters in a simple scene, you can better connect them to their environment and context, and also deepen their relationship to one another. In this case, I thought that our protagonist's race car would be a great addition to the final illustration.

Make a series of sketches until you find one you think works, always focusing on the attitude of your characters. They should interact with the elements of the background in a way that will add to their personality and story.

10 Take your sketch and clean it up, trying to keep the freshness of the original, but correcting any mistakes you see along the way. As you can see, every element you add to your characters, from the sidekick's briefcase, to the protagonist's helmet, or the car's wheels, is specific to the context in which your characters live, and to their personalities. Never stop asking questions about your characters: what clothes would they be wearing and how would they wear them? Would they button their jacket or leave it undone? Would they tuck in their shirt or leave it out? Each answer adds personality and specificity to your designs. The references you collect early on will help you achieve this believability.

With the cleaned lines, the scene further takes shape

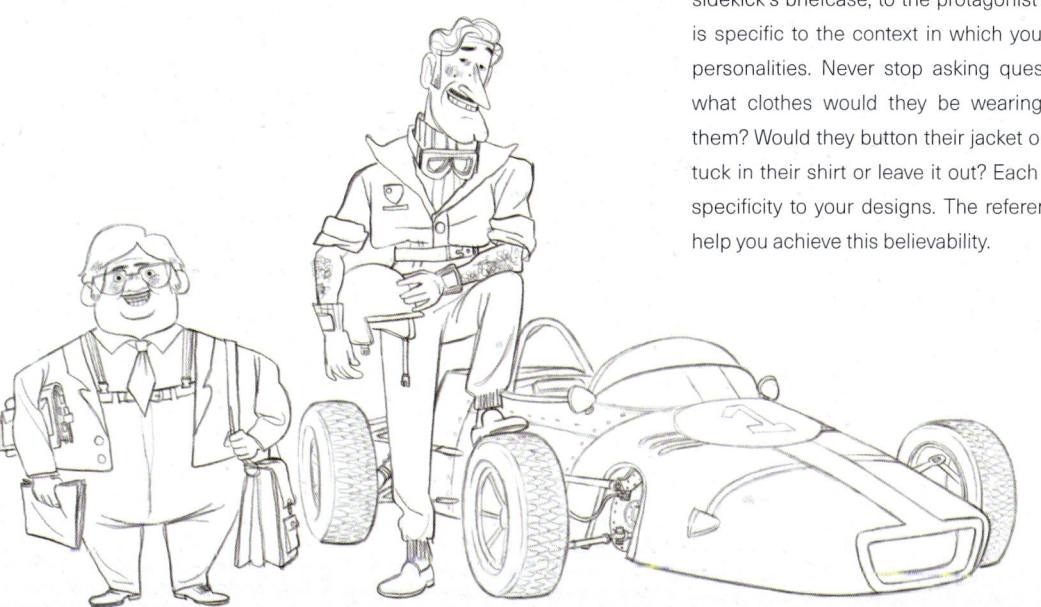

11 Add a basic colour to your illustration and focus on how this choice reflects your character's personality. My protagonist is the most famous driver in the world and he really enjoys his status, so I choose a bold red suit that shows his confidence. His car matches his colours and the sidekick wears the car's colours in his suspenders and tie, which shows his great admiration for the protagonist, and brings homogeneity to our image. Every little detail counts!

Use colours to help enhance the narrative moment

12 Continue to add all the details mentioned before, such as sparkles in the hair, colour variations in the face, lights and shadows, texture, and so on. Remember to use your references again at this stage. For example, to paint and stylize the reflections on the car, you need to analyse how they look in real life.

Use real-life references to add details such as reflections and paint sheen

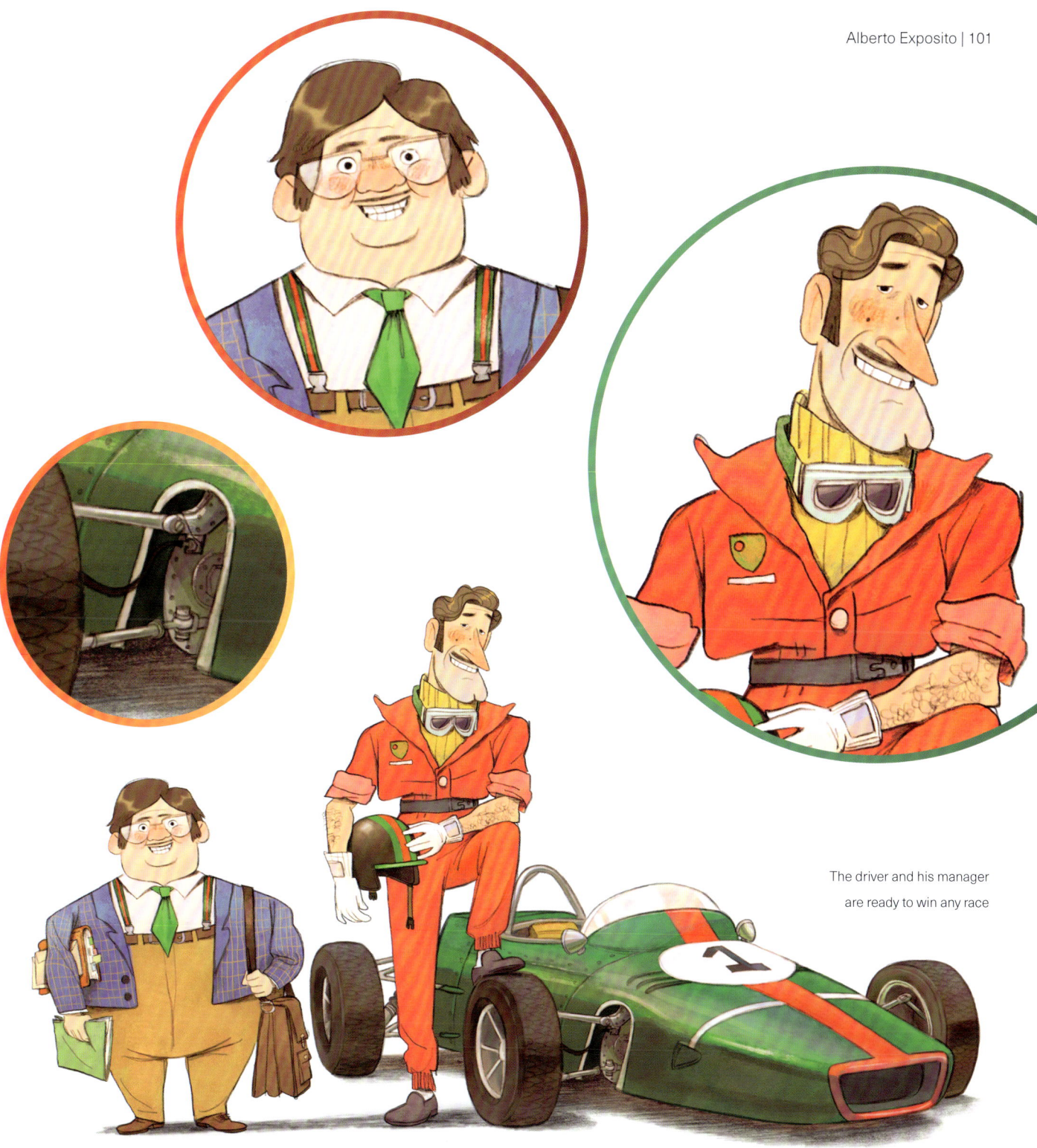

The driver and his manager
are ready to win any race

The illustration is finished and the most important thing is that I enjoyed the process – if you enjoy your work, it will show in your designs and illustrations. Don't stop being creative and keep coming up with new ideas that you enjoy. What I admire most about many of my favourite character designers is the freedom with which they draw – you can really see how much fun they had. Ideas are usually more important than the quality of our drawings. A well-drawn but boring design will never beat a creative and original one.

Exaggerate the shapes, proportions, and poses, and try every idea, no matter how silly or crazy it seems. Never stop creating and, don't forget, have fun drawing!

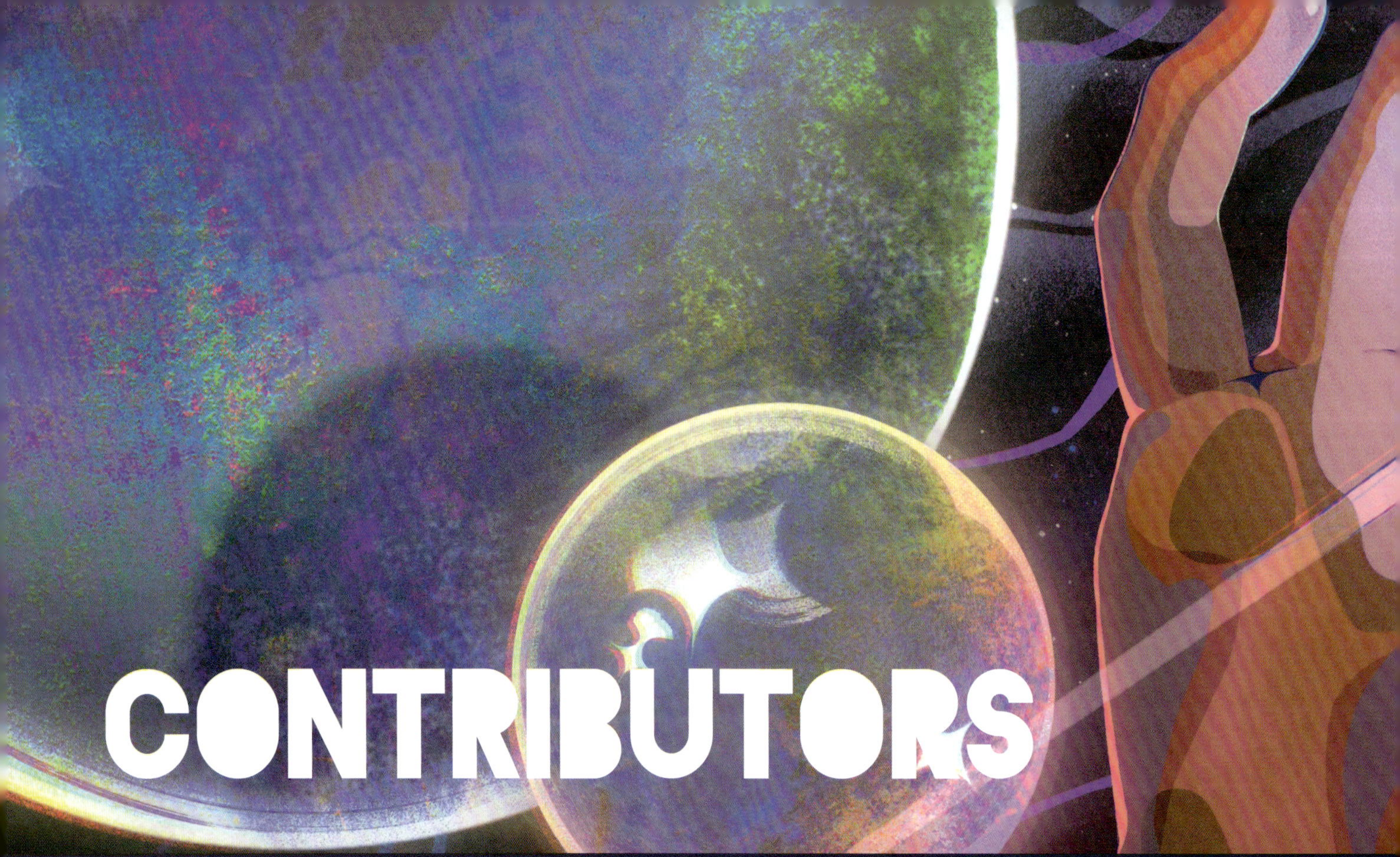

CONTRIBUTORS

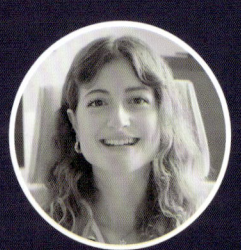

ISABELLA AGOSTI
Illustrator & Character Designer
isabellaagosti.com
Isabella is a freelance artist from Italy. She loves designing characters and illustrating compelling stories to let their personalities shine through.

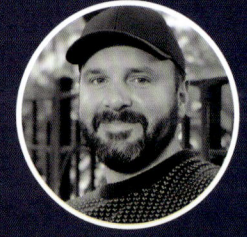

TOM BOOTH
Story & Art at Made Up Games
madeupgames.com
Tom is an author and illustrator of children's books, and a designer for animation and games. He lives in Portland, Maine, with his wife and son.

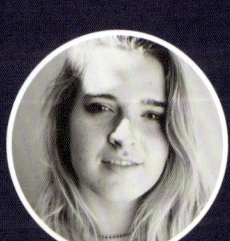

LARA GEORGIA CARSON
Senior Designer
larageorgiacarson.com
Lara is a Canadian illustrator based in Vancouver, BC. She works as a designer for animated TV and a freelance illustrator in her free time.

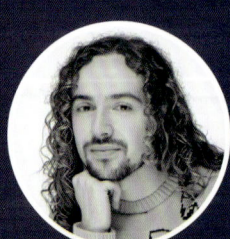

KÉVIN CERQUEIRA
Freelance Character Designer
theartofwill.fr
Kévin is a freelance character designer and illustrator from France. He loves creating diverse and expressive characters that tell their own stories.

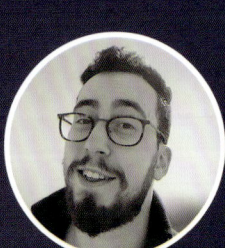

SCOTT EPSTEIN
Character Designer & Vis Dev Artist
scottepsteindesign.com
Scott is a Los Angeles-based artist working in feature and television animation. He loves to create whimsical and comedic fantasy characters and environments.

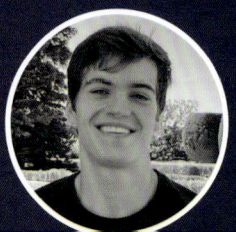

ALBERTO EXPÓSITO CAMPOS
Character Designer & Illustrator
albertoexposito.org
Alberto is a character designer and illustrator from Cáceres, Spain. His work is known for its warmth and the expressive nature of his characters and scenes.

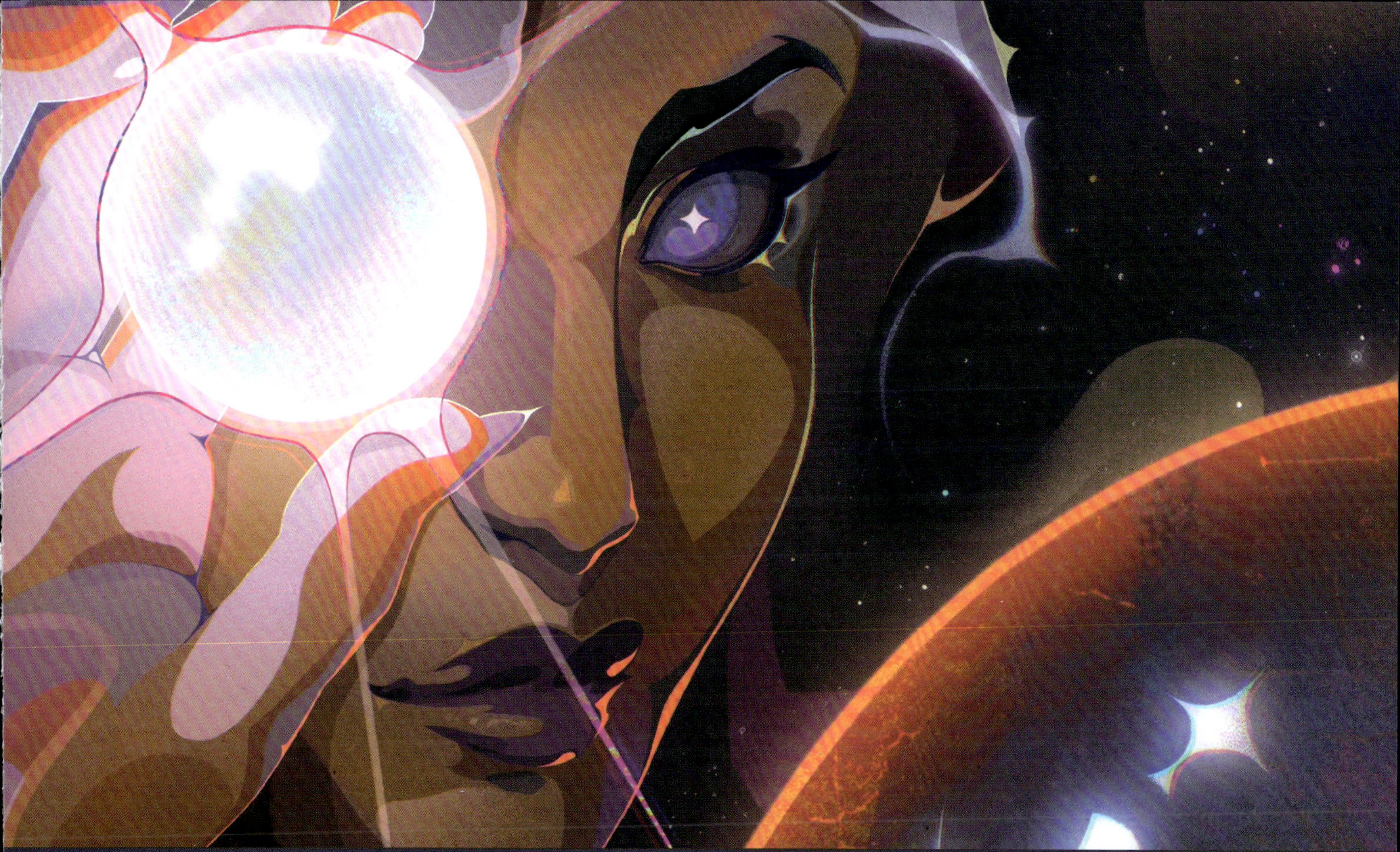

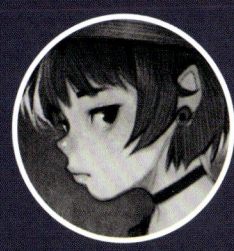

SIMONE 'SIMZ' FERRIERO
Artist
instagram.com/simz.art
Simone is an Italian illustrator and comic-book artist. His work is focused on fantasy, sci-fi, and the concept of slice-of-life scenes involving witches and ghost cats.

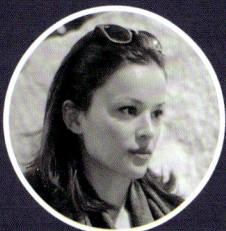

SEDA KIR
Illustrator & Character Designer
artofseda.com
Seda is an illustrator who works for various clients all over the world. She has been playing with colours and lines her whole life and is happy to have made it her career.

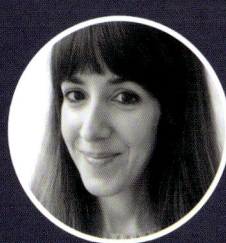

LIDIA MORALES
Character Designer & Concept Artist
lidiamoralesart.com
Lidia is a professional artist with extensive experience working in video games and animation, focused on bringing unlimited creativity to every project she works on.

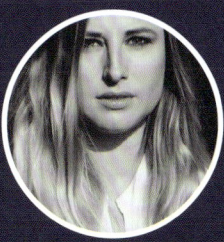

ANNE NEYENS
Freelance Artist as Annie Mation
mrsanniemation.com
Anne is a Belgian concept artist and illustrator living in The Netherlands. The majority of her art is character based, telling stories through personality.

Image © Lara Carson

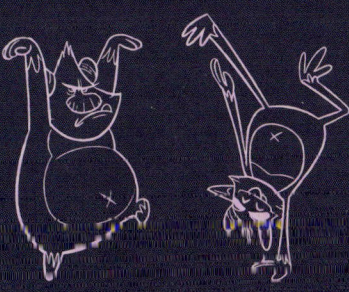

50%
of net profits donated
TO CHARITY

In 2022, 3dtotal Publishing became successful enough to make a pledge to donate **50% of its net profits to charity**. This continues to be possible due to the incredible support from all our customers, employees, and partners. At the time of printing, we have donated over $1.62 million (USD) to charity.

We focus our giving on three charitable areas: **environmental, humanitarian, and animal welfare**. We use organizations such as Effective Altruism and Founders Pledge to guide who we help within these causes. Some ways of doing good are over 100 times more effective than others, so donating this way hugely increases the impact of our contributions.

**See 3dtotal.com/charity
for full details.**

3dtotal Publishing